T0012596

"Mixing tender and rigorous res
archive with lyrical and polemical
from silents to slashers, this wonderful book excavates ___
history of the moving image to discover its potential future."
MARK ASCH, AUTHOR OF *CLOSE-UPS: NEW YORK MOVIES*

"A powerful intervention to the often fraught concept of
representation, one that shines through its nuanced and
thoughtful prose. Moving, invigorating, and readable. I
devoured it with immense joy."
GRACE BYRON, WRITER AND POET

"An instant classic in the field of queer film studies."
ANDREW CHAN, AUTHOR OF *WHY MARIAH CAREY MATTERS*

"A thoughtful, revelatory, and rewarding read from two of the
most essential critics working today."
ASHLEY CLARK, CRITERION COLLECTION

"Caden Mark Gardner and Willow Maclay have created something crucial for our times that will no doubt become one of
the classic texts of cinema history and criticism."
MILLIE DeCHIRICO, CO-AUTHOR OF *TCM UNDERGROUND*

"A superb work of film history... lively and thoroughly
researched, a treasury of astute film criticism, and a portrayal
of the highways and byways of trans (legal; medical; political)
that is both engaged and dispassionate. A definitive treatment of the subject."
MOLLY HASKELL, AUTHOR OF *FROM REVERENCE TO RAPE*

"One of the most important — and exciting — works of long-
form film criticism of this century thus far."
ALEXANDRA HELLER-NICHOLAS, AUTHOR OF *1,000 WOMEN
IN HORROR: 1895-2018*

CORPSES, FOOLS, AND MONSTERS

CORPSES, FOOLS, AND MONSTERS

The History and Future of Transness in Cinema

Caden Mark Gardner

and

Willow Catelyn Maclay

Published by Repeater Books

An imprint of Watkins Media Ltd

Unit 11 Shepperton House

89-93 Shepperton Road

London

N1 3DF

United Kingdom

www.repeaterbooks.com

A Repeater Books paperback original 2024

1

Distributed in the United States by Random House, Inc., New York.

Copyright Caden Mark Gardner and Willow Catelyn Maclay © 2024

Caden Mark Gardner and Willow Catelyn Maclay assert the moral right to be identified as the authors of this work.

ISBN: 9781914420580

Ebook ISBN: 9781914420597

CONTENTS

PREFACE
What Are Trans Film Images?

This collaboration — a critical examination of trans film history and its images — was born out of the paucity of positive, progressive, or nuanced trans film images in mainstream film, as well as a serious dearth of trans voices within film culture. There are certainly important trans historians and scholars, such as Susan Stryker, Cael M. Keegan, and Jules Rosskam — to name a few — but outside of the walls of academia, discussion of the histories of trans film images in broader culture is lacking. This may be symptomatic of trans film images being regarded as a small subset of queer cinema. It might also be due to distribution, for films with nuanced trans images tend to not be afforded the same level of distribution as films following cisgender characters and images, or films with more overt but simplistic trans images made by cis people.

Body Talk was a series of dialogues we started in 2018. The series focused on mainstream and widely circulated films such as *The Silence of the Lambs* (1991), *Boys Don't Cry* (1999), and *Paris Is Burning* (1991). *Body Talk* started during the Trump administration. Sadly, throughout this period, many mainstream narratives around trans persons, our rights, and our representation were reactive and toxic. Given this background of prejudice and exclusionary politics, publishing critical discussions about dominant and widely known trans film images felt urgent. Many of the mainstream films we discussed were regarded as "game-changers" by the mainstream, and some received the industry's highest accolades. But they were very much imbued with all too familiar tropes and clichés of trans people on-screen. It was in revisiting Kimberly Peirce's *Boys Don't Cry* for *Body Talk* that we hit our breaking point:

> I don't think movies are the be-all, end-all for social change or anything of the sort, but there's certainly something symptomatic in the American psyche where for the most part the only times we've been on screen are to be murdered, turned into a joke, or a tragedy of failed transition. The mainstream isn't interested in our livelihood or our goals. It's a lost highway of corpses, fools, and monsters.[1]

This book was born from that edition of *Body Talk*. From that point on, we felt a duty to go deeper, beyond the mainstream offerings, to try and mine through older, often obscure films and on-screen portrayals that were only beginning to become available to a larger audience and that allowed for a more varied and nuanced look at transness. Neither of us could have anticipated the number of films both old and new that would be covered in this project. What has excited us the most in recent years has been seeing the emergence of trans filmmakers from all corners of filmmaking who have made deeply personal, political, and bold works that are interwoven with their trans identities. They point towards new ways to see trans people on-screen while also connecting to our disparate pasts, across generations. But trans cinema is not yet a fully-fledged subgenre and has instead been a scattering of images that are often recycled by non-trans filmmakers. What, then, are "trans film images?"

Trans film images make up a significant portion of the average person's media diet of trans people, in films that do not fall into the category of "queer" or "trans". These films range from studio comedies like *Soapdish* (1991) to Harmony Korine's off-beat independent breakthrough *Gummo* (1997) to Danny Boyle's sensational drug film *Trainspotting* (1996) or John Carpenter's action sequel *Escape from L.A.* (1996). The majority of the trans film images within these films are rarely consequential to the plot. In the instances when they are, they are often used as a slight against a male character's masculinity: being "fooled" by a trans sex worker, for instance, or to call into question a female character's femininity by "revealing" her past "secret" life before transitioning. The duration of these trans film images may be a single scene, existing in the frame for a matter of seconds. Yet, there is something memorable about each of them, especially for trans viewers who, while growing up, found them in often widely celebrated and circulated films. Trans viewers hold and carry many of these film images in their memories and their unconscious relationship to cinema, even if the films themselves have faded. These images serve as reminders of how the world has often seen us.

"Trans film images" is consciously abbreviated as a term. "Trans" can mean "transvestite," "transsexual," and/ or "transgender" within this book — as identities, they fall under the umbrella of transness. Many of the older films covered use different language, terms, and concepts. Trans men and women, cross-dressers, intersex, and other gender non-conforming individuals were often pathologized with now-outdated medical language and there are dialogues about shifts in language among trans people within many of these works, particularly in the non-fiction films. This complex relationship between language and the image should, however, not deter us from examining these older works: they can still present a powerful image and distillation of the past, and it is necessary to reckon with the limitations of these films and images in the context of their respective periods. These films mattered: they were foundational to how trans people are seen in the mainstream.

This book places many of these films and images within their periods to give context to the dialogues, societal perceptions, and institutions surrounding trans people. Much of the research for this book and many of the films themselves explore trans medicine's power and influence in America and how it filtered into early trans narratives. This is primarily why Christine Jorgensen is the jumping-off point — the confluence of trans medicine as a phenomenon and her celebrity created the prevailing image tied to these modern, transformational procedures. There were trans people and gender non-conforming identities across the world that preceded Jorgensen, but the proliferation of trans film images from the post-World War II period onward is tied to trans medicine and the avatars of that period, with Jorgensen being among the most influential.

Corpses, Fools, and Monsters functions as an admonishment of the ways the mainstream has presented trans lives on-screen through harmful stereotypes and tropes, and in that respect the book was written to serve as a critical history of the trans film image, much as Vito Russo's *The Celluloid Closet: Homosexuality in the Movies* has done for gay and lesbian representation. Paradoxically, as co-authors and cinephiles, we have each found levels of empathy, sympathy, and relatability to these on-screen "monsters," both literal and figurative, and that has also informed how this book explores the nuance of these trans film images and their complicated resonance for the trans viewer.

This book would not have existed without the work and research of trans scholar, professor, and filmmaker Susan Stryker. In an essay that was performed as a monologue at California State University, Long Beach in 1993, "My Words to Victor Frankenstein Above the Village of Chamounix," Stryker likens herself and the trans body to Mary Shelley's *Frankenstein*. The trans film image resonates through Stryker's words:

> The transsexual body is an unnatural body. It is the product of medical science. It is a technological construction. It is flesh torn apart and sewn back together again in a shape other than that in which it was born. In these circumstances, I find a deep affinity between myself as a transsexual woman and the monster in Mary Shelley's "Frankenstein." Like the monster, I am too often perceived as less than fully

human due to my embodiment; like the monster's as well, my exclusion from human community fuels a deep and abiding rage in me that I, like the monster, direct against the conditions in which I must struggle to exist.[2]

Trans film history and its language also exists in the margins, among human beings who are prone to isolation due to society having historically considered them monstrous. Stryker's essay remains a bedrock of theory and criticism regarding the trans film image and its possibilities in going beyond the boundaries and limits of direct representation. James Whale's *Frankenstein* (1931) and other adaptations of Shelley's story offer an appealing connection to the struggle of transness. A trans person can be drawn to film works that are outside the bounds of common trans narratives because they see their own embodiment paralleled in them. Stryker's embrace of "the monster" speaks to the trans experience; dysphoric rather than euphoric. This is the central conflict in looking at the history of trans film imagery: the images widely circulated in mainstream culture versus the images trans people sought to claim as their own. Trans viewers individually can be drawn to different narratives, film frameworks, and genres, but collectively there have been consistent titles and filmmakers that have been embraced over the years, ranging from Jonathan Glazer's *Under the Skin* (2013) to the oeuvre of David Cronenberg and the subgenre of "body horror," finding commonality through images often more ruinous than aspirational. While some of these filmmakers have engaged in direct representations of transness on-screen, it is the adjacency their works have to transness as a concept that has resulted in their films being venerated within trans cinephile circles.

While this book functions as a thorough critical, cultural, and historical look at trans film images and emerging trans cinema, it should not be confused with a directive, decree, or definitive repository of every trans film image put forth. *Corpses, Fools, and Monsters* is not about can-

CORPSES, FOOLS, AND MONSTERS

onizing or de-canonizing certain films. Its primary aim is exploring trans people's complicated relationship with their film images, with critical and historical consideration given to all the films presented; to develop a conversation about what constitutes *truthful* trans film images and where and how that truth manifests.

CHAPTER 1
The Legend of Christine Jorgensen

Pre-Jorgensen Trans Film Images

Prior to Christine Jorgensen's celebrity in America, trans images in the mainstream were largely rendered through cross-dressing and gender play on-screen. This was partly an extension of stage performance: the tradition of male and female impersonators on the vaudeville stage or in theatre, where works ranging from Shakespeare to J. M. Barrie's *Peter Pan* featured cross-gender casting. One early example — from Hollywood's silent film period — of how male and female cross-dressing interact with society and culture at large is Sidney Drew's *A Florida Enchantment* (1914).

A Florida Enchantment is the story of a woman named Lillian Travers (Edith Storey), who is given a magical seed that will transform whoever consumes it into the opposite sex for a brief time. The structure of this film is similar to pioneer filmmaker Alice Guy-Blaché's earlier *Les Résultats du féminisme* (*The Consequences of Feminism*) (1906), in which men and women all throughout society wake up to find that their sociological roles have been reversed. Although both films are dated — such as featuring minstrel characters — they nonetheless present feminist concepts in a sly manner by exposing sociological differences between sexes. *A Florida Enchantment* does make cross-dressing a source of humor, but it also incidentally shows how both trans femininity and trans masculinity are received.

Lillian takes the seed and "becomes" a man, donning a

cap and a suit and going by the name of Lawrence. As Lawrence, the character flirts with the girls and even kisses a few, gets into fights, and proves she can be just as rowdy as any of the boys. While it is all played for laughs, the viewer nonetheless sees a character transition, and through that transition unlock some part of herself. It would be a stretch to refer to her as a trans masculine archetype — when the seed wears off, she treats her traipse through masculinity simply as a much-needed vacation — but there is still something resonant about a female character stepping across the gender binary.

If there is a positive aspect to Lillian/Lawrence's journey, however, the same is not true for their suitor, Dr. Frederick Cassadene, played by actor-director Sidney Drew. Travers encourages Cassadene to take the seed and become a woman, and Cassadene's story essentially mirrors Travers'. While the film allows Travers to be able to pass as a man, Cassadene, as a woman, is chased out of town by furious baton-wielding cops — possibly a comment on the fact that cross-dressing was largely treated as an illegal activity during this period. This initial depiction of societal revulsion at images of potential trans-femininity is visible in the mainstream throughout film history — in broad comedies, this is primarily situated as the folly of a "man" in a dress, whose concepts of femininity are garish and become the subject of ridicule.

There were early examples of the trans-image beyond American cinema, most notably in Germany, the country itself having become synonymous with sexual liberation during the Weimar Republic. Ernst Lubitsch's comedy of the sexes, *Ich möchte kein Mann sein* (*I Don't Want to Be a Man*) (1918), presents Ossi (Ossi Oswalda), a tomboy fed up with the rules and regulations of her sex. She is not interested in being dignified or waiting around for a man to come along and lock her into marriage. She wants to be where the boys are, to smoke and drink, cuss and flirt with whomever she pleases, and she finds it completely unfair that she is not allowed to express herself in whatever way she wants.

In contrast to the malicious humor in *A Florida Enchantment*, *I Don't Want to Be a Man* is playful with the conventions of a comedy of this type; Lubitsch's directorial style is light and his filmmaking smartly intertwines gags, reaction shots, and a zeal for the comedic. There are numerous innovative shots, such as one that uses perspective and depth of field to display a decadent ballroom flooded with dancers that Ossi crashes in drag. A few of the finer Lubitsch touches in this film involve Ossi's governess (Margarete Kupfer) puffing away at a cigarette while an intertitle reads, "Girls shouldn't smoke," or a flock of male tailors circling around a more conventional-looking woman than Ossi, arguing amongst themselves who gets to measure which part of her body for a dress. Here, the conceit of a character changing their sex is treated as a lark, a moment of dress-up, and gender euphoria.

When Ossi is seen for the first time, she is in the middle of a poker game with a gaggle of men and wearing a very baggy skirt and loose-fitting top meant for comfort. When the game is broken up by her governess, who insists that such an activity is unsuitable for a lady, she decides to do the most rational thing: to become a man. She does not come to that decision immediately, however, and spends a lot of time moping about her bedroom and asking God why she was not born a boy. This is one of the rare films from the era that numerous trans-masculine people can point to and say they too have been there. Lubitsch manages to foster empathy for Ossi instead of turning her predicament into a joke. Ossi is the tomboy archetype, but she has some elements of trans masculine longing that reach beyond freedom of behavior and into questions of identity, giving her a more nuanced depiction of gender play which gestures towards transness in a truthful manner.

I Don't Want to Be a Man feels liberated from many of the conventions associated with the gender-swap comedy, with

Ossi evoking the initial euphoria and troublesome road-blocks that come in the early stages of transition. The way that Ossi fights with her suspenders when she is putting together her suit, or fumbles with her tie, and huffs with frustration at the way her chest seems to get in the way of the outfit, is something that trans people are intimately familiar with, and the film plays it not for humiliation or shame, but as a gag. Compare the frustrations that Ossi has with her suspenders to the joy that spreads across her face when she puts on a top hat — she yearns to have such a sense of freedom felt throughout her entire body.

The masculine traditions that Ossi is taught by her would-be love interest, Dr. Kersten (Curt Goetz), are some of the more interesting elements. He is none the wiser that his new "brother" is the girl he spent the first act of the film flirting with, and Ossi is quite pleased that she passes as a man in the eyes of someone who knew them previously as a girl. The tension in the film resides in whether Dr. Kersten sees this young man as a man, or if he knows it is Ossi in drag but humors their efforts. Lubitsch does not give away the answer but imbues it with comedy and walks right up to the edge of what was acceptable in a movie of this type when he has Kersten and Ossi casually kiss one another multiple times in a drunken stupor. It is comedic, but deepened by the secret of Ossi's momentary experience of trans masculinity in this potentially queer romantic entanglement. Ultimately, Ossi and Kersten end up together after she reveals to him, while still in a tuxedo, her long feminine hair.

Reinhold Schünzel, a German director and actor who appeared in Lubitsch films, with 1933's *Viktor und Viktoria* directed another example of a film that played with gender against the backdrop of the Weimar Republic. *Viktor und Viktoria* is a farce about a struggling actress, Susanne (Renate Müller), who reinvents herself by presenting as the female impersonator "Mr. Viktoria" and the series of professional and romantic entanglements that result. The film was a hit and has been remade many times, first in 1934 by Schünzel himself in the French language (*Georges et Georgette*), and then in English by Victor Saville in 1935's *First a Girl* (starring husband-and-wife pairing Jessie Matthews and Sonnie Hale). Later, in 1957, there was the West German remake *Victor and Victoria* by Karl Anton, and, most famously, Blake Edwards' *Victor/Victoria* (1982) starring Julie Andrews and Robert Preston.

In Schünzel's film, Susanne's confidante Viktor (Hermann Thimig) goes along with her plan because he himself has been performing in drag while down on his luck. Their shared secret is a tension in the text, although this is less due to fear of reveal and more tied to Susanne's relationship to Robert (Anton Walbrook). Her romantic feelings for Robert develop while, in male drag, rejecting the advances of female admirer, Ellinor. Ultimately, Susanne leaves her tuxedo behind and walks into Robert's arms in a dress, leaving Viktor scrambling to save the stage act, having to do an awkward improv dressed as a Spanish Contessa. His performance is well-received due to it being perceived as a comedy. After the performance, the police confront Viktor in his dressing room for performing as a female impersonator. The authorities then announce that Viktor is a man rather than a woman. The stage company breaks into laughter at the absurdity of this being seen as unlawful, with Schünzel in many ways presenting how ridiculous it is to criminalize such gender-play performances.

An issue that lingered in producing queer, non-conforming images, especially in Hollywood, was the moral and puritanical crusades that often occurred in response to them. But even with the existence of the Production Code (also known as the Hays Code) and studio self-censorship from the 1930s, cross-dressing on-screen was not perceived as a point of moral outrage if it was tied to comedy. Indeed, it persisted for decades: Jack Lemmon and Tony Curtis in *Some Like It Hot* (1959), Cary Grant in *I Was a Male War Bride* (1949), and Bugs Bunny in numerous *Merrie Melodies* animated shorts, best represented in Chuck Jones' master-piece, *What's Opera, Doc?* (1957), with the iconic cartoon rabbit portraying Valkyrie Brunnhilde.

The flipside of male-led cinematic cross-dressing was represented by Katharine Hepburn in George Cukor's 1935 *Sylvia Scarlett*. Hepburn, much like Curtis and Lemmon later in *Some Like It Hot*, is on the run with her embezzler father, and takes on a disguise, transforming from Sylvia Snow to Sylvester Scarlett. As Peter H. Kemp put it in a 2002 retro-spective of the film in *Senses of Cinema*:

> ...the film takes Katharine Hepburn's star-image to levels never touched before or since. When narrative circumstances compel Hepburn's Sylvia to clip her braided plaits and transform into Sylvester, the film's diegetic arena becomes, for more than half the plot's duration, a tantalizing field for all kinds of ambiguous play.[1]

The film is about crossing over in more ways than one: gender, geographic borders, and genres; a playfulness that has made for an enduringly strange film. Despite the fact the film plays on Katharine Hepburn's star persona — she wore slacks in public and had long been rumored to have a queer sexuality — this was a film that both she and Cukor were deeply embarrassed by. Test screenings were not kind to it; there was reported booing and walkouts pertaining to a scene in which Maudie (Dennie Moore) finds Sylvia's Sylvester so irresistible that she lunges over to her for a kiss while helping Sylvia don her mustache.[2] The aftermath of the kissing scene comes after a rather abrupt transition wipe, giving the appearance that more happened than just a kiss, and that those elements were cut.

Despite knowing this will just be a brief exploration of inhabiting the male gender rather than fully living it, Sylvia as Sylvester is still more appealing on-screen than when she is fully presenting as female. Hepburn's co-star Cary Grant is the hyper-masculine cad and con artist Jimmy, and they share palpable on-screen chemistry, even as Jimmy becomes clued in on the character's gender charade. As film critic Michael Koresky characterized it, there is a sense of "deflation" when Grant leaves the film, as Sylvia — after being a player in Jimmy's con games — ceases to be Sylvester.[3] With its lead reverting back to her feminine appearance, this is ultimately how *Sylvia Scarlett* got away with so much. Even though Sylvia presents male to deceive and evade detection, she is not caricatured by Cukor, himself a gay man who would later dabble in more gender-play on-screen with an imaginary sequence in *Adam's Rib* (1949) where there is visual gag of actors Judy Holiday, Jean Hagen, and Tom Ewell all presenting in drag.

While the aims of these films were not exclusively about presenting characters changing genders, nevertheless, for many viewers there was something deeper that resonated with their sense of self. These instances of gender-play were "contained narratives" in which, by the film's conclusion, characters would revert to their initial gender presentation. These plays on gender were never meant to be permanent, but the concept of gender on-screen was forever altered with the news of Christine Jorgensen and her "sex change." In the wake of Jorgensen's reveal, the proliferation of images relating to gender, real and fictional, shifted with new possibilities onscreen.

Christine Jorgensen: Print the Legend

"It was like watching a B-movie, except it was about me!"[4]
Christine Jorgensen in a 1986 public access television interview with Ron Niles regarding the media coverage of her transition

In terms of both medicine and culture as it related to transness, America lagged behind several countries by years, if not decades. Germany had long been the leader in the fields of gender and sexuality. Dr. Magnus Hirschfeld had written and published studies about gay and trans individuals in the early twentieth century and opened the Institute for Sexual Science to treat patients with a trans identity, including performing surgeries. The Institute was also a cultural hub that hosted lectures, discussions, and film screenings.[5] Hirschfeld was dubbed "The Einstein of Sex"[6] and earned worldwide recognition for his work, but when Hitler came to power in the 1930s, the Institute became an instant target. The aim was not just to close the Institute but to eradicate any trace of its mission, and in 1933 the Nazis destroyed the Institute's books, research files on patients, and papers. Hirschfeld — a Nazi target for his Jewish heritage as much as for his scientific studies — died in exile in 1935, shortly after the Institute's destruction. It was an undeniable setback in trans medicine, but that did not stop the rest of Europe from making important advances in medical intervention for trans people, even as the United States dragged its feet on setting up systems and treatments around mental health more generally.

Despite the legend that surrounds her, Christine Jorgensen was not the first American to express a desire to want a "sex change," and certainly not the first to live as a different gender than that assigned at birth. One pre-Jorgensen figure was trans man Dr. Alan Hart, famed for his work on X-ray photography screenings to treat tuberculosis, who had a hysterectomy in 1917 and officially socially transitioned to male while under psychological evaluation and observance. Dr. J. Allen Gilbert would write of Hart in a medical journal that he had taken an "exit as a female and started as a male with a new hold on life."[7] Hart would also take synthetic hormones when they became available in the 1920s, decades before Jorgensen. Hart's procedure was done in secrecy, identified in Dr. Gilbert's writings under the patient code name "H," although despite the covert nature of his transition, Hart would face being outed in the years after.[8]

Even if America lagged behind Europe in surgical inter-

vention, Jorgensen's opportunities to seek out her procedures were made possible by networks of American trans
and cross-dressing people and respected sexology research-
ers in the preceding decade of the 1940s. Sexologist Dr.
David Cauldwell had a paper on transsexualism published
in a sexology journal in 1949.[9] Trans pioneer Louise Lawrence worked with Dr. Alfred Kinsey's famous and influential research on sexual variance and referred Kinsey to many
cross-dressers across America, including those who were
patients of one of the foundational figures of trans medicine in the United States, Dr. Harry Benjamin, a German
exile who was inspired by Dr. Hirschfeld's work.

Trans women patients who were considered fit for surgery by multiple medical professionals during this time,
however, often did not receive it. This was due to medical interventions involving the "changing of the sex" still
being taboo and a potentially "law-breaking" procedure
— existing laws around "medical mayhem," a short-hand
for the removal of "healthy organs" (tied back to soldiers
who intentionally self-injured on the battlefield), had been
invoked in more than one instance in the 1940s to halt
trans surgeries in the United States. It became an effective
legal maneuver to prevent access to trans surgeries domestically.[10] As a result, such surgeries were a rare and deeply
secretive process, even post-Jorgensen.

These institutions of government bureaucracy and medical boards invoking medical mayhem laws did not stop
individuals who sought such treatment; most went abroad
to countries like the Netherlands, Sweden, Denmark, and
Morocco, which had surgeons who were more experienced
and involved in creating the standard procedures of trans
surgeries for decades to come. But it would be ahistorical to
deny the significance and cultural legacy of Christine Jorgensen, who is rightfully seen as a pioneer. To borrow from
John Ford's *The Man Who Shot Liberty Valance*, "When the
legend becomes fact, print the legend!"

Most of the media clamor and intrigue surrounding Jorgensen — with headlines such as "Ex-G.I. Becomes Blonde Beauty" published on December 1st, 1952 in *The New York Daily News* — turned her into a global phenomenon. Due to the public ignorance around the procedure, Jorgensen's sex change led to speculation on whether she could now produce eggs or potentially carry a child to term, especially as many other medical "miracles" such as artificial insemination and sperm banks were also entering mainstream public consciousness.[11]

Jorgensen had an undeniable star-quality, and while not a "bombshell," fulfilled notions of traditional femininity in a way that made any accusations against her of transgressing sex and gender norms seem absurd. For years she stuck with her look: a blonde bouffant wiglet that made her more closely resemble First Lady Pat Nixon than a Marilyn Monroe or Rita Hayworth, and with a force of personality that allowed her to ride the waves of celebrity up until her death in 1989. While she made a reasonable living performing in nightclubs, her talent as a stage or screen presence was modest at best. Despite the founding of the Erickson Educational Foundation (EEF) by Texas trans scion Reed Erickson, which helped make advances in trans medicine domestically, there were not strong community apparatuses, causes, or campaigns for trans rights that Christine Jorgensen could be the national face of. Whether in the newspapers, a Movietone news bulletin, or a television interview centered on her transness, she often had to reintroduce herself to the public repeatedly through the years, giving updates on the ways her life had and had not changed. The "performance" for Christine Jorgensen primarily involved re-telling her story, in having to "live out loud" when she was left without the choice of returning to a conventional life.

Doors did open for Jorgensen. In her famous filmed 1952 press conference at New York's Idlewild Airport (now known as JFK International Airport) after returning to America, she noted how she was offered a movie contract, in which she feigned interest but remained circumspect about her potential stardom. She remained disciplined in what she sought and expected from the media industry, waiting until 1967, nearly fifteen years after her first procedure, to publish her autobiography. It was even reported that she was approached to perform in a film that one could not imagine existing without her story making such waves: Edward Wood Jr.'s *Glen or Glenda* (1953). This film is one of the earliest attempts to translate a popular true story into a trans film image. The film is not without its own set of quirks, and through Wood's unique, at times surreal perspective, becomes a bold take on transsexuality and cross-dressing in public and private life.

Glen or Glenda: A Strange and Curious Subject

Transness and its variances were adopted as subject matter by the movers and shakers of exploitation and B-movie cinema after Christine Jorgensen made headlines. This trend produced works such as William Castle's *Homicidal* (1961) and Doris Wishman's *Let Me Die a Woman* (1977), but the first of these was *Glen or Glenda*. Released a year after Christine Jorgensen's transition became public fodder, the film has long been a notorious work, but it presents itself as a fair, "seeing-all-sides-of-the-issue" picture on the topics of transness and cross-dressing. As stated in the film's opening disclaimer:

> In the making of this film, which deals with a strange and curious subject, no punches have been pulled — no easy way out has been taken. Many of the smaller parts are portrayed by persons who actually are, in real life, the character they portray on the screen. This is a picture of stark realism — taking no sides — but giving you the facts — all the facts as they are today...
> You are society... JUDGE YE NOT!!!!

While Wood's authorship and their own relationship to cross-dressing has long served as a source of speculation, the man who pushed hardest to exploit headlines about Christine Jorgensen was *Glen or Glenda* producer George Weiss, who initially approached Jorgensen to directly use her story, and she rebuked him.[12] *Glen or Glenda* went through multiple possible titles, with *I Changed My Sex* as one, and publicity one-sheets circulated with the title *I Led 2 Lives: Based on the Lives of Christine Jorgensen*.

Made quickly and released in 1953, *Glen or Glenda* has endured not so much for its opening text's plea that people "judge not," but as one of the most notorious "bad" movies ever made. However, the film portrays Wood's Glen dressing up in skirts and angora sweaters as more than mere "eccentricities," and rather as an earnest, anxious, at times introspective act, thereby acknowledging the high stakes of pursuing such personal expression.

While dated in its language and use of medical jargon through the character of Dr. Alton (Timothy Farrell), the film nonetheless makes an explicit separation between those who cross-dress and those who would physically transition. *Glen or Glenda* eagerly explores the differences and conflicts between the then separate categories of transvestism and transsexualism. The film proposes that Glen can have a fulfilling life that conforms to cis-heteronormative masculinity while still having the "character" of Glenda as part of his identity. There is an undeniable poignancy in the scene where Barbara (Dolores Fuller, Wood's real-life girlfriend) takes off her angora sweater and presents it to Glen in a moment of understanding, allowing him to embrace that side of himself through her love. It is also to *Glen or Glenda*'s credit that it addresses how the criminalization of cross-dressing has been responsible for the death of at least one character, Patrick/Patricia, even if the film does not outright call for decriminalization. In the film's conclusion, Dr. Alton advises that "Glenda must be transferred" to Barbara for Glen to "healthily" no longer express his cross-dressing side. The couple follow through on this advice and have their "happy ending." Glenda "disappears."

It cannot be sugar-coated that the film has an awkward, at times incoherent, moralist streak in which the threat of doom for Glen and other "not so fortunate Glens" lingers if they cannot make the *right* decision for themselves. Glen is anxious about what his identity says about him. He imagines being on public trial for being a "gender outlaw" for his cross-dressing and wonders if there is more to it than just a love of feminine dress. There is a scene that features a roar of thunder over an insert shot of a newspaper headline about a sex-change operation, and it is used to cast doubt on that procedure being the right trajectory for a person in Glen's position. Instead, Wood redirects the Glen character into being open about his cross-dressing to those closest to him and proposing that he can thereby maintain a "good life" without making such a drastic change. Nevertheless, the film does feature somebody who would best be served in undergoing such a change.

The film's story of the transsexual Alan/Anne feels siloed in an almost protective way, going to great pains to avoid suggesting that the panic and anxiety that hinders Glen/ Glenda and other characters is comparable to Alan/Anne's life story. But Wood ties Anne and Glenda together on a symbolic level by having both be connected through a motif of the film: when they each catch sight of their own reflections in a department store window when presenting feminine. Anne is played by an unknown, credited as "Tommy" Haynes, a likely pseudonym that provided anonymity to the performer, which leads one to speculate that the performer was themselves transsexual. Anne never speaks in the film; instead, her whole story is told by Dr. Alton in voiceover. On one hand, this gives Anne's story a documentary-like quality, but it also renders her voiceless — a subject who can only be understood through the framework of medical gatekeeping. Glen and the other cross-dresser characters, in contrast, are given full expression in scripted dialogue and with a larger amount of screen-time dedicated to their story. In that respect, Anne also shares a connection to Christine Jorgensen in having her story and image mediated through scientific language and media speculation that rendered her as much a scientific phenomenon as a real person. This is not the only connection Anne shares with Jorgensen. Anne is given a backstory about being an effete young boy who went off to fight in World War II and then got an operation to fulfill their lifelong dream of living as a woman.

An unavoidable question regarding *Glen or Glenda* remains Ed Wood's gender identity. The film would not be a one-off for Wood in terms of performing in drag, with Wood later appearing in his 1970 film *Take It Out in Trade* in female dress, and he authored numerous pulp paperback books centered around cross-dressing. In the years after the film's release, Wood would submit to American female impersonator publications under the persona of "Shirlee," photographed completely made up in dresses and angora sweaters.[13] Wood was fully involved in these close circles of cross-dressing with hardly any attempt to hide their male identity. But *Glen or Glenda* does clearly show his anxieties about his gender at the time in laying out the risks in both society's reaction, as well as the reaction of his loved ones. Wood knows he cannot be the "happy story" of this personal narrative. The film's shift from Glen/Glenda into the other trans film image, Anne, becomes the necessary uplifting, albeit imperfect, trans film image.

Irrespective of Jorgensen's refusal to collaborate with Wood and Weiss on the project, the film remained notorious for decades and was indelibly associated with her and the trans film image itself. That alone grants *Glen or Glenda* a significance above and beyond questions of its qualities as a film. It is also a time capsule of Eisenhower-era conformity, and the inner conflicts among those who wish to be able to truly express themselves, and that extends to the much maligned but courageous and trailblazing writer-director and star of the film, Ed Wood.

Christine: A Celebritization

Christine Jorgensen would not publish her autobiography until 1967, while American trans pioneers like Tamara Rees and Charlotte McLeod self-published or sold the rights of their stories to pulp magazines soon after they were outed in the newspapers. In the time between her public transition and book deal, there were some notable changes in American life for trans people. The year before her memoir was published, Dr. Harry Benjamin published *The Transsexual Phenomenon*. The Erickson Educational Foundation was founded in 1964. Trans societies, newsletters, and publications like Virginia Prince's *Transvestia* were fully active, although discreet. *Transvestia*'s rival publication *Turnabout* (run by Siobhan Fredericks) was not just publishing magazines to networks of trans women and cross-dressers but also had a publishing imprint that put out novels and novellas. Gender clinics were opening across major American cities and universities. Geoff Brown's novel *I Want What I Want* (1966) became a popular work in both cross-dressing and trans circles in the years after its publication. Christine Jorgensen was no longer the sole reference point of transness and gender variance. But there was still something to Jorgensen's mystique in having been "the first," which allowed her to get her memoir, *Christine Jorgensen: A Personal Autobiography*, published by the prestigious Bantam Books years after she first made headlines.

The memoir was quintessentially Christine Jorgensen in her frankness and self-deprecating humor, speaking highly of her tolerant, loving parents, and her love of photography and filmmaking with her aspiration of wanting to make documentary non-fiction films — one of her earliest jobs as an ex-GI involved working in the cutting department for RKO–Pathé News as an editor.

Christine Jorgensen: A Personal Autobiography doubles as a showbiz and trans memoir. Jorgensen makes it clear she preferred making dignified appearances on-camera and on-stage as opposed to salacious ones. Reviews of her stage show had some brutal responses, and she references in her book how certain pans from the trade papers left her thinking that she had "laid one of the biggest eggs in show business history."[14] She questioned if the movie business was even for her and began to regard Hollywood as her nemesis rather than as an opportunity, and yet the film rights were sold and *The Christine Jorgensen Story* was going to be made. Little did Jorgensen know, however, a major public figure had seen her story and flipped it on its head with his own tale about Hollywood, taste, gender, sex, and power, which would also go from the page to the silver screen. Gore Vidal's *Myra Breckinridge*, published a year after Christine Jorgensen's memoir, was an instant success. The film adaptation of the book was also, in a twist of fate, released in 1970, the same year as *The Christine Jorgensen Story*.

Myra Breckinridge and the Salacious Trans Imaginary

"Gore Vidal doesn't know what a transsexual is. He created a sadistic homosexual. He doesn't tell a story. He knocks everything and never sees any good. He's an overblown stuffed shirt who does nothing but write trash!"[15]

Christine Jorgensen on Gore Vidal and *Myra Breckinridge*

By the mid-1960s, Gore Vidal had been a prominent cultural figure and public intellectual for several years, having worked on successful productions in theater and in film as a studio contract screenwriter, most famously with *Ben-Hur* and *Suddenly, Last Summer*, as well as publishing well-received historical fiction with his breakthrough gay novel, *The City and the Pillar*. His 1968 novel *Myra Breckinridge* tells the story of Myron Breckinridge, who flies to Denmark to undergo a sex-change operation, becoming the beautiful, voluptuous, sex-crazed Myra in the process. The film adaptation would follow the plot mechanics of the novel with a few notable departures, such as Myra's operation not being in Denmark, but instead a public spectacle at an unknown hospital in Hollywood, in an operating theater lit like a movie set. Myra (Raquel Welch) goes to her uncle Buck Loner's (John Huston) Hollywood acting school, where she pretends to be her own widow and claims that it was in Myron's will that she receives half the school, or $500,000. Myra's identity becomes the subject of investigation for Buck, who ultimately finds out that there is no death certificate for Myron. Myra later discloses to her uncle her trans identity through a peepshow-esque upskirt reveal.

While in Hollywood, Myra seeks to destroy "traditional manhood" by "realigning the sexes" in terms of power balance. She crosses paths with Leticia Van Allen (Mae West), a talent agent who has a gender-roles-reversed casting couch where a gaggle of men line up for her. Myra becomes obsessed with a pair of young lovers named Rusty (Roger Herren) and Mary Ann (Farrah Fawcett), each of whom she believes personify the traditional man and woman. One night, Myra lures Rusty, ties him to a table and anally rapes him with a strap-on. The assault causes Rusty to have a nervous breakdown and abandon Mary Ann. Myra uses the pair's breakup to move in on Mary Ann herself, with whom she engages in a love affair, but Mary Ann rejects a more serious relationship, stating she prefers men. This throws a wrench in Myra's pursuit of fortune, fame, and upending of sexual norms and, largely, the story's narrative trajectory. In the film, a manifestation of Myron (played by film critic Rex Reed) runs Myra down in a car. While in the novel Myron does transition, the film employs the narrative trope of the dream-ending, upon which Myron awakens in the hospital after a car accident, not gender reassignment, with Mary Ann at his bedside as a nurse. Looking at his bedside table, Myron sees a magazine with Raquel Welch on the cover, reduced to being a mere dream avatar of his trans-feminine imaginary.

The novel was a satire of the gender norms and hyper-masculine mores of both old and new Hollywood and plays out on the page as something of an in-joke that got out of hand. As a satire, *Myra Breckinridge* cannot really be seen as a typical trans narrative in comparison to a memoir like Jorgensen's, or to Wendy Ross in Geoff Brown's *I Want What I Want*. According to Vidal, it took him a considerable amount of writing before he made Myra a trans woman. Gay author Christopher Isherwood (*Berlin Stories* and *A Single Man*), to whom Vidal dedicated the book, considered the novel closer to self-portraiture of Vidal in its depiction of a tyrannical, self-assured personality with a voracious sexual appetite that matches their wit, intellect, and love of the past.[16] The book was written during the highpoint of the counterculture and gestured subversively at low-culture and queer camp with some instantly recognizable references to those in the know — for example, Myra's surname being taken from Ed Wood player, Bunny Breckinridge (famously played by Bill Murray in Burton's *Ed Wood*). The book was panned, with *Time Magazine* asking, "Has literary decency fallen so low?"[17] Nonetheless, it was a bestseller, with the lewdness that critics and literary circles condemned being the main draw for readers.

Myra Breckinridge, the film, went from being the talk of Hollywood to one of the most misbegotten disaster projects of its era. The film was a zany, postmodern, and self-referential satire essentially aimed at Hollywood at a crossroads, with the Old Hollywood studio system as people knew it collapsing and the New Hollywood of the Seventies on the horizon. It is notable that film industry scion Richard Zanuck — who paid Vidal a six-figure sum for the film rights — wanted to make it as a Twentieth Century-Fox film, believing that adapting a hit contemporary novel was an opportunity to get with the times. The pre-production for the film stressed its potential as a box-office winner, with A-listers including Elizabeth Taylor, Barbra Streisand, Anne Bancroft, and Jeanne Moreau rumored to be vying for the role of Myra.[18] The role was actively sought. Even cross-dressers and trans women, including a then twenty-five-year-old Candy Darling, tried out for the part of Myra.[19] George Cukor was approached to direct and was favored by the film's co-screenwriter and co-producer David Giler (who later worked on the *Alien* film series and *The Parallax View*).[20] In retrospect, it can only be imagined what Cukor would have done with this film, especially given that he had played with gender norms so audaciously in *Sylvia Scarlett* decades before.

The film was eventually helmed by British director Michael Sarne, who was better known as a pop singer. The on-set tensions and his erratic behavior during the making of the film became the stuff of legend. The film's explicitness, vulgarity, formal messiness, and heavy-handed symbolism was expressed most concisely in a sequence replete with cutaways to old Hollywood movies in which Myra, dressed in a Stars and Stripe bikini, sexually assaults Rusty with a strap-on dildo. Such a scene also made it earn the reputation of being among the worst films ever made. Perhaps the film's most salient commentary is that machismo and traditional masculinity needed to be discarded, subverted, and transgressed not just on an industry level but on a personal level too. Although nobody would ever confuse Vidal for a feminist, let alone consider *Myra Breckinridge* a feminist work, his critiques of the patriarchal structures in both the old and new Hollywood were certainly shared by many feminists.

Myra Breckinridge does not commit fully to its trans film image, functioning as a contained, temporary narrative of trans embodiment, using the public interest of the Jorgensen story as a springboard. Yet the film holds the fantastical imaginary of trans femininity up as both an idol and as an anarchic subversive sally against gender norms. With its inserts of older work that tested the limits of copyright laws, a deliberate clashing of many film styles and featuring several generations of Hollywood stardom from Raquel Welch to John Huston and Mae West, it is riotous, outrageous, shocking, tedious, and impossible to defend in matters of good taste. With all that, even if it trades on the public's salacious fascination with Jorgenson, it is still an essential work in discussing Hollywood's interest and limitations in addressing the trans film image. Its transgressive quality as a novel drew people into making the film, but in execution *Myra Breckinridge* showed how Hollywood at the time could only muster a sense of pranksterism rather than earnestly devote any serious considerations in producing a trans film image.

A Biopic and its Discontents

Where *Myra Breckinridge* represented a failed foray into New Hollywood, *The Christine Jorgensen Story* was built on the shoulders of the old guard and made under the auspices of United Artists, although its press notes show that it was via UA's Exploitation Department.[21] Christine Jorgensen was a technical advisor on the production and took the role so seriously that she and her family loaned out heirlooms and jewelry pieces to the actors. Produced by the prolific Edward Small (whose credits included everything from *Witness for the Prosecution* and the Elvis Presley headliner *Frankie and Johnny*), Irving Rapper — best known for his work with Bette Davis, including on her widely regarded career-best film, *Now, Voyager* (1942) — was chosen to tell Christine Jorgensen's story.

In theory, Rapper seemed a good fit for the project. While never an auteur at the level of his contemporaries, such as George Cukor or Raoul Walsh, his films were sturdy vessels for his actors; he worked multiple times with Bette Davis, and in other films with the likes of Ginger Rogers, Kirk Douglas and Barbara Stanwyck. His films were functionally star vehicles — particularly his work with Davis. In interviews and press notes, it was always suggested that Rapper was hired because of his "sensitivity" as a director.[22] It is true that *The Christine Jorgensen Story* is sensitive and attempts a base-level empathy, but Rapper's images are dull, and the direction is neither creative nor engaging enough to drive the narrative forward. He does not have a Bette Davis to fall back on.

Instead, John Hansen plays Christine Jorgensen, both before and after transition. Physically, Hansen is a conventionally good-looking young American man with broad shoulders and sandy blond hair — he looks like a football player, and in no way resembles Christine prior to her medical transition. Hansen was in his first film role, and it shows. His acting leans on broad, melodramatic flourishes, as does the film with an unsubtle orchestral score and an equally unsubtle metaphorizing of Christine's gender anxieties — best epitomized in a scene during Army basic training where the tortured lead cannot stop seeing images of girl's dolls while in this highly masculine, dangerous environment. Christine considers suicide by drowning, but after coming out about her gender identity to a female friend, goes on her journey to understand her condition and change herself for the better.

In essence, the film is a glorified TV movie with the didactic intent of teaching tolerance about a sexual minority that had rarely been given space in the public discourse. It is difficult for any issue film — or biopic for that matter — to escape the limitations of their genre, and *The Christine Jorgensen Story* fails both as art and as a document of Jorgensen's transition. The film has some moments of trans-femininity that feel authentic, such as the flashbacks to her youth where childhood wonder and feminine longing collide with Jorgensen in adolescence (played by Trent Lehman) not understanding why they cannot have what they want. Ultimately, the film failed to retain any longstanding interest as a cultural object in the public sphere or in cinephile spaces and, at best, remains a curiosity, as do many other films about transness from the early 1970s. The film lacks the enduring images and performances that Jorgensen's story deserves.

Where *The Christine Jorgensen Story* did have real significance, however, was in setting the template for stories of
transness, with later films using the structure of her biopic
as a narrative model — becoming the dominant storytelling
mode for the next five decades in mainstream filmmaking.
Biographical details, such as her wish to play with dolls at a
young age, her inherent femininity as a child, and the scientific basis for her transition — rooted in hormonal imbal-
ance and a potential intersex diagnosis — became hallmarks
of what was expected of trans women looking to medically
transition in real life. It was not just that Jorgensen was the
trans person that most Americans knew, but that her story
became the life trajectory that trans women were expected
to inhabit, and it is only recently that what is understood as
the transition narrative of a trans woman has become more
variegated.

When Susan Stryker made the short film *Christine in the
Cutting Room*, it was a speculative work where it was not just
imagined that Christine Jorgensen was speaking directly to
the audience, but that she had also, through her training
with film news reels, edited and put together this montage
of images to highlight the "Age of Anxiety" of the 1950s, of
which she was one of the most notable products. "I had been
a photographer and filmmaker who became a performer,"
this Christine Jorgensen notes in how the spectacle of her
existence launched her as a celebrity. Images of Julius and
Ethel Rosenberg, civil rights unrest including lynchings, the
mushroom clouds of a nuclear bomb, colorized television
commercial presentations, scientists, cartoons, Godzilla,
kitschy UFO special effects, and Jorgensen herself, both
in the public eye and intimate photos of her vacationing,
holding a camera, eager to capture an image for her own.
The public image of Christine Jorgensen versus the private
image are wrestled with during the short, and Jorgensen,
as imagined by Stryker, firmly asserts her place in history
through cutting narration:

I was the bomb dropped on the gender system that blew up the body's meaning. I was the destroyer of binaries for a world split in two. Knowledge imploded into a black hole of knowability, and its radiation spawned mutant amalgamations of fact and fantasy like me.

In a way, Stryker's version of Jorgensen takes a verve of approaching the atomic age and its semiotics much like the novel *Myra Breckinridge* took in its protagonist's fervor for the Hollywood Golden Age. *Christine in the Cutting Room* postulates what Jorgensen, if given the opportunity to make films rather than have her image and story ripped off by others, could have done.

There has not yet been an attempt as bold as Stryker's to reintroduce Jorgensen in a way that flips the script, where the subject is now confronting the viewer. There was the HBO Max mini-series *Equal* in which trans actress Jamie Clayton (*Sense8* and *The L Word: Generation Q*) dressed up and spoke in Jorgensen's unmistakably mannered transatlantic accent, but her story was among many in that series and was presented like a living history museum reenactment in breaking the fourth wall to the viewer.

Christine Jorgensen showed us the limits of celebritization around transness that continued to cycle with newer faces from different corners of the world becoming the trans figure *du jour*, albeit predominately white Western trans women. Jorgensen set the blueprint for how many trans stories would be told in various forms of media. It is a testament to her influence. But it also shows how the media so often defaulted to her because she had no choice but to negotiate her image with public fascination from the onset. One of her last filmed appearances before her death in 1989 would be in Lee Grant's 1985 America Undercover documentary, *What Sex Am I?*, where she is seen as the respected elder figure of the wide array of trans people interviewed. Perhaps one day somebody will move forward to tell her entire life story through her passing. John Hansen in a blonde wig leaves a lot to be desired when considering the legend of Christine Jorgensen. She was the lodestar and reference point for all things transness for so many years, even after her death; an avatar of transness in the United States and the world.

CHAPTER 2
On the Cusp of Stonewall:
Trans Film Images in the 1960s

During the 1960s, trans film images became more varied. A consistent source of these images were B-movies that often presented trans bodies as fetish objects and the subject matter as a taboo. No doubt, many of these images were exoticized, but in certain collaborations and in some instances, there was a progression away from abstract, exotic notions of transness towards giving trans people a voice. The decade started, however, with many trans film images whose provocative allure was the film's *raison d'être*.

One source of interest in trans images was the fascination with modern medicine as gender clinics began to pop up across North America. Another was the rise of trans celebrities, particularly non-American trans women who were initially known for being female impersonators, such as Coccinelle (Jacqueline Dufresnoy), Bambi (Marie-Pierre Pruvot), and April Ashley. All worked and performed in Paris, France as cabaret showgirls at places like Madame Arthur's and Le Carrousel de Paris, which also featured numerous other trans women, many of whom also started as female impersonators — in fact, many programs from the time show the performers in and out of female dress. Just like Christine Jorgensen, Coccinelle and Bambi made headlines when both trans women went to Casablanca to go under the knife of surgeon Dr. Georges Burou, one of the most in-demand surgeons of the era, credited with inventing modern "bottom surgery."[1]

What made Bambi and Coccinelle distinct was that their bodies were on display as performers, and their transness was tied to their allure as showgirls. This was in marked contrast to other publicly significant trans women of the time, such as ex-military vets like Christine Jorgensen or English trans woman Roberta Cowell (whose transition predated Jorgensen's and received an equivalent fanfare). The pin-ups of trans women and cross-dressers in publications like *Female Mimics*, which featured and sold many photos of Bambi and Coccinelle, meant that their bodies and images were not simply objects of desire, but aspirational for many.

Stardom was similarly not afforded to Bambi and Coccinelle in a way that led to a serious future in screen acting. However, they did become trans film images, primarily in travel films that promoted the tourism of Paris. For example, Coccinelle's appearance in 1959's *European Nights* (Alessandro Blasetti), a hybrid of documentary and scripted dialogue in the tradition of many filmed musical revues, which highlights her as the centerpiece of a musical number. Similarly, performance as exhibition, with a hint of exoticism, was the trans film image for Bambi in films like Vittorio Sala's *Costa Azzurra* (1959). (Coccinelle would later appear in another of Sala's films, 1962's *Beach Casanova*.)

The majority of Bambi and Coccinelle's subsequent appearances through the 1960s were as "themselves" and rarely explored or gave any deeper context to their work as performers. One exception was Coccinelle's appearance in the 1962 Argentine film *Los viciosos*; after giving an erotically charged performance of the pop song "Twist Lessons," there is a sequence in which she is followed backstage and asked questions by a male member of the press that turns into a professional interview.

The other side of these film appearances for both women, as well as many trans women and cross-dressers who undertook sex work at this time, was the world of Mondo and sexploitation. Bambi appeared in the "nudie" film *Day of a Stripper* (1964) and the famous Mondo filmmaker Mino

Loy's movie *90 notti in giro per il mondo* (*90 Nights Around the World*) (1963), while Cocinelle appeared in the "shockumentary" *Mondo Inferno* (1964), co-directed by Sergio Leone collaborator Antonio Margheriti, which juxtaposed the exoticism of transness alongside modern slavery, snake charmers, and bullfighting in a travelogue of the extremes. Even Christine Jorgensen participated, appearing in the 1962 Filipino musical film *Kaming Mga Talyada: We Who Are Sexy* (directed by Tony Cayado). Susan Stryker describes Jorgensen's involvement as "offering different possibilities for pleasure and identification," and elaborating a theme that is equally applicable to the trans film images of Bambi and Cocinelle, "enacting a culturally legible womanliness divorced from a biologically female sex, becomes decorative or ornamental, beautiful in an aesthetic sense, but no longer reproductively functional; she exists solely as image and spectacle."[2] Their scenes were often brief but highlighted promotional material to act as a draw. In moving with the more sexually liberated times, trans film images were shifting beyond the demure Christine Jorgensen and into more sexualized realms.

These types of Mondo films, which actively promoted trans film images, were shot exclusively by cisgender outsiders. There were very few instances of true collaboration that happened between director and performer. Bambi would have more say, collaborating in old age with director Sebastien Lifshitz on a biographical documentary titled, simply, *Bambi* (2013), which is a treasure trove of archival footage and intimate home movies from her showbiz years.

"Transploitation" as Autobiography: *I Was a Man*

Ansa Kansas is rarely discussed in trans or cross-dressing circles today. This is a loss, as her later-in-life transition story makes her 1967 autobiopic, *I Was a Man* by journeyman filmmaker Barry Mahon. The film was not only a novel film for its time, but one that, despite all its quirks as an exploitation work, reveals enduring truths about those who cordon off their lives as trans people until it becomes untenable.

I Was a Man begins with a white-jacket sequence (a scene where a doctor describes something in a matter-of-fact way). The doctor describes Kansas as a "hermaphrodite" who could potentially adopt cross-dressing, transsexualism, or homosexuality as a way of dealing with their non-normative biology. Kansas is cast as herself and portrays her own life story as a Finnish immigrant in New York who worked a blue-collar job but had a "secret." While presenting as a man, she works in a heavily masculine field as a sea merchant and often finds herself working in the domestic space of the ship's kitchen, but on occasion goes out with the fraternal group of sailors at bars. While the men scoop up girls, Kansas struggles to interact and engage in the typical masculine carousing, and later cannot perform in the male sexual role. When Kansas is alone, she goes out, spending a day in Coney Island in a dress, makeup, and wig. But at close quarters, she is deeply cautious, in one scene running into a closet with a nightgown she has bought when a friend stops by.

Kansas sees a doctor to "end this masquerade," reframing the idea of transness as a masquerade by stating that, for her, dressing as a man is the true disguise. The doctor notes her anxiety and sadness, but remarks on her being middle-aged and therefore too old to transition — a legacy from the Jorgensen story and other trans narratives produced at the time, whose subjects were in their twenties. Kansas is steadfast in her belief that it is not too late and so she returns to her native Helsinki to transition. Back in New York, she comes out to friends and coworkers who are surprised but generally understanding, some of them retrospectively realizing why she conducted herself the way she did. Her life as a sea merchant ends and she becomes a nightclub act, during which she tells stories reframing her experiences with the lightness of touch and humor that permeates *I Was a Man*. At the end, over a scene of a school yard of children playing, Kansas states she is happy and hopes for a better future where those younger than her can get the same kind of help she did.

The film's poignancy and earnestness are unusual for its time in that the transition narrative not only incorporates a real trans woman but allows her to tell her own story. It is important to note, though, that the presence of the trans person in the exploitation genre was often merely to serve as a fetish object with little agency or internality, and usually without involving a trans person in the trans role. In that regard, *I Was a Man* is a rare but notable exception.

Two Queens Enter, One Leaves: On *She-Man: A Story of Fixation*

"The film that you are about to see has to do with a better understanding of our fellow man. We have gathered the information as intelligently and as honestly as within our power and potential. And would like to portray to you as intellectually as our medium will permit in the findings of our research."

Dr. Louis C. Pessolano, M.D., introducing *She-Man: A Story of Fixation*

She-Man: A Story of Fixation (1967) has reappeared recently, largely due to the interest of cinephiles, including Danish auteur Nicolas Winding Refn, who helped in its being restored. In 1967, then unknown Canadian director Bob Clark (*A Christmas Story* and *Black Christmas)* took on the task of making a B-movie full of famous American female impersonators in the notoriously swampy, humid Florida summer as his feature-film debut.

The film follows the pattern of the exploitation B-movie with a focus on transness by having a white-jacket figure open and close the film by speaking directly to the camera. This was a common way for sex and shocksploitation films to be granted legitimacy and evade censorship. However, even before the viewer gets to the film's white-jacket figure of legitimation, it opens with a real-time scene of a silhouette of a female impersonator undressing behind a partition and putting on masculine clothes as an exotic lounge music score plays.

She-Man follows an American soldier on leave named Albert Rose (Leslie Marlowe) vacationing in Florida. Suddenly, he gets taken to a dark room, where he is confronted by a mysterious, shadowy vampish figure with a long cigarette who has compromising information on him. This figure wants a year of Albert's life in exchange for suppressing this information.

"Do I have a choice?" asks Albert.

"No!" The villainess purrs as the lights come on and a curtain opens to reveal a female impersonator named Dominita (played by New York City and Club 82 female impersonator fixture Dorian Wayne). She toasts Albert to "A year of change" with a champagne glass. Wayne's performance presents a fascinating forerunner to Divine's Babs Johnson and Dawn Davenport characters in *Pink Flamingos* (1973) and *Female Trouble* (1974), with a dash of the Disney villain Maleficent from *Sleeping Beauty* (1959). Wayne would work as a Broadway dresser, never getting a bigger role than this, although she did direct home movies of herself and various female mimic friends in drag that bear comparison to the Gay Girls Riding Club movies put out by Ray Harrison in Southern California's underground film scene.

On the surface, Albert's transformation in *She-Man* conforms to the typical "force-femme" narrative that was often associated with sex fetish communities and publications at the time, although the feminization he undergoes does include hormones. What is notable about *She-Man*, however, is that Albert Rose, who becomes Rose Albert, is not the only character in the film who goes through a "year of change." A female character is put into a "butch" transformation to live as a man. There are other queer-coded and gender non-conforming individuals who work under Dominita as well, all of whom share the common issue of being at the mercy of Dominita and her blackmail, even in some cases doing her bidding by spying on others. The set-up in some ways anticipates John Waters' *Desperate Living* (1977), with Dominita's Florida estate as the precursor to Queen Carlotta's oppressive Mortville.

What also makes Albert's "force-femme" narrative interesting is the fact this is not simply a "man in a dress" being traumatized by a "violent transvestite." He accepts his change and becomes a polished female impersonator. Given Albert's role as the protagonist of the story who ultimately takes Dominita down, you cannot say the effectiveness of his transformation was due to being brainwashed. As Rose Albert, Marlowe's performance becomes a lot more entertaining and physical compared to the lumbering, stiff Albert Rose viewers are introduced to at the start of the film. It is clear within this gender-play that Marlowe much prefers performing as a woman, which adds a certain complication to the text, something connected to the fact that the role of Albert is played by another real-life female impersonator, Leslie Marlowe, who was just as much of a presence in the New York scene as Wayne was. The film ends with Albert defeating Dominita and falling in love with one of Dominita's lackeys, Ruth (Wendy Roberts), along with an incoherent postscript by the white-jacket. But in this decisive moment of good prevailing over evil, Albert's victory comes while being Rose.

Rose, however, remains the dominant image of the film, defeating Dominita not by dominating her through masculinity, but by going toe-to-toe, high-heels-to-high-heels, with her in drag, and strongly resembling Dominita's own old Hollywood look, countering Dominita's riding crop whip by smacking her with a purse. Dominita's wig comes off, yet Albert does not slip out of his Rose wig in victory; instead, in a mannered lisp with pursed lips, he reveals Dominita's real backstory as an Army deserter (whose self-inflicted gunshot is implied to be an attempt at self-castration) to everyone who was under her control. Dominita is a "violent transvestite," and yet it is not polite society that takes her down, but instead her mirror image, a double of her own creation. In this enclosed world of outsiders, *She-Man* feels liberated from the normative forces of the status quo: a film that exists within its own enclosed trans-universe.

Question Time: *Queens at Heart*

When *She-Man* was released to adult movie theaters, it had a lead-in: the documentary medical film *Queens at Heart*. Its origins are still unknown — there is no official credited director — nor is it known how exactly it was funded. The original negative was lost, with its recent preservation being achieved through remaining projection prints. The authority figure in this film is a folksy personality named Jay Martin, presumably a television newscaster with no white jacket or medical degree to his name, who interviews four trans women picked from Drag Ball Beauty Contests across the country. Their names are Misty, Vicky, Sonja, and Simone. Martin talks directly to the audience to explain that they are going by first name only as these are drag queens who are "breaking the law."

Queens at Heart was released a year after the Compton's Cafeteria Riot, a pre-Stonewall riot primarily led by trans women and cross-dressers in August 1966 at a late dining establishment in San Francisco's Tenderloin District. The Compton's Cafeteria Riot is still not given its proper due in LGBTQ history, and many details of the event remain hazier than the Stonewall Riots. Compton's "screaming queens" — as they were later known, thanks to Susan Stryker's film with Victor Silverman, *Screaming Queens: The Riots at Compton's Cafeteria* (2005) — came under fire because cross-dressing as a "masquerade" was still a criminal offense in San Francisco at the time. This group of trans women and cross-dressers, many of them sex workers attempting to patronize the Compton's Cafeteria, were met with hostility from the space's management.[3] The cops were called, and instead of suffering another embarrassing, potentially life-ruining trip to the paddy wagon, the queens fought back. Coffee was thrown at officers, in addition to tables, utensils, and salt-and-pepper shakers. Protests and pickets then followed against Compton's and against the violence perpetrated by the San Francisco police. The Mondo film *Gay San Francisco* (1970), likely the first film to reference Compton's, described this major moment in trans resistance: "So frequent were the fights between screaming queens in the 2:00 to 3:00 a.m. period that police — even in permissive San Francisco — had had enough and asked an all-night cafeteria to close by midnight!"

Queens at Heart, likely filmed in 1965, captures pre-Stonewall queer life with scenes of vividly colorful drag balls and competitions. There are unfortunately no soundbites provided from these events, with the dialogue consisting solely of Martin's questions and the queens' varied answers, although no current version of *Queens at Heart* includes any answers from Misty. They are all given the same questions: "When did they 'first know' they were different?", "What do they want?", "Who are they attracted to?", "Who knows about their life?", and "Was there anything in the 'earlier days' that proved to be a significant moment that led them to where they are now?" In its twenty-minute runtime, *Queens at Heart* explores several multifaceted issues surrounding transness and trans films images. Sonja, for instance, details how her body has responded to hormones, mentioning that almost no man she has dated really cared about her identity and how her budget is spent entirely on her wardrobe. Simone is upfront that she has lived a "double-life," with one notable detail being that she wore makeup when she faced the Vietnam War draft board to be turned away, underscoring how cross-dressing was made into a joke in the television show *M*A*S*H*. In that series, cross-dressing character Max Klinger (Jamie Farr) actively sought a Section 8 discharge (to be discharged for being seen as 'mentally unfit' for service, which was often used against LGBTQ service members and draftees) to avoid getting drafted.

Simone mentions putting in the extra effort to hide her feminine side from her parents and siblings, a situation that will have been complicated by the fact that she has just started hormones. Both Sonja and Simone reveal an interest in surgery, with Simone specifically mentioning she wants to go to Casablanca and get the modern Dr. Burou treatment in preference to seeing an American surgeon. The only time the film deviates from its claim to be educational is when Martin asks Simone to talk about giving fellatio to men. Simone is easily the most dominant trans image in the film and responds playfully to Martin's questions about her figure and physicality. When she tells Martin she is six feet tall and he remarks that she is one of the taller drag queens he has seen, she immediately responds in a moment dripping with star-power, "But I am one of the more beautiful ones, darling!" as she smirks, chewing gum.

Vicky, in contrast, is the most anxious presence: quite visibly uncomfortable on camera, trembling and emotional, stressing how medical transition is necessary for her as it is "a step away from loneliness and suicide." A filmed reenactment shows how she must balance living in two worlds and how she goes into "male drag" for her job as a hairdresser to "conform to conventions" and accumulate money for her operation, all while feeling like an imposter. Cameras follow her on the streets of New York where she looks at women in envy and at store windows getting excited about the displays of women's clothing from dresses to undergarments. Initially constrained by its own formal conventions in being structured around a set of questions, Queens at Heart opens in these little moments of the everyday, which for a moment add an extra dimension to these trans film images, de-exoticizing them and emphasizing their autonomy and humanity. Even with some dated features, Queens at Heart is still a valuable, insightful look of trans women of the past.

A Day in the Life

"You know the saying, 'Behind every good man, there's a woman!'"
Trans subject in *Behind Every Good Man*

The possibilities in trans film images, beyond being merely transition tales or stories from the subcultures of a particular time and place, were already being explored in the 1960s. As a UCLA film student, Nikolai Ursin (who would later be a cinematographer for a number 1970s gay pornography films and the experimental films of Bruce and Norman Yonemoto) shot a hybrid of documentary and scripted fiction to depict the everyday life of a trans woman, much like the sequence with Vicky in *Queens at Heart*. *Behind Every Good Man* (1967) is a stunning eight-minute document focusing on a trans woman of color that, in 2022, was added to the National Film Registry in the United States and was restored by the UCLA Film and Television Archive.

In the first half of the film, viewers encounter a montage of a black trans woman walking the streets of Los Angeles and trying on clothes, alongside reaction shots of men who gawk at her as she walks by. She speaks openly about wanting to marry a man in her narration and the film takes that aspiration seriously. The subject exchanges looks with a man and they hit it off as Dionne Warwick's version of "Reach Out for Me" plays. The intensity of the conversation causes her to miss her bus, but results in a date.

The second half of the film shows her at home, dressing up, going from underwear to her dress, makeup, and wig as Dusty Springfield's "Wishin' and Hopin'" builds up anticipation for what this candlelit dinner-date holds. She narrates how she in many ways eschews gender norms, such as walking into the men's bathroom only to be apprehended by an undercover cop very casually, not unlike Ansa Kansas mentioning being arrested in her act in *I Was a Man*. It later becomes clear that she is staying in for the night and expects the man, the same man that made her miss her bus, to show up for dinner. The heroine waits in her candlelit apartment as her record player plays "I'll Turn to Stone" by the Supremes. Will a man come into her space and stay there? Will he ever come? It is left unclear how much he knows about her and if such knowledge has led to cold feet on his part. With the fleeting sense of being stood up washing over the subject, it becomes a quietly heartbreaking ending. The trans film image is shown wanting to be loved and cared for, but the reaction society has to a black trans woman, of anti-blackness and anti-transness, shows the vulnerability in having such needs and desires.

A Time of Separate Categories

In the twenty-first century, the gay, lesbian, and bisexual communities have taken a more conscious role in working with the trans community — after decades of a tempestuous relationship — by affirming the trans community's place in their broader, big-tent coalition. But what is often missed in such coalition-building is the complicated histories in the nuances of trans identity. In many ways, the use of the term "transgender" rather than the term "transsexual" was itself a reparative action designed to bring together small groups of people under a larger umbrella. It is important to outline how transness today is a consolidation of many identities and groups that were previously separate. The Stonewall Riots are seen as the dawn of a new age for gay liberation, but both prior to Stonewall and after, LGBTQ rights remain a complicated issue due to various groups in some cases having hostile relationships.

Some of these divisions are exemplified by two famous patients of Dr. Harry Benjamin: Christine Jorgensen (who only sought the attention of men after she transitioned and spoke openly about not identifying with the gay community at any point before her transition) and Virginia Price (a trans woman who initially identified as a heterosexual male cross-dresser), who he saw as the archetypes of the "transsexual" and the "transvestite" respectively.[4] For decades, these were treated as separate categories by the medical establishment, and within the category of transvestite there was further separation by sexuality — those who cross-dressed but were attracted to men, and those who were attracted to women.

The problem with this kind of categorization is that it fails to see how these two individuals exist within a larger spectrum. The trans women in *Queens at Heart*, who all came from the gay community but then lived as transvestites and had an interest in getting surgeries, are just one example that complicates Benjamin's taxonomy of transsexual and transvestite.

This shows that, while an important figure, as a man of his time there are a lot of complicated aspects to Benjamin's role in trans medicine. Most of this was tied to cross-dressing being considered a crime of masquerade across the country. Another was that the categories of homosexuality, transvestism, and transsexuality were seen as disorders, something which made the arguments for medical intervention in the case of transsexuals more controversial. With the publication of *Transsexual Phenomenon* in 1966, Benjamin created the Harry Benjamin International Gender Dysphoria Association (HBIGDA) as a broad organization that could supply legal, medical, and psychological programs and research for transgender people in need. This would later be known as the World Professional Association of Transgender Health (WPATH). WPATH still exists today and, since 1979, has provided the medical protocols for transgender people known as the "Standards of Care."

While it cannot be overstated how important it was for these protocols and apparatuses to be put into place and to build a system of professional care within the United States, it was a system immediately vulnerable to bigotry, biases, and gatekeeping. Over the coming years, Standards of Care became a lightning rod for controversy in the arbitrary ways the goalposts would often be moved from one trans patient to the next. In the 1960s, the "perfect" transsexual often had to be sexually attracted to the opposite sex. To be seen as a candidate for invasive surgeries, trans women would have to only be with men and trans men only with women. This created many problems for designated "transvestites" who had predilections for wanting these surgeries. Often, they were simply told to stay in their category of "cross-dresser."[5] But in the 1960s, in addition to battles against medical gatekeepers, these struggles led to inter-community battles and conflicts among the small groups running against the currents of the big-tent activism of other minority communities.

Divisions between cross-dressers and trans women were reinforced, less due to an inherent animus between these communities, and more because, as we have seen, the medical community that dealt with issues on gender sought to separate them into the categories of "transvestite" and "transsexual." However, certain privileged people in powerful positions did also try to impose these divisions on the community, one being among the most significant figures of the trans and cross-dressing movements in the mid-twentieth century, Virginia Prince.

Prince advocated for cross-dressers rights, but in turn wished for straight cross-dressers to distance and separate themselves from cross-dressers who identified as homosexuals and away from transsexuals; she advised her cross-dresser groups and readers of her publication *Transvestia* to follow her lead. This included controlling membership of one of her groups, the Foundation for Personality Expression (FPE).[6] She famously went to the discreet upstate New York cross-dressing enclave in the Catskills known as Casa Susanna to explicitly state this to the close company in attendance (which included numerous patrons who would later transition). This specific interaction, and Prince's overall complicated legacy, were featured in Sebastien Lifshitz's documentary, *Casa Susanna* (2022).

Prince came from money and had marriages and relationships with women, hence her status initially as a heterosexual transvestite. She was not without virtues, such as risking potential obscenity felonies to keep *Transvestia* running.[7] But Prince saw the rights of straight cross-dressers as separate from the rights of the gay liberation movement, whether they were homosexual men, street queens, drag queens, or gay cross-dressers, which was, in retrospect, baked into the respectability politics of that period that Jorgensen and many trans pioneers abided to. But unlike Jorgensen, Prince was also something of a hypocrite; she made her own feminizing hormones and altered her body, much like the trans women from whom she wanted to distance herself. She would later be part of the great gender variance and trans umbrella, right alongside the people she had previously pushed away. By 1968, Prince had dropped out of identifying as a straight cross-dresser and was living fully as a woman.[8]

Prince's active gatekeeping and exclusionary practices on a community-level were not widely embraced even among her own ranks, however. Many alternative trans and cross-dressing publications popped up in the 1960s, such as *Turnabout*, whose contributors included Darrell G. Raynor, the pseudonym of renowned science-fiction writer and cross-dresser Donald A. Wollheim, whose 1966 cross-dresser book *A Year Among the Girls* became such a sensation it was later republished in 1968. In an even more significant turn of events, many *Transvestia* readers, contributors, and FPE members did go on hormones and transition, regardless of Pierce's decrees. Prince would later admit her mistakes, although tensions between herself and her trans peers, as well as younger trans people, continued up until her death in 2009.

Virginia Prince remains a difficult figure to discuss. To acknowledge her role in trans history requires balancing her controversial and outright wrong beliefs with all her groundbreaking, courageous work. In many respects, Prince was as consequential as Jorgensen. Though her notoriety was built on an insistence on discretion, she appeared on television talk shows and briefly in the documentaries *What Sex Am I?* and *Transexual Menace*.

The lingering discussion around the topic of surgery and hormones bears witness to the fact that these categories of cross-dresser/female impersonator/female mimic and trans woman were not static for those who belonged to these groups. This area is discussed in very frank and open terms in Frank Simon's *The Queen* (1968).

The Queen and Sowing the Seeds of Post-Stonewall Queer History

The Queen is a pre-Stonewall presentation of 1967's Miss All-American Camp Beauty Pageant, featuring drag queens in the moment before gay liberation but after the publishing of Christine Jorgensen's autobiography, Benjamin's *Transsexual Phenomenon*, and *A Year Among the Girls* and *I Want What I Want*. Over its hour-long run-time, *The Queen* gives viewers a backstage pass, capturing a turbulent world where sex, gender, and race collide rather than merely offering escapism. It is a keenly observed overview of a particular moment in American life.

The Queen was produced by Lewis Allen, whose body of work was not focused on *cinema verité* but instead Broadway shows (everything from *Annie* to *A Few Good Men*) and films including Francois Truffaut's English-language debut *Fahrenheit 451* (1966), Shirley Clarke's *The Connection* (1961), John Huston's adaptation of *Annie* (1982), and Jonathan Demme's *Swimming to Cambodia* (1987).[9]

It was released by the fledgling film distributing arm of Grove Press, which had earned a reputation as a maverick, uncompromising book publisher of prominent works of radical politics and the counterculture. Allen's reputation, along with that of the other producers, Si Litvinoff and John Maxtone-Graham, helped with the organization of press screenings, and as a result, provided the film with significant press coverage despite it being given an X-rating, ensuring it was reviewed in *New York Magazine* and *The New York Times* on release.

The figure that director Frank Simon primarily follows in *The Queen* is drag icon Flawless Sabrina (also known as Jack Doroshow), whose makeup and wig application is immortalized on the film's poster. Sabrina was not just a figurehead for drag balls but a crafty, ambitious organizer who, through National Academy — a national drag organization that she founded — ran 46 drag pageants over the course of a decade. *The Queen* shows how drag pageants were hitting a peak: attracting a broader, more mainstream audience and gaining attention from the likes of Andy Warhol, who saw her drag pageants in his native Pittsburgh, and with Sabrina herself becoming a photo subject for Diane Arbus.

Sabrina is a natural in front of the camera. She works her act on-screen but also serves as a thoughtful, nurturing force for the participants of the pageants she organizes. These were not just contestants she was fostering; she also employed several queer people who were having their only opportunity to be among people like themselves for such an event.[10] Once the show starts, the viewer is treated to an audience that includes New York icons of the period: Warhol (a judge of the pageant), Arbus, Rona Jaffe, Terry Southern, and George Plimpton. The set-up features a live band and Warhol superstar Mario Montez performs as a maudlin court jester with deliberately off-key singing. Even with its transgressive elements, the pageant is polished, and the audience looks to be little different to Truman Capote's high society Black and White Ball of 1966. But aspects of class and race are inescapably present. Most of the young queers will have to search their pockets to afford a Greyhound bus ride home; the closing image of the film is drag queen Rachel Harlow holding her crown and her suitcase as she awaits her ride. Meanwhile, the cis spectators go back to their penthouses, second homes, or art studios, and the ball has been just another evening of bizarre entertainment they were told to attend by those hipper than they were.

When New York queen Crystal LaBeija walks off stage once it is announced she is placed only as the pageant's third runner-up, it punctures the spectacle and underlines the personal stakes in the competitive nature of the balls. She exclaims angrily to the camera about the process of the pageant, arguing that racism and colorism led to her placement as third runner-up, calling out the judges favoring the more conventional pageant queen Rachel Harlow and that conventionality being tied to race.

"I have a right to show my color, darling! I am beautiful, I know I am beautiful!" Crystal exclaims.

Simon wisely never adds any further editorializing to LaBeija's protestations about the pageant's process, letting Crystal get her words in while Harlow takes the crown. LaBeija's confrontation plays less as an effort to be disruptive for the sake of getting attention and more as a kiss-off, seen today by modern reviewers as a read and throwing shade. In a striking contrast to the trans woman of color in *Behind Every Good Man*, who retreats into the solitude of her personal space, Crystal LaBeija and her confidante Lottie (later known as Lottie LaBeija, identified by her sash as Miss Fire Island) walk defiantly out into the night.

Crystal LaBeija did not just give up. Ultimately, within the next decade, she would be running House of LaBeija and the rise of Houses for modern ball culture scenes, accelerating as disco became the soundscape of queer people and people of color alike. It is the ballroom connection to *Paris Is Burning*, in which House of LaBeija is featured prominently, that gives *The Queen* an even greater historical importance beyond being a significant cultural snapshot of its period.

Flawless Sabrina, meanwhile, would have her last pageant on Fire Island in 1969, discomforted by how mainstream the endeavor had become and returning to the underground scene. Later, she worked as an advisor to Hollywood productions that included the New York-set

Midnight Cowboy (1969) and *Myra Breckinridge*. She would become a subject and trans film image in her collaboration with trans filmmaker Zackary Drucker in the short, *At Least You Know You Exist* (2011). Sabrina was the matriarch of her chosen family — an activist, an advocate, and mentor figure to trans and queer youth, fighting for trans rights and inclusion until her death in 2017. Many of the major figures in *The Queen* would return to their various circles, living as outsiders in the drag and performance spaces. *The Queen* developed a cult legacy — its poster appears in John Waters' *Pink Flamingos* — and it became a staple in queer circles and video stores for years. Its recent restoration and re-release in American cinemas introduced it to a new generation of queer viewers, and it has since been discussed alongside Jennie Livingston's *Paris Is Burning*, the two films representing invaluable time capsules of New York trans and drag images that are connected in setting and participants.

Transness as Cinematic Form: *Funeral Parade of Roses*

Directed by Toshio Matsumoto, *Funeral Parade of Roses* is a Japanese film from 1969 set in the Shinjuku district of Tokyo, a notorious area in the late Sixties due to its propensity for gay host clubs. Art Theater Shinjuku — one of the theatres connected to Japan's Art Theatre Guild (ATG) — spearheaded a nationalized independent film movement, which sought to create a new wave in Japan's national cinema, with directors such as Yoshishige Yoshida, Akio Jissoji and Nagisa Ōshima reacting against the cinema of the past and reconstituting Japanese film through the politics of the time. These directors were reevaluating what the Japanese cinematic form could be beyond the melodramas of Mikio Naruse, Kenji Mizoguchi and Yasujirō Ozu, or the samurai-filled period work of Akira Kurosawa and Masaki Kobayashi. Matsumoto was among the directors from the

ATG who wanted to change the shape of Japanese cinema through a radical melding of documentary, avant-garde, and narrative forms.

The ATG were a New Wave movement as explosive as its French or the Czech counterparts, imbuing their filmmaking with political and formal ingenuity. With the rise of television in Japan, cinema attendance declined, and the studios responded by shifting into subject matter they would have never previously considered, such as pornography and gory violence.[11] The ATG stood separate from these concerns and embraced experimentation and politically motivated filmmaking. *Funeral Parade of Roses* helped inaugurate a new type of Japanese cinema that took cues from Alain Resnais and Jean-Luc Godard. For Japan, the 1960s was a period of great social and economic upheaval — with rapid economic growth and technological advancement alongside radical student movements and the polarizing Westernization efforts as the nation sought to resituate its identity after the U.S. occupation of Japan ended in 1952. Amongst all of this, Japanese cinema became an outlet that would express these questions about Japan's future. Matsumoto finds both a powerful metaphor for the wider Japanese moment and a possible identity in those who rejected the gender binary and lived in a playful and eroticized in-between.

Funeral Parade of Roses is a loose adaptation of *Oedipus Rex* and casts numerous gay personalities and actors from the host clubs of Shinjuku. As with other directors in the Japanese New Wave, Matsumoto was a film theorist and had a cinematic philosophy that he dubbed "neo-documentarism," which was an abstracted version of neo-realism. This style took thematic documentary subject matter that was played straight but combined with exaggerated elements of dramatization to capture both objective realities along with internal subjective states of characters, critically commenting on the cinematic and media apparatuses' expressive techniques. *Funeral Parade of Roses* is the fullest expression of Matsumoto's theory.

In the late 60s, and in Japan, gender non-conforming individuals were all clustered under the umbrella of "gay." In the case of the characters in *Funeral Parade of Roses*, they are given the attribution "gay boy," not unlike the "femboy" label that has taken root in some modern queer spaces. Under the phrase "gay boy," twinks are slotted alongside cross-dressers and transsexuals, and pronouns are applied loosely to these characters without strong preference or identifiers. They are instead an embodiment of gender variance through the way they express themselves.

Funeral Parade of Roses introduces viewers to Eddie (played by a beautiful actor simply credited as Peter) during a sexual encounter with her boyfriend Gonda (Tsuchiya Yoshio). Eddie's soft, sloping body is accentuated by a tracking shot across her skin in close-up. The eroticism of the introduction is capitalized upon through a wonderful abstract image of Eddie's legs being pulled apart slowly as Gonda kisses her from below. The cinematography is blown-out, blindingly white, and fades in and out, with dissolves emphasizing the texture of their bodies clasping each other. Matsumoto does not call attention to the fact that Eddie is completely flat-chested. This is ostensibly a heterosexual moment between a man and a woman but is complicated by the divergent facts of Eddie's biology, visible, but not disruptive, to their intercourse. This is a new sexual representation, which positions the trans film image as a revolutionary, avant-garde symbol of liminality. Eddie's body is representative of new potential definitions of what sexuality could look like on-screen, the flux of Japanese identity as it becomes modern, and a tool for Matsumoto to present his theoretical idea of new cinema. This is all made possible through the expression of a body that is androgynous and trans feminine, and forces the audiences to confront assumptions of gender, sexuality, and cinematic form.

Funeral Parade of Roses exemplifies how visual language can be formed around the discursive ideas of gender non-conformity. By blurring the lines between documentary, fiction, and the avant-garde, Matsumoto makes a broader point about not only gender, but cinematic form. Matsumoto's technique incidentally introduces a practical way to apply the concept of gender-genre to filmmaking. If concepts of non-binary thinking are applied to the visual grammar and communication modes of various cinematic genres, any film, or subject could be queered through that expression. Through the disruption and reformation of existing cinematic concepts, *Funeral Parade of Roses* reveals that gender identity and experimental filmmaking can be in communication with one another. Representation is necessary, but films and filmmakers must also understand how trans people move and experience life, and then communicate that visually. *Funeral Parade of Roses*, with its many abstractions, digressions, and guerilla filmmaking in the gay district of Shinjuku, communicates this in a powerful way.

Funeral Parade of Roses is not only an academic enterprise, but a playful one. At a gay bar, Eddie is locked in a battle with another hostess named Leda (Ogasawa Osamu). This is a symbolic conflict, which not only speaks to the complications that were arising in what a Japanese woman could be, but also in the possibilities of how Japanese cinema looked and felt. Leda stands in front of a mirror and asks who is the fairest of them all and Eddie walks into frame. Leda also has a romantic connection with Eddie's lover Gonda, and she is worried she is getting too old to hold down her man, while Eddie is hip, has beat fashion, and her idea of a Japanese woman is modern and westernized by rock'n'roll. Leda, by comparison, resembles a geisha, and her appearance evokes the melodramas of the past, not the exciting possibilities of the Japanese New Wave.

Matsumoto also uses a few traditional documentary techniques to counterbalance the stylized, erotic love triangle between Leda, Eddie, and Gonda, presenting the queerness of the Shinjuku region and adding an element of authenticity to a film that explores the tension between artifice and reality. In these talking head segments, denizens of the gay scene are asked why they are a gay boy, why they want to be a gay boy, or how they see their future. The answers are varied. Some say they do it because it is fun, others say it was because they would otherwise be miserable, and none have a grasp on what their future entails. To further complicate the mimesis of the film, Matsumoto also interviews his actors. The questions they are asked shift them between the actor's perspective and that of the character. Peter says he feels like Eddie. He thinks that she is just like him, except for the incestuous desires of the *Oedipus Rex* portion of the picture. Osamu says that she is a woman but is not interested in going all the way and having "the surgery," as she likes herself as she is. These responses seem quintessentially modern, in contrast with American expectations of cross-dressing and transsexuality of the Fifties and Sixties, and its narrative pattern of medical intervention and resolution through surgery.

The stark difference, when comparing *Funeral Parade of Roses* to American exploitation films of the period, is that *Roses* does not create an exposition around transness, avoiding some of the clumsier aspects of trans storytelling. The effect of Christine Jorgensen's public profile was a strain of medical and psychiatric realism in movies about transness. Typically, white-jacket characters are given long expository sequences explaining transness to the audience in blunt, sometimes contradictory terms. There was a worry of perversion in the American mode of trans film images, and these doctors were introduced to stave off concerns from censors, or a confused American public. *Funeral Parade of Roses* is a much more liberated work, by comparison.

Funeral Parade of Roses is also radical in that it shows that movies about trans people can be fun, profane, and irreverent. Eddie has two other cross-dresser friends that she hangs out with and many of the film's most iconic and long-lasting images come from these scenes. In one sequence, the friends go to a shopping center and stroll into the men's bathroom with no problems. There is one shot of the trio together at the urinal like a backwards-facing police line-up. A man walks by these urinating transsexuals with a confused expression, wondering if he has the wrong room, and gives up when he sees the urinals. It is funny and does not dehumanize trans people. The film does not center an offended bystander. It is a political image without explicitly calling attention to the politics therein.

When the gals leave the men's room, they walk up the block and run into a gang of cis girls who insult them by calling them "fags." Eddie and her dolls react with faux contempt and call the cis girls ugly. All of it is very catty and foreshadows the transgender concept of throwing shade. None of it is serious, and when fists start being thrown and purses are swung, music that's reminiscent of the Benny Hill television program starts looping over the soundtrack, and the speed of the frame increases to emphasize the comedy. This is a film of multifaceted tones and ideas, and some of its brightest and best moments come in the simple, casual ways that Eddie and these other queer characters carry themselves and how they treat the conflicts around transness as a joke. It is proto-punk and anarchic *and* gave the film a notable cultural legacy and currency. Stanley Kubrick was reportedly inspired by this film about gender rebels when he constructed the look and feel of his adaptation of *A Clockwork Orange* in 1971.[12]

Funeral Parade of Roses is also restless in how it veers from one form and into another as numerous topics and ideas take shape. This is also representative of how Eddie experiences the world. Eddie has an epiphany in an art gallery while looking at portraits of deformed faces when, in voice-over, a man is heard relaying the theme of the gallery installation. "Behind the face is a mask, and behind that mask is another mask." This is a simplistic philosophical reading of how people present themselves, but for Eddie it rings true, and she struggles with her secrets. While *Funeral Parade of Roses* is often hilarious, and even more frequently sexy, it ends as a psychodrama in the vein of Roman Polanski's *Repulsion* (1965) during its final revelations. Eddie's origin story contains an all too familiar trope. She comes from an abusive family with an emasculating mother, and an incestuous father. Eddie's gender inversion stems from this, and it causes a crisis for the character in the final act. The real twist is that Eddie has, in an inversion of the Oedipus myth, murdered his mother and unknowingly laid with his father, and like Oedipus, Eddie blinds herself as punishment. Despite its conclusion, *Funeral Parade of Roses* has not been consigned to the genre of tragedy. Instead, it remains an incredibly exciting, refreshing, unforgettable film that is a record of its time and place, and that shows the radical potential of the trans film image, serving as metaphor, provocation, and object of desire all at once.

CHAPTER 3
Post-Stonewall Transness from the Underground to the Mainstream in the 1970s

Mirror, Mirror: *I Want What I Want* and *Sister Hyde*

"*Wherever you go in the world, you find the greatest barriers to understanding between people are barriers of communication. Yet people have shown signs, though slowly, in recent years of being more aware, more sympathetic and tolerant of unfortunate minorities. They are willing to accept ideas which ten years ago were completely taboo. Permissive society is one thing, but also forgotten these days is taste. I believe if unusual and controversial ideas are presented with good taste, the public finds them not only interesting but acceptable.*"

I Want What I Want producer, Raymond Stross[1]

"*God made man in his own image — and he blew it!*"

I Want What I Want

Like in the United States and the rest of Europe, there were news items in Britain about people who transitioned and people who were outed. One was April Ashley, a successful showgirl and model who became a national celebrity when the dissolution of her marriage to Arthur Corbett, Lord of Rowallan, made her a tabloid and talk show staple, becoming one of the most famous trans women in Britain.

Geoff Brown's *I Want What I Want* was originally published in 1966 at the rough midpoint of a decade in which Britain and the British Empire were undergoing radical changes. Not unlike *The Christine Jorgensen Story*, it was delivered to the screen too late after its publication, in 1972, failing to retain the impact and freshness of the original work. Yet, *I Want What I Want* remains an interesting cultural artifact today to the extent that it is not exclusively tied to clinical narratives about transition. The year before *I Want What I Want*, Hammer Film Productions released a trans spin on a classic horror story: *Dr. Jekyll and Sister Hyde* (Roy Ward Baker). Merging the classic Robert Louis Stevenson story and the real-life Jack the Ripper murders, the film very much feels of the post-*Psycho* horror lineage in the secretive split identity crisis of its villain. It is instructive to discuss the two films together, both given their proximity in terms of release and the fact that, however unintentionally, *I Want What I Want* follows many beats one would find in a Hammer Horror film, especially in how it presents transition, reveals, and dysphoria on-screen.

I Want What I Want boasted considerable talent in front of and behind the camera. It was produced by Raymond Stross, who had success with other novel adaptations that contained LGBTQ themes, such as the controversial *The Fox* (1967) and *The Leather Boys* (1964) with Gillian Freeman, author of *The Leather Boys*, adapting the screenplay. Gerry Turpin's cinematography is polished, as is the costume design and art direction that captures the colorful swinging Sixties, and the film was directed by renowned theater director John Dexter. Overall, *I Want What I Want* is a competently realized film that sets the stage for many trans narratives to come: a fractured fairy tale of a solitary, alien trans figure who, through many traumatic confrontations, decides to take matters into their own hands.

The cover for the novel *I Want What I Want* is one of the most widely circulated and referenced trans images of its era: protagonist Roy looking into the mirror and seeing their true self Wendy in the reflection. It remained as the film's poster and is forever synonymous with the trans mirror scenes trope. When Wendy starts to really embrace her feminine side publicly, the film presents a near shot in a real-time scene of her dressing up and applying makeup in front of viewers. The length of this sequence highlights her mistakes in her makeup applications, overdone and gauche, to adapt to modern, conventional femininity and its expectations. It is a bizarre choice by the film given that, within the film's own timeline, Wendy had already been dressing up and presenting as a woman prior to this scene. The film and its excessive score introduce Wendy's interest in feminine clothing with a tremble, suggesting it as a taboo, with the risk of being found out.

In *Dr. Jekyll and Sister Hyde*, however, we see the instant ecstasy of a sex change and a celebratory image of the trans feminine. Dr. Jekyll (Ralph Bates) seeks eternal life, but in mixing female hormones in his elixir (because women typically live longer), he becomes Edwina Hyde (played by former Bond girl Martine Beswick). When looking into the mirror for the first time, Beswick's Hyde initially shudders and looks away, but then something fascinating happens. First, she is greeted with an admiring stare from a male character who is near speechless at her beauty. Then Hyde takes another look at the mirror and begins to admire her female features, gives a wide smile, lets out a laugh, and starts striking poses and playing with her hair. The music in the transformation scene mirrors Jekyll's pained face and bodily contortions, but when Beswick enters as the trans film image, the music becomes sweepingly triumphant. In giving the film a glowing review for *DRAG Magazine*, trans woman and critic Linda Lee made this closing remark about the transformation moment: "When one sees him [Dr. Jekyll] drink it [the formula] and change from an ordinary-looking man to quite a beautiful girl, one can only sigh and wish it were that easy."[2]

In *I Want What I Want*, Anne Heywood, who is a cisgender woman, plays the lead character Roy/Wendy before and after her social and medical transition. As Roy, Heywood looks closer to a Dorothy Arzner butch lesbian-type than a suave gentleman in ascots, trousers, and overshirts — as though only a bob wig and shoulder pads were added for Heywood to play the character before their change with no real effort to present more masculine features beyond thick eyebrows. As Wendy, Heywood is made up with a certain lack of refinement in her wigs and makeup, veering close to female drag. In *Dr. Jekyll and Sister Hyde*, had the filmmakers decided to simply put actor Ralph Bates in a dress, the film would have been closer to the other on-screen Hydes, and the film's legacy and reception among trans viewers would have been closer to that of DePalma's *Dressed to Kill* (1980). Here, though, the trans film image is transfixing and seductive.

Trans viewers then and now find Beswick's reveal scene rewarding compared to other trans narratives, largely due to the film promoting its "twist" from the outset. Every trailer and poster of the film led with the fact that this was the story of how a male doctor turned into a beautiful woman. Despite *Dr. Jekyll and Sister Hyde* being a radical take, making the central transformation about a change of sex, it stays grounded in the essentials of the story. Presenting as Dr. Jekyll's sister, Edwina Hyde, she begins to murder people. In switching bodies between Jekyll and Hyde, the two personas enter a war with each other for their personhood. And there is another remarkable mirror moment in this conflict over the body. Dr. Jekyll's attempts to suppress his Hyde side become increasingly difficult and the switches between the two become more involuntary. In one moment, he contorts and collapses, and in the next has transformed back into Sister Hyde. In an act of defiance, she addresses the mirror with commanding relish — "It is I who exists, Dr. Jekyll! Not you! It is I who will be rid of you!" — with the transformed seeking to extinguish remnants of the past self.

Wendy's "reveal" moment comes early on in *I Want What I Want*, in a scene in which her playboy father first sees her in a dress, filmed in the dark of a home study and scored to elicit a jump scare. The way the scene is written robs Wendy of perspective within her own story, especially given the book is written from her point of view. In comparison to the book, the film in many ways infantilizes Wendy, portraying her as a victim rather than a self-possessed individual "*wanting to be a woman*" but struggling to "*really be a woman*." This is very much of the time in which the film was made, but it is a barrier for many modern viewers. The father is simply painted as the villain and the film stumbles in trying to show nuanced, "honest" conversations between Wendy and other characters, such as her sister, whose liberalism and open-mindedness Wendy tests and who proposes a cod-Freudian explanation for Wendy's transness, tied back to the loss of their mother. In a visit to her doctor, she is lectured about being "a normal woman" who can attract the attention of a "normal man." Compared to how Ansa Kansas asserts herself to get the care she needs in *I Was a Man*, Wendy is completely at the mercy of the doctor. The gatekeeper holds the most power in this picture.

But against the doctor's orders, Wendy attempts to live stealthily (perceived as a cis woman) until Frank (Michael Coles), a potential suitor, wants to have sex with her, only to realize she is trans. He assaults her, knocking her down along with a standing mirror that breaks into pieces. The only trans image she felt ownership of — her reflection — is now beyond her control and broken. She decides to pick up the shards and, out of desperation, castrate herself. She miraculously survives and, in the hospital, is rewarded with the procedure she always wanted. No such assault happens in the book, no mirror is broken, and Wendy does not wake up healed from a surgery. Instead, it ends with her falling down the stairs due to her weakened state from swallowing dozens of aspirin in a suicide attempt. In the film, the trip to the hospital is considered the "happy ending" that

Wendy Ross earns in exchange for her suffering. It ends differently for Edwina Hyde.

There is no reverting back to normalcy in *Dr. Jekyll and Sister Hyde*, which ends with one last surprise "reveal." The two dueling sides end in a stalemate over the body. Jekyll, trying to evade police, cannot escape Hyde and falls to the ground with a group of onlookers watching. The Jekyll/Hyde corpse is found to be an amalgamation of male and female characteristics. Although sex change is a feature of the film, that it also ends on this non-conforming body rather than the Hyde side fully disappearing from the narrative is fascinating. The image of the body vexes the surviving characters the moment they lay eyes on it and it resonates as a trans film image even more than the transformation scenes in a certain respect, echoing real-life instances of the deaths of many trans people whose bodies — modified with gender-affirming-care or otherwise — are found by those not privy to their trans identity. In death, these bodies become a topic of salacious fascination, and birth speculation as to how the person lived alive. They were not monsters or murderers like Sister Hyde, just everyday, private people.

A common trope in many trans narratives is that, for a trans person to be sympathetic, they must be pushed to the brink; it is the way in which trans characters "earned" their humanity. *I Want What I Want* is one of the earliest films to build its entire narrative around that trope. Sister Hyde, however, is never portrayed as being a tragic victim for wanting her femininity, but her assertiveness into wanting to control her body and destiny becomes an aspiration that can never be attained, instead ending in an unfulfilled hybridization. Thus, the end of *Dr. Jekyll and Sister Hyde* can be read as a glimpse of society reacting to a trans body; shock, bewilderment, and repulsion, with the trans body disempowered and voiceless.

Recurring Trans Film Images: The Evolution of Jenifer Michaels

The trans people that featured in films, particularly in non-fiction, would often go on to become "recurring images" across several other forms of media. In the 1970s, Jenifer Michaels became a recurring trans film image navigating the complexities of transition and sex work. Through these documented snapshots of her life, there is a visible evolution in her presentation and comfort on camera. She starts as a fidgety person who is flushed and grappling with her gender expression and rapidly transforms into somebody with movie star-level charisma.

Not much is known about Jenifer Michaels, beyond the fact that she had deep ties to sex work and the pornography world in Los Angeles. With her trademark red curly hair, she is visible in a party montage set to Joe Cocker's "Feelin' Alright?" in Tom DeSimone's gay porn classic, *Confessions of a Male Groupie* (1972). She also had a part in the large ensemble cast of the James Bidgood-like bisexual sex farce *Sex & Astrology* (1971). What became of her after the 1970s is unclear; though with her history of drug addiction, her time spent in prison, and the looming HIV/AIDS epidemic in the following decade, it is unlikely that she is still alive today.

Michaels makes an appearance as an effeminate gender-questioning individual named Jimmy in a segment of the Pat Rocco film *Sex and the Single Gay* (1970). This segment was called "Changes," and due to its significance has commonly been excerpted from the rest of the film and featured as a standalone. The excerpt is not unlike *The Queens at Heart* interview section, and it has often been criticized by modern viewers for the intrusiveness of the questions, alongside Michaels' clear level of anxiety on camera.

Rocco attempts to tease out the similarities and differences between being gay or trans, both of which, at the time, could result in being arrested, fired, or institutionalized. Rocco did not come from the mainstream, television news, or the medical field and was, through his own work, one of the most important documentarians of the 1970s gay liberation, particularly in Los Angeles, where the gay community was under siege from the Los Angeles Police Department. In the same year as *Sex and the Single Gay*, Rocco also released *Sign of Protest*, a short about confronting homophobia and hostility at a West Hollywood bar. The interviewer this time is not Rocco, but William King, a middle-aged Charles Durning type, and despite Michaels being introduced as "an admitted transsexual," the segment uses her male name and pronouns.

Categorization and labels are the crux of King's early questions to Michaels, asking about sexual preference between men or women, her gender identity, and whether she identified as a homosexual. On the last question, Michaels immediately states that if she had simply identified as gay, she would never identify as transsexual, which she does; though she also says that the categories of male and female were gray areas for her. She stumbles occasionally, for instance, in saying that female impersonators mock women, though arguably does so to make it clear that this is not what she and other trans-identified people are doing. The conversation catches many of the existing tensions among transsexuals, transvestites, drag queens, political lesbians, feminists, and gay men.

King also asks Michaels about whether she wants to get the "complete operation." Michaels states that it is her "intended purpose... to change"; that to identify as trans would mean medical transition is the intended goal and how people not being supportive of her wishes of transition upsets her so much that it would send her "into a tremor" when talking about it in therapy. She notes how most of her lack of support came from men she was involved with, leading her to speculate that her seeking transition "threatened" their masculinity. When King asks her how this has impacted her mentally, Michaels gives one of the most memorable lines about transness from this era: "Well, people who think LSD is a trip should try taking hormones!"

On the questions of how she views her role as a woman going forward, her answers show a more gender-queer aspect, but are also informed by men and women of this era who were rejecting traditional roles. Michaels states she hates bras and prefers to lean into her natural beauty, evoking some lines from the women's liberation movement, and demonstrating how transness shifts along with wider culture rather than remaining a static or fixed form. This is tantalizing, because the cultural associations of transness at this time were still fixed on the Christine Jorgensen model of the traditional beauty modes of the Eisenhower 1950s. The "Changes" section of *Sex and the Single Gay* ends with Michaels in more masculine attire — dress shirt, boots, and striped slacks — walking around Hollywood Boulevard only for the scene to cut to her putting on makeup in a public women's bathroom. She leaves in a skirt, sweater, vest, and with a bandana around her neck. The short ends with a montage of her interacting with a man, walking in a garden, on a swing, with the maudlin song written for the film, "Changes," playing as she removes her sweater and lays topless beside a creek, cementing her as an anti-conformist individual who marches to the beat of her own drum.

It is evident from Michaels' next appearances in Penelope Spheeris' *I Don't Know* (1971) and *Hats Off to Hollywood* (1972) that she is a lot more comfortable on-camera. This is perhaps due in part to her greater familiarity with the filmmaker. Michaels, who was still going by Jimmy, had struck up a romantic relationship with Spheeris' sister, Linda, a lesbian who was, to the surprise of many, drawn to Michaels. In fact, Linda provides narration in the opening sequence of the two walking the street together:

What could be more perfect than love with Jimmy? Man together with woman, just how Mother Nature ordered it. Finally, I had fallen in love with a man. It was the way out, it was the last chance for both of us. Of course, he had his problems, most of it with his identity. But I had similar problems and I somehow knew we could help each other. I remember when I first saw him. I loved him. I thought, "Only if he loved me too."

Linda calls Michaels "Jimmy" and uses male pronouns, but from all appearances, Michaels is fine with this. The title *I Don't Know* is just as much a reference to Linda's love life and her direction after this whirlwind romance as much as it is about Michaels' station in the spectrum of gender. When Linda recalls asking Michaels if she wanted to go to the Gay Liberation parade in Los Angeles, Michaels told her, "I'm already liberated!" But Linda also references the multiple times that Michaels tried to kill herself with sleeping pills, once exclaiming to Linda, "How can I live in this condition?" Linda Spheeris claims Michaels had opportunities to get surgery through research programs but turned it down, with Linda speculating that maybe "he likes just being the unique person that he is." Michaels is held by the woman who loves her but cannot quite understand her struggles in transness and gender identity. Penelope Spheeris in turn presents a revealing interview with Michaels, who says she has a wonderful time with Linda, but does not see long-term relationship potential, let alone marriage. It is an illuminating moment that Michaels only sees Linda as a friend and one where the viewer is more clued in than Linda on the state of things, undercutting the self-assurance of Linda's narration.

Michaels' sex work in the fetish space where she presented as both male and female for magazines is also a topic of discussion. It is referenced first by Spheeris' disapproving brother Andy who, despite his long hippie hair, is traditionally masculine. He fixes cars and casually calls Michaels both a "faggot" and a "fool." They have testy interactions for much of the short whenever they are in the same room, with Spheeris and her small crew of UCLA student filmmakers being protective of Michaels. Andy never quite escalates to becoming a physical threat, just somebody who has his own insecurities (he would later appear again as a biker in *Hats Off to Hollywood*, the unrequited crush of gay man Dana Reuben) and there is a moment where Michaels uses a common retort among cross-dressers and street queens at the time, immortalized by the effeminate cross-dresser Lindy (Antonio Fargas) in the film *Car Wash* (1976): "Honey, I'm more man than you'll ever be and more woman than you'll ever get!" What makes *Hats Off to Hollywood* and *I Don't Know* a broader point of interest beyond their trans film images is the fact that they were very much the forerunners to Spheeris' enduring and critically celebrated documentary film, *The Decline of Western Civilization* (1981).

Hats Off to Hollywood is a hangout film that follows the travails of sex work amid a counterculture on its last legs in 1970s Los Angeles. Viewers are reintroduced to Jenifer Michaels in a low-cut blouse, without a bra, wearing bell-bottoms and sporting a black eye as a cover of "Dream a Little Dream of Me" plays. Yet, she is no worse for wear compared to the other main character, a flamboyant man named Dana Reuben in a bandana with glitter all over him clutching a Raggedy Ann doll. In their chance meeting, Michaels and Reuben forge a bond that is strictly platonic but becomes increasingly co-dependent. Reuben lives on disability and is a free spirit who covers up his more controlling tendencies. Michaels is mindful of how she is perceived and talks openly about being trans. Things shift from a buddy hangout movie to something seedier when Reuben begins to goad Michaels into turning a trick to help him out financially. In turn, he gives her housing, as his disability checks cannot pay for food. When Michaels enumerates the risks involved in sex work, Reuben shrugs it off: "There's a risk in everyone's life!" and Michaels tersely counters with her own truth, "I take a risk by just walking out the door!" There are montages of Michaels getting into cars to turn tricks and even a tender shot of her and a john in bed. Reuben claims in the narration that Michaels does not just "hook" for him, but that she does it for herself and likes it. Michaels immediately contradicts this with her own sardonic testimonial: "I hate to hook! Sometimes, I would rather die."

Sex work for trans women is often a tool of survival and can be a ticking clock of hard outcomes, such as violence, death, or incarceration — and this happens to Michaels. She is returned to Reuben with bad news: she was arrested for sex work, and because she refused to be an accessory for the police's sting operation to arrest more sex workers, she has a prison sentence looming. The film shifts tone from a tale of Los Angeles' hedonistic eccentrics to a social realism, becoming surprisingly touching in the process. Reuben also reveals his past as a drag queen who did sex work that ended in arrests to show he is not as aloof as he often appears to be with Michaels. What is remarkable about Michaels' perspective on going to prison is that she sees it as an opportunity and doesn't consider being incarcerated with men a problem — she is the "closest thing to a woman" for many of them. She finds the fact that she can have a guaranteed room and a meal in prison as a privilege for a trans woman who struggled to find secure housing and food. That statement manages to undercut the illusions that policing sex work impedes sex work. It also presents the bleak realization that if governments guaranteed people income, food, and housing, then prison would cease to be necessary for non-violent offenders such as Michaels.

Jenifer Michaels' trans film image over the course of "Changes" in *Sex and the Single Gay*, *I Don't Know*, and *Hats Off to Hollywood* shows a progression in how a trans subject can both take control over their image while also showing vulnerability and real, very common experiences. This is partly achieved through the shift from the formal interview set-up to working multiple times with a filmmaker she knew well. It is a loss that Michaels was never able to carve out a more conventional acting career in film. Other trans film images would emerge in non-fiction spaces and even become recurring, with windows into their lives peppered across multiple film titles, but few were as appealing as Jenifer Michaels.

The Warhol Superstars: Pioneers Without a Frontier

Women in Revolt (1971) was a satire of the growing women's liberation movement by Paul Morrissey and Andy Warhol, starring Candy Darling, Holly Woodlawn, and Jackie Curtis. Warhol's "Factory" upended conventional modes of artistic expression and was at the forefront of numerous avant-garde practices. Darling, Woodlawn, and Curtis became forever associated with Lou Reed (who had interacted with all of them during his time with the Velvet Underground) after his popular solo song, "Walk on the Wild Side," told their story and cemented them as muses of the classic rock canon. Darling, Curtis, and Woodlawn were stars, and their continuing relevance and legacy in the trans community has turned all three into idols for new generations. They were all markedly different from one another. Darling had an intoxicating Old Hollywood glamor that contrasted with the seedier New York art world she inhabited. Woodlawn was wildly expressive and had a profound sense of sarcasm and irony. Curtis, the most genderfluid and genderqueer, took cues from James Dean and was also the most mysterious and temperamental of the trio. The combination of these screen presences made for a unique portrait of transness as a salacious, satirical embodiment of womanhood in *Women in Revolt*.

Radical feminist Valerie Solanas has been seen as the likeliest source of inspiration for *Women in Revolt*. Previously a presence at Warhol's Factory, and even a friend of Candy Darling, Solanas attempted to kill Warhol with a gun in 1968, later dramatized in Mary Harron's *I Shot Andy Warhol* (1996). Despite their friendship, Solanas never considered Darling a woman in the way that Solanas herself was, viewing her more as a hyper-feminine gay man. If Solanas and

Warhol had anything in common, it was in the ways they viewed Darling, Woodlawn, and Curtis, with Warhol even making cruel remarks over the years about Darling, saying in the BBC documentary *Walk on the Wild Side*, "These drag queens... they don't really know what girls go through. They've never had a period. They take these pills, but they can't tell. They don't know what it's like to be a real woman."[3]

This is a dehumanizing and regressive commentary from Warhol, but he also took a shine to each of them and had a level of admiration for their creative pursuits. Warhol was a contradictory figure, and *Women in Revolt* is a contradictory film. Despite this attitude towards their gender identity, however, he also saw them as trailblazers. He did not put the full weight of his influence behind any of them, but he understood their screen potential and their verve as captivating personalities, saying they were "pioneers without a frontier,"[4] which suggests a revolutionary possibility in all of them. He was correct in this regard, and the trio have retained their importance as icons of an era.

There is a tension within *Women in Revolt* where the concept and the magnetic presence of the performers renders any poisonous attitude of potential transphobia unimportant. The ingenuity of all three manages to wrangle the film out of the intended joke of "men" playing feminist women. Instead, it creates a portrait of illicit transness that is rare in cinema, with a notable exception being the proto-punk idealism of *Funeral Parade of Roses*, itself influenced by the New York underground filmmaking that Warhol and his Superstars became synonymous with.

In *Women in Revolt*, Jackie (Jackie Curtis) is fed up with men and has started an organization she hopes will finally liberate women everywhere called P.I.G. (Politically Involved Girls). Curtis is a political lesbian and a virgin prude with the heart of a degenerate. She has a male "slave" who tends to her every desire, but whom she also abhors. Like most of Paul Morrissey's work, this is an X-rated film that contains copious nudity, sexual content, and a scatological sense of humor that foreshadows the work of John Waters.

Curtis's best friend is Holly (Holly Woodlawn), and in contrast to Jackie, Holly is a nymphomaniac. She ripples ecstatically in most scenes and her cartoonish introduction presents her as a trans version of Daffy Duck. Holly is in the middle of sex with a nameless man; her face is hidden and all that is visible are her scrawny arms flailing at the mass of his hunky flesh. She complains that she cannot breathe, ripping and pulling at him to get off her. When he finally moves, Woodlawn jolts up to look directly into the camera with her eyes crossed and tongue sticking out, as if to say, "Yuck!" All of Woodlawn's scenes contain a biting contempt for the social mores of the patriarchal world, and she is like a careening pinball bouncing off naked men and women wherever she goes.

Darling's character could not be more different from the others. She plays Candy, a well-off woman who comes from "good breeding." Holly and Jackie think it is a wonderful idea to contact Candy to see if she will funnel them money for their political organization, but she believes it is a better idea if she takes her nest egg and runs off to Hollywood to become a big star — a classic Hollywood Blonde. These dreams of stardom were like Darling's own. There is a scene with a talent executive who is promising major things for Candy, but only in exchange for sexual favors.

The film can be shocking in how little it cares for morals or basic decency, and Darling, Woodlawn, and Curtis shine when their personalities are given free rein to improvisational, profane comedy that is biting, shirks respectability, and remains highly quotable. The trio see the film as a lark and present their most extravagant ideas about cis womanhood. Warhol and Morrissey's satire now has an ironic effect for modern viewers, where these images play out as less tied to their reactionary origins and instead present the novelty of trans-as-cis acting.

Women in Revolt was not Holly Woodlawn's first picture

with Paul Morrissey. The year before, she had starred along-side Joe Dallesandro in *Trash* as the sexually frustrated girlfriend of a heroin addict. Unlike *Women in Revolt*, *Trash* is not a comedy but a genuine art film meant to evoke the stagnation and quiet desperation in the lives of addicts. It was shot on 16mm and then later blown up to 35mm, and through exquisite close-ups of the actors' bodies and their faces, the film has a wonderful sense of textural intimacy, but there is no explicit eroticism between the characters. Joe's drug habit causes him problems in sexual perfor-mance. Though Holly's character wants sex, it is not the driving force of her character, as it is in *Women in Revolt*. She spends most of the film rummaging in dumpsters for furniture. Morrissey plays it for poignancy rather than laughs, showing Holly speak of these discoveries softly with sweet enthusiasm. There is a scene where Holly wants Joe to help her bring home a drawer chest she found in front of a church, but he thinks it is all junk. His response wounds her, for her womanhood is found through this rummaging and the things through which she can create a semblance of domestic life. The film is called *Trash* but for Holly that word does not mean what it means for most. For her, it is her life. It is her identity.

Morrissey shoots the underseen parts of a ravaged New York City, and even though he adopts a social realist mode, there are many painterly compositions that stand out, such as one of Holly laying nude in her earthy, brown apartment on a bed she fished out of a dumpster. *Trash* is deliberately slow, with Joe wandering around the streets at an organic, natural pace. He has given up on a normal life and lets his drug habit dominate his choices — content living in the rhythm of getting high, coming down, getting sick, and then getting high again. His performance is curious and beguil-ing because he spends so much of the film half asleep but remains captivating. Morrissey made the choice to compose *Trash* in long passages where little happens beyond broken, slurred conversation, due to Joe's drug usage.

In *Trash*, Holly's character is a cisgender woman, but unlike in *Women in Revolt*, the film aims to be social realist rather than satire. Woodlawn in real life was often rebellious and fluid about her gender identity, sometimes purely out of survival, although in her own words she was "destined to be a woman."[5] Her public persona was often playful and sardonic with an innate sense of performance that could be broad but also layered. *Trash* and *Women in Revolt* are two distinct performances that show off Woodlawn's range. She earned critical praise for her work in *Trash*, with the great director George Cukor even arguing for Woodlawn as a Best Actress in a Supporting Role nominee for the Academy Awards that year.[6] There was a grassroots movement to place Woodlawn among the stars, with buttons made and with Woodlawn photographed in one of her fur coats holding a cat, her Oscar campaign pin visible. Nothing ever came of it, but it would have been a deserved nomination.

In the documentary *Beautiful Darling* (2013), actress Julie Newmar says of Candy Darling that she had a Marilyn Monroe quality and Newmar assumed that she could have been a star if those in power in Hollywood had allowed it. When Darling was a child, she wrote to Kim Novak, who responded positively. Darling was so moved by the gesture that she kept that letter with her for her entire life. This letter was reassuring for Darling and reaffirmed her belief in her own womanhood. Darling wanted nothing more than to be a fixture of Hollywood and presented herself in the way of old glamor. She wanted to be beautiful and timeless in the way that her heroes were. She has become that icon — immortalized by artists like Lou Reed, the Smiths, and ANOHNI, to name a few, over the decades. But also, for many trans women, Candy Darling is what Kim Novak had been for Darling herself.

Darling and Jackie Curtis made their screen acting debuts in 1968's *Flesh*, a Joe Dallesandro vehicle and their first official film with Morrissey and Warhol. Darling's notoriety and associations with Warhol's Factory and New

York nightlife in general landed her a cameo in Alan J. Pakula's Academy Award-winning *Klute* (1971), alongside Jane Fonda. She and Fonda became fast friends, and the two were potentially going to star in a picture of Warhol's that would have eviscerated Hollywood called *Blonde on a Bum Trip*, but nothing ever came of the film beyond scattered ideas and rough plotting built around the murder of glamorous celebrities like Fonda. Darling was going to play the murderer. If this would have happened, it would have made for a fascinating twist on the trope of the trans serial killer, because it would have been a satire in the hands of Warhol. Darling's best role, and the one that most strongly highlighted her abilities as an actress, also came in 1971, in Mervyn Nelson's *Some of My Best Friends Are....* In this film, Darling's status as a trans woman, her acting abilities, and the fragility of her own glamorous creation of herself intersect with one another in a way that none of her other film roles ever did.

Some of My Best Friends Are... is a Christmas film, where all the lonely souls of the gay and lesbian community convene at a gay bar called the Blue Jay. Over the course of the evening, patrons wander in, all of them are looking for connection on an otherwise somber evening. The Blue Jay is all they have, and like most people around Christmas, they want to be with their family. This is an ensemble film, with the camera roving around the crowded bar eavesdropping on conversations and hook-ups and observing the outright desperation of all these patrons looking for solace. In the early 1970s, the barriers that prevented queer people from living openly and freely were still very much in place; even post-Stonewall, you could still be jailed for cross-dressing in public or dancing with someone of the same sex. Violence hangs over everyone, and the tensions of a nascent political movement introduce a new kind of queer anxiety in the trans film image — the closet has cracked open slightly, but not entirely. Darling plays a young woman named Karen, who sits alone at the bar, staring off into space. She is lonely, emblematic of her lack of conversation with the other patrons, and she feels marginalized, even in this supposedly welcoming setting.

Karen is a character that is in stark contrast to Darling's star persona; she is lacking confidence, introverted, and transparently bashful about her appearance. She does not have her look together, something vitally important for trans women to feel comfortable, and something that was of utmost importance to Darling in her daily life. Karen lives on the edge of passing as cis and that knowledge worries her. She technically is at a gay bar made up primarily of gay men, which is a better option for her as opposed to a straight one where those anxieties surrounding passing and appearance would be further amplified. There are reasons to believe she is more comfortable with gay men because, in addition to probably first identifying as a gay male before her trans identity, she is there for the same reasons they are in wanting safety and a sense of community. But she sticks out in her awkwardness. There are other women at the Blue Jay, but they are outgoing and have platonic connections to the male patrons. Karen is a stranger.

This internalized transphobia is easily read on Darling's face. Karen spends most of her time consuming fruity "girly drinks" at the farthest end of the bar. When the camera finds its way over to her, she is often isolating herself, and there is a great deal of emotion contained in Darling's lonely, wayward eyes. Karen is not having a good evening. She is so preoccupied with how she looks and everyone's perceptions of her. She feels there is an inevitability to her trans identity being "found out," leading her to constantly run to the bathroom to add powder to her face or apply a new coat of lipstick at the bar in between drinks. This constant upkeep of her appearance is exhausting and takes its toll on her throughout the evening. Darling very much understood the psychological dimensions of Karen's burden in real life, and such futility tied to passing, as her real-life relationship to overusing female hormones had negative effects on her body.

To evoke a sense of community, there are several moving parts and involved plot mechanics in *Some of My Best Friends Are...*, but Karen is the only character who is given the chance to have an internal monologue. In a particularly striking scene, a drunk hustler approaches her and asks her if she wants to dance. The hustler is looking to hook-up with any woman he can, also crumbling under his own internalized homophobia, and is so stoned that Karen seems like a good option. He calls Karen beautiful. Her sadness lifts, and she starts repeating to herself that if he thought she was beautiful then she must be a woman. During this monologue, Karen is lit by a hazy glow, Old Hollywood-style, and morphs into a fantasy version of herself. She now looks like a movie star, like Candy Darling.

In the fantasy, Karen's hair is bleached blonde and white like ash, flowing around her in deep, curving locks, and she is wearing a beautiful orange gown that hugs her body in all the right ways. Even the rock music in the club shifts into something more elegant, with instrumental exotica lounge music used to soundtrack her moment of gender euphoria, but it is short-lived. The hustler grabs Karen by the ass, and the jarring cut back to reality is harsh, the look on Karen's face screaming, "What if he finds out?" The hustler then reaches his hand up Karen's dress and then the moment shatters — he no longer sees Karen as a woman. He rips off her wig and beats her. She retreats into the men's room, and with that choice, her gender identity is obliterated.

The loss of Karen's wig is a symbolic death. Without that long hair, she is robbed of femininity. In this moment, Darling is seen without the dress and make-up, shedding all the external constructs of her femininity for the sake of the role, a truly brave and bold performance — one that could have potentially removed her from the category of "woman" in the eyes of the filmmaking industry. All that is left of Karen is the essence of her femininity. A pall of silence hangs over the Blue Jay, as the gay men wait for Karen to come out. When she does, the silence continues; she no longer resembles the person she was in her wig and makeup. It is like a forced detransition and a closeting all in one, and the tragic irony is the Blue Jay is supposed to be safe. If it is not, then where can someone like Karen realistically go?

After this scene, there is no life behind Karen's eyes, or in the way she carries herself. She is like a wounded animal trying to find a corner of the room to lay down and die. She finds her way back to the farthest end of the bar, where a man talks to her gently, but Karen is emotionally and mentally checked out. There is an honesty in this scene that is all too rare in movies about trans people. Karen's worst, most agonizing reality has come true. Later that night, she will have to walk home, all alone, in her body, with its worst realities visible in her appearance. She has no safety net. *Some of My Best Friends Are...* affords Darling as Karen the interiority to communicate her aspirations to the audience, but the film remains circumspect in noting that few will understand or accept this character's trans identity. The film pities and humanizes Karen while providing Darling a role that showed a commitment to social realism and a bold step forward for her craft as an actress, which she never got to show on film again.

In contrast to the tragic, realistic role in *Some of My Best Friends Are...*, Darling appears in a more avant-garde film framework in Werner Schroeter's *The Death of Maria Malibran* (1972). Here, Darling is treated like an ethereal being and a stand-in figure for the doomed mezzo soprano singer after whom the film is named. The visual language is impressionistic and highly stylized and Darling is lit frequently in gold and amber, with the close-ups finding great beauty in the contours of her face. This is a role where Darling does most of the heavy lifting through facial articulation and lip-syncing. Notably, she also performs to the camera, singing in her quintessential breathy voice to the Mabel Wayne–L. Wolfe Gilbert song, "Ramona." Schroeter eschews dialogue in favor of a diegetic operatic soundtrack and other musical collages set to Mozart, Stravinsky, Maria Callas, Puccini, and Janis Joplin alongside his compositions, which are expressionist, hyper-emotional, and built upon surreal sequences without linear narrative. Darling's transness is not at the forefront of her role; rather, she is incorporated into the pantheon of great female beauties and artists' muses such as Magdalena Montezuma and Ingrid Caven. But the film is not without its missteps, such as when Schroeter presents Darling performing in blackface for one brief interstitial.

There is a note of tragic foreshadowing in Darling's appearance in *The Death of Maria Malibran*. She is the only character who is told that she is a "brave child and sometime... something great will happen to you." Darling would not live to see herself break the glass ceiling of what trans actors could produce and how they were used, but she was gaining momentum. She continued working and supporting Jackie Curtis as a playwright, starring in *Heaven Grand, Amber Orbit*, and *Vain Victory: The Verisimilitude of the Damned*. She had caught the eye of the great playwright Tennessee Williams, who gave her a role in his *Small Craft Warnings*. She and Williams hit it off, but Darling was exhausted by life. She struggled with her mental health, and even in these happier moments, suffered the indignity of not being allowed to use either bathroom on set. She was given a broom closet, which she decorated with a star — defiant to the end.

In 1974, when Darling was nearing her death, something attributed to black-market hormones, she wrote to Warhol: "Unfortunately, before my death I had no desire left for life... I am just so bored by everything. You might say bored to death. Did you know I couldn't last? I always knew it. I wish I could meet you all again."[7] She had Peter Hujar photograph her at the end of her life, a series of stunning black-and-white images with a skeletal, but still striking Darling, framed by funeral lilies. Darling died of lymphoma on March 21st, 1974. She was 29 years old. Darling was, and still is, an icon for many trans people. Though her life and career were short-lived, her legacy in the trans community is one of near martyrdom. Jackie Curtis, who was still writing and directing plays, would die of a heroin overdose at 38 in 1985. Woodlawn would make numerous appearances on the stage and film and television before passing away from cancer at age 69 in 2015.

The legacy of Candy Darling, Holly Woodlawn, and Jackie Curtis is still deeply felt in the trans community. Most of the films in which they star are obscure, underseen, and under-discussed, but their images endure. They showed that there was a way to become yourself, and that the self was not a static creation, and its progression was wayward rather than linear — a becoming. For cinephiles who have come across their work in the years since, their iconoclastic star power is unforgettable.

Dog Day Afternoon: A Sleazy Littlejohn Becomes a Robin Hood at the Movies

Dog Day Afternoon's categorization in the queer film pantheon has shifted over the years. Initially, it was understood as a gay film about two male lovers, but its modern reputation is of a film where the plot is set in motion by the lover of a trans woman robbing a bank to assist in her surgery — which is the true, correct reading. Its status as an award-winning mainstream classic was conferred in large part thanks to the story being taken directly from the headlines and because many figures in New York's gay scene knew or were friends with the principals before the life-changing 1972 Brooklyn Chase Manhattan bank heist took place.

Dog Day Afternoon reinterprets the story of trans woman Elizabeth Eden and her husband John Wojtowicz. Eden and Wojtowicz's marriage ceremony on December 11th, 1971, received a considerable amount of media coverage given that the wedding was not legally binding, and had difficulty finding a venue. Lee Brewster's *DRAG Magazine*, a New York publication that was equal parts queer activism and culture, covered the wedding, featured the wedding party and showed Eden in her wedding gown with the kind of spread more typical of a celebrity in major magazines.[8] The wedding was also filmed by the Gay Activist Alliance (GAA), whose founders included *The Village Voice* columnist and gay activist Arthur Bell. Was it a prank subverting the Institution of marriage? Or simply a powerful symbolic ceremony for two sexually liberated people? Either way, considerable effort, money, and time was invested into this event. The couple had peers and friends in the queer community. But Wojtowicz was viewed by other GAA members at the time as a "looney-tune" at best, and at worst somebody who took advantage of people for the purposes of his sexual appetite, as gay activist Randy Wicker would later recall.[9] For Eden, Wojtowicz would end up being a mix of both eccentric and exploiter, with the charm of the former quickly evaporating.

In *Dog Day Afternoon*, Al Pacino portrays Wojtowicz, now renamed Sonny Wortzik, as a sympathetic, accidental criminal, in over his head, but street-smart, and decent enough to know how to treat women and the elderly right. He makes idle chit-chat with the ladies of the bank, sends the elderly hostages out first, and calls for a doctor when one of his hostages, who is diabetic, begins to have a cardiac event due to the sweltering August heat. There is a long history in the movies of criminals that are worth rooting for, dating back to Jimmy Cagney's time at Warner Bros. playing blue-collar gangsters who had their reasons for engaging in crime, and Pacino's Sonny Wortzik harkens back to these earlier characters.

The real Wojtowicz was different, and while it is not unusual for films based on true stories to take dramatic license, especially to create audience investment in the characters, the blurring of lines within *Dog Day Afternoon* colors its legacy. Wojtowicz was interviewed while in prison by *The Village Voice* after the release of the film, and he dismisses the romantic notions of Pacino's portrayal.[10] In the jailhouse interview, he is coarse, arrogant, and has an ego about his own legend. He treats the bank robbery like an exaggerated fishing story where the stakes rise ever higher as time passes. He is brusque when asked about the rumor of the bank robbery being staged to pay for his lover's sex reassignment surgery. He does not deny that it was part of the plan to use the money for Eden's operation, but he states that overall it was a mafia-planned robbery that went horribly wrong. When asked about Eden again, and if he believes that she is a woman (she had since had vaginoplasty), Wojtowicz replied, "Naw, she's still a man." Eden was given some space in this interview to tell her side of the story and she is described in *The Voice* as being smarter than Wojtowicz, having settled with Warner Bros. in a lawsuit that netted her a great sum of money, and when she is asked if she still loved "Littlejohn" (Wojtowicz's nickname), she replied, "Never did."

This is not the story that *Dog Day Afternoon* tells (which screenwriter Frank Pierson adapts from the *LIFE Magazine* piece on the bank robbery that had a gay pun in its title, "The Boys in the Bank"[11]), and because it is so distanced from the reality of the real Liz Eden and John Wojtowicz, it has the odd sense of feeling separate from its origin as a fable all of its own. *Dog Day Afternoon* is a strange beast, but it has held its place in the larger canon of trans film images and the film world due to the fairytale quality of its romantic gesture told through an all-time great performance from Al Pacino that presented the real John Wojtowicz as a better man than he was.

Pacino's ability to balance and exploit how he is perceived as an actor is why the film has sustained. In the 1970s, it was seen as a genuine risk for him to take on this role of "playing gay," especially as his character is not tortured by his sexuality in ways like Marlon Brando's repressed Major in *Reflections in a Golden Eye* (1967) or Dirk Bogarde's closeted barrister in *Victim* (1961). As Sonny, Pacino had to walk the fine line between queerness and aspiring to a vision of being a "man's man" for robbing a bank. In finding that balance, Pacino makes Sonny a very curious character, and *Dog Day Afternoon* becomes a film less about the act of robbing a bank than one where the perception of someone can change instantaneously if the public believes them to be queer. This is what happens when it is eventually revealed that Sonny is married to Leon (Chris Sarandon), who is based on Liz Eden. It is also a metatextual component where Pacino could have very easily been read as queer for portraying this character. Initially, Sonny is another anti-hero in the typical mode of male characterization in American movies of the 1970s. He is fidgety, nervous, and seems prone to violence, but he has a plan. When he and Sal (John Cazale) hold up the bank, they begin to build momentum as cult heroes when the public gathers outside, cheering them on and mocking the police, because in the wake of the riots and murders at Attica Prison, no one is trusting law enforcement — another instance where the film gestures at real events. Local news stations are building up the story, and there is a circus around the bank. When Sonny walks out, he is greeted with applause, his name is chanted, and the people love him, but a pall falls over the crowd around the halfway point of the film when Leon appears, and they realize this guy they have rallied around is queer.

Pacino does not play Sonny as a stereotype, and he also does not overly pronounce any femininity in his sweaty, disheveled, nervous body language. Outside of a line or two, where he slips into girl talk with the clerks, there is nothing outwardly identifiably queer about the way that Pacino approached the role. He masks his intentions, and it is a type of closeted performance that is structured around a reveal, but the difference between *Dog Day Afternoon* and other trans films with a reveal is that it does not hinge entirely on a twist, but that the reveal deepens the character dynamics of all involved. Sonny's anxieties are not with being found out. In fact, when Sonny asks for his wife, he had to have expected Leon, even though he was also married to Angie (Susan Peretz), because when Leon appears, he is happy. He shouts "happy birthday" to her from across the street and has a broad smile spread across his face. While *Dog Day Afternoon* strays from the truth, there is some authenticity to be gleaned in the way that it expresses itself, and because Pacino's performance is so balanced, it snuck under the radar of discriminating moviegoers.

Leon, by contrast, cannot hide their queerness. When Sarandon was preparing for the role, he tried to replicate the body language of a New Jersey housewife, often put-upon, and acting as though in need of a fainting couch. Leon is someone prone to picking fights, and the image of her, stubble-faced, flat-chested, and in a bathrobe, created a very incongruous sense of femininity. It is not at all how Liz Eden looked at the time. Eden was tall and conventionally attractive; in her wedding photos, she looked as though she could pass as cis, and was even compared to screen actresses Katharine Hepburn and Dolores Del Rio in *The Village Voice*. But casting directors Michael Chinich and Don Phillips had little interest in casting someone who looked like Eden. John Waters collaborator Elizabeth Coffey auditioned for the role and was told she did not "look the part," despite being a trans woman.[12] Through Sarandon, and the choice to cast him, Hollywood continued to push forward images of trans women as merely men in dresses, with Pacino and Sarandon initially widely perceived in the film as gay men.

With Sarandon's presence, *Dog Day Afternoon* presents a world where queerness is primarily embodied by gay men. When the crowds disperse after the reveal of Leon, there is a tracking shot through the remaining protestors who are causing problems for the police, and most of them are gay men — some are in dresses. The film's plot has now become a "gay cause," echoing gay liberation protests at the time and Wojtowicz's own ties to gay activism. While Sarandon's casting falls into a negligent category, *Dog Day Afternoon* still feels like an important moment in the history of queer cinema.

Pacino and Sarandon, admittedly, have chemistry with one another, which is impressive considering they are placed in two different settings for most of the film. When they share a phone call with one another late in the film, the full depth and quality of their relationship is felt in Pacino's exasperation and Sarandon's choice to pry and make fun of Sonny, centering Leon's concerns in a passive way that nonetheless takes up space. While listening to their conversation, it is evident how and why they fell in love with each other, as there is a certain codependent element at the center of their dynamic. In the 1970s, Pacino was particularly excellent at portraying exhausted, damaged psyches without going over the top — but it is also easy to feel that they are doomed. It is perfect for the movies, where romance is better left to suffer or flame out entirely. Their chemistry further complicates a reading of the film, because while *Dog Day Afternoon* fails as a trans picture, it was initially perceived as a gay one, and accepted by the studio and audiences alike. This was progress, but the kind where you win the battle and lose the war. Over the final image of the film, an intertitle says, "Leon Shermer is now a woman living in New York City" — the shooting script attempted to honor the character's trans feminine identity by having the title card be, "Leon is now a woman named Lana"[13] — which is vague and speaks to a confused conception of transness centered on surgeries.

The real Elizabeth Eden fell into trouble the moment news circulated of her ties to Wojtowicz, as it outed her as a trans woman, which took a toll on her already fragile mental health. She told Lee Brewster in *DRAG Magazine* that she was evicted from her apartment due to this unsolicited notoriety.[14] She did make visits to Wojtowicz in prison, acknowledging his generosity for her surgery, but the relationship became a deeply one-sided dynamic. Eden moved out of New York City and up to Rochester, New York, where she lived until her death from AIDS-related complications at the age of 41 in 1987.

Every so often John Wojtowicz's mugshot goes viral on social media with the story that he did it to pay for Elizabeth Eden's operation, which casts him as a trans-amorous Robin Hood. In some ways, viewers — and this even includes trans people — are compelled to project the image of Al Pacino's Sonny onto Wojtowicz rather than looking at the real man. And it made sense, Pacino was a once-in-a-lifetime movie star whose popularity made this story completely accessible to a broader audience. In *Saturday Night Fever* (1977), there is a moment where John Travolta's Tony Manero is looking into the mirror casually chanting, "Attica! Attica!" This testifies to the film and character's cultural staying-power as a hip anti-hero, and demonstrates that Hollywood's anxieties about a major actor playing a queer role were unfounded.

But there are deeper intricacies and complications in the real relationship between Wojtowicz and Eden, one mired in misgendering, despite the fact the man in question bragged about paying for the surgery to affirm her as a woman. He was a "chaser" who wanted to have control and ultimate say over her, with the payment of her surgery in many ways functioning as a transaction for that control. Eden chose to love herself and never reconnected with Wojtowicz in any significant way again. She lived a quiet life away from the tabloids that proved to be too costly of a spotlight for her. She never got to give her full side of the story away from "Littlejohn", versus the way Wojtowicz was repeatedly allowed to self-aggrandize for several decades after the event, and in the recirculation of his story, even years after his death, in the 2013 documentary, *The Dog*. Wojtowicz will always win in terms of public image because people see the gallantry of Al Pacino in his story. Eden, however, is tied to a less-than-flattering trans film image, a stubble-faced Chris Sarandon, with poorly plucked eyebrows and unkempt hair, clutching a robe.

My Words to Dr. Frank N. Furter: *The Rocky Horror Picture Show*

"I'm just your average man... and your average girl, really. I'm the tranny next door!"[15]

Richard O'Brien, creator of *The Rocky Horror Show*,
in a 2015 interview on BBC's *Newsnight*

There were few bigger underground hits in the 1970s than *The Rocky Horror Show*, which premiered in 1973 in London. It was made in a time of heightened sexual freedom and expression, influenced as much by the androgyny of glam rock as older cult films, an homage to the B-movies and horror classics of yesteryear. Its creator Richard O'Brien has suggested its enduring popularity is due to it combining elements of myth and fairytale, a mix of Hansel & Gretel with the Book of Genesis, in which the serpent that seduces the modern Adam and Eve takes the form of an androgynous alien scientist, the most iconic character in the whole production: Dr. Frank N. Furter.

The whole show and Dr. Frank N. Furter was the concoction of Richard O'Brien, who would also play the role of Riff-Raff on the stage and screen. O'Brien remains a controversial figure, as they would identify as a third gender non-binary and, in their own words, as trans,[16] but not without their own troubling, harmful statements regarding the affirmation of other trans people seeking to be seen as women or men over the years.

The film version, Jim Sharman's *The Rocky Horror Picture Show* (1975), moves forward the trans image of Dr. Frank N. Furter (Tim Curry), the "Sweet transvestite, of Transsexual, Transylvania." Recent productions both on-screen and on-stage have raised debate on whether *The Rocky Horror Show* is transphobic or not due to the outdated, clinical language in the lyrics to the song "Sweet Transvestite." Attempted corrections have ranged from revising the lyrics (such as in the television show *Glee's Rocky Horror* tribute episode) or casting transgender actress Laverne Cox in the role of Dr. Frank N. Furter in a 2016 live-for-television production. In the latter telecast, the song "Sweet Transvestite" contained the original lyrics, with Cox indicating that, much like any art that uses outdated language, it is always important to contextualize them.[17] What is seen as bad or poorly aged now in trans film images was in the past considered important, radical, and accessible.

For many who came of age during the film's 1975 release and after, *The Rocky Horror Picture Show* was one the first trans film images they ever saw. And while Dr. Frank and their minions are killed at the end, the iconography and appeal of *Rocky Horror* comes not from the Adam and Eve squares Brad (Barry Bostwick) and Janet Weiss (Susan Sarandon), but from the transgressive gender-queer image of Curry in a black corset, huge white pearls, fishnets, and scare queen makeup, parading their body as a locus of seduction and desire. That image is the draw in *Rocky Horror*, allowing non-conforming individuals to be liberated through entertainment and art by crossing over into the domain of the misfits. Dr. Frank is an outsider, an alien who has traveled everywhere to find a place for themselves because their desire to create a human lover was rejected by their home planet's society. They are an outlaw within science and gender, marginalized as a body and a subject. When not in a corset, Dr. Frank is in a green dress that also functions as a medical scrub with a pink triangle stitched on it — a re-appropriation of a symbol previously used by Nazis against LGBTQ prisoners during the Holocaust into a symbol of gay defiance, pride, and liberation.

The 1970s were a time where trans and queer film images were frequently conceived as violent menaces, such as the rapist hillbillies in *Deliverance* (1972) or the unbalanced cross-dressing con artist in *Freebie and the Bean* (1974). Vito Russo noted in *The Celluloid Closet* that this was the product of the end of the production code. Explicitness of figures and themes of queerness were often portrayed negatively rather than just coded, erased from the narrative, or pushed to the margins as in earlier times, deeming the output of 1970s Hollywood a continuation of "the freak show aspects of homosexual villains, fools, and queens."[18] But Dr. Frank N. Furter transcends ever being labeled a villain. Calling *The Rocky Horror Picture Show* "the gayest film yet ever released by a major studio,"[19] and recalling how the 1970s became a time of gay panic with Anita Bryant's homophobic "Save Our Children" campaign, Russo specifically relished the moment in which Tim Curry performs "Sweet Transvestite." Russo called it "the essence of what every parent in America fears will happen if our sexual standards are relaxed," because it makes widely perceived deviances "tangible" and "visible."[20] Even though the film initially did poorly at the box office, Russo noted its second-act success as a cult hit and moneymaker as something to be incredibly optimistic about, because those who are going to these shows, largely young people, are clearly craving what *Rocky Horror* is presenting to them, not just in the visibility of what could be out there in terms of gender presentation but an immersive, communal, experience of like-minded individuals.

In a Year of 13 Moons and Personalizing Queer Tragedy

German auteur Rainer Werner Fassbinder is widely embraced in queer cinema circles today for a prolific career that included such films as *Die bitteren Tränen der Petra von Kant* (*The Bitter Tears of Petra von Kant*) (1972), *Faustrecht der Freiheit* (*Fox and His Friends*) (1975), *Querelle* (1982), and his update to Sirkian melodrama, *Angst essen Seele auf* (*Ali: Fear Eats the Soul*) (1974). His legacy can still be seen in many contemporary queer works such as the films of Todd Haynes and Ira Sachs through to João Pedro Rodrigues' excellent trans film *Morrer Como Um Homem* (*To Die Like a Man*) (2009) and trans filmmaker Lyle Kash's *Death and*

Bowling (2021) — a film full of visual callbacks to Fassbinder's work.

Fassbinder's 1978 feature, *In einem Jahr mit 13 Monden* (*In a Year of 13 Moons*) (1978), tells the story of the final days of a trans woman, Elvira Weishaupt (Volker Spengler). It does not have the same level of acclaim as his other films, due perhaps to its limited availability, but also perhaps because it is an intense, thorny film about human relationships with a very troubled, vulnerable trans film image at its center. It is widely perceived as Fassbinder's most personal film, having been rushed into production while Fassbinder was mourning the suicide of his lover and frequent actor in his films, Armin Meier.[21]

In a Year of 13 Moons begins with a foreboding vision of cosmic influence, opening with a text that raises the question of predestination and Fassbinder's searching for some deeper structured reason behind the act of taking one's own life:

Every seventh year is a Year of the Moon. People whose lives are strongly influenced by their emotions suffer more intensely from depressions in these years. To a lesser degree, this is also true of years with 13 new moons.

When a Moon Year also has 13 new moons, inescapable personal tragedies may occur. In the 20th century, this dangerous constellation occurs six times.

One of these is 1978.

The film opens at daybreak, when it is still safe enough for hustlers on the streets to cruise. There is a silhouette of a figure in leather who is revealed to be Elvira, in leather man drag. She is found out and beaten up by gay men. Her body is that of a woman and yet, for a moment, her gender-play fooled these men — introducing a complicated, multi-layered take on the trap narrative ("trap" is slang for those who present as one gender only to be "revealed" as the opposite). Her trans identity is not why she is beaten; rather, she is assaulted because she is perceived as a woman entering a male space through male "masquerade." Elvira had been wearing a woman's slip and corset underneath male attire, later explaining she did not choose a male presentation to revert, but because it feels "less shameful" to cruise when in men's clothes. It is alarming, risky behavior that her abusive lover at home, Christoph (Karl Scheydt), is completely unsympathetic towards once she returns home. In starting from this point, Elvira's trans film image is deeply knotty and multifaceted in demonstrating that transition is not in and of itself a gateway to happiness.

After one final abusive fight between Elvira and Christoph, in which Christoph threatens to smash Elvira's face in the mirror, he leaves their apartment. Later in the same day, Elvira takes sex worker Rote Zora (Ingrid Caven) to her former place of work, a slaughterhouse. And in what has become one of Fassbinder's most infamous scenes, the camera tracks through the factory following the process of one cow after another being killed and butchered. Elvira, a former butcher (the real-life Armin Meier's prior occupation), is completely desensitized to the environment, while Zora and, by extension, the vast majority of viewers who have never been inside a slaughterhouse, view it as plainly disgusting and jarring.

Narrating over this slaughterhouse scene, Elvira mentions her trip to Casablanca to Zora, a shorthand for getting an operation with Dr. Burou. Readings of the film often argue that the procedure Elvira underwent is being framed as analogous to the butchering of the cows.[22] Such readings are just outright transphobic, built on the implicit belief that every gender-affirming surgery is the butchering and mutilation of the body.[23] Elvira herself never speaks of her body in such terms and neither does Fassbinder. In fact, a sizable portion of the film goes into more depth on her getting the operation in Casablanca;[24] very few characters comment on her and she passes to the extent that the gay hustlers only see her as a cis woman. It seems to be, if anything, an incredibly effective procedure in physical terms, but psychologically perhaps it is another story.

The slaughterhouse scene, while deeply disturbing, does not function as a commentary on gender-affirming surgeries but rather on the film's very visible themes of exploitation, the interpersonal, and desensitization to cruelty. It is made clear, through the bombastic, heightened way Elvira speaks of her past relationships, that she fully acknowledges being driven by masochistic impulses, but nonetheless has felt exploited by others and that exploitation is in many ways rooted in her prior life. Elvira next goes to the monastery where she was raised as an orphan. With Zora in tow, she visits her past life where she discovers that having the story of her childhood presented in plain speech is more brutal than anything she witnessed in the slaughterhouse.

A tracking shot of Sister Gudrun (Lilo Pempeit, Fassbinder's real-life mother) pacing around the church courtyard is a barn-burning testament to her recollections of the orphaned child abandoned and forgotten by their birth mother. She recalls the child she remembers as Erwin, an individual who tried hard to please the other nuns, and whose intense yearning to be loved was heartbreaking. It causes Elvira to collapse. Sister Gudrun's ultimate summation shows Elvira as a survivor who is irreparably informed by the trauma of their life, and by embracing the masochism of it, can "thoroughly enjoy the horrors of this hell instead of being destroyed by them." *In a Year of 13 Moons* sees Elvira finally reaching her limit. The film has the intensity of a volcanic rupture waiting to explode.

Elvira's unrequited love, Anton Saitz (Gottfried John), is the film's ultimate villain; an ardent, exploitative, capitalist and speculator who is utterly indifferent to Elvira. Some Fassbinder scholars prefer to project Fassbinder onto Elvira, but arguably, he can equally be read as Saitz, a powerful eccentric of many appetites who loves to control, dispose of, and discard those around him without a second thought. There is a moment of Zora channel-surfing a television that shows newsreels of Chilean dictator Augusto Pinochet, Maurice Pialat's *l'amour fou* classic film *Nous ne vieillirons pas ensemble* (*We Won't Grow Old Together*) (1972), and an interview with Fassbinder himself in which he is being casually dismissive and arrogant about the questions of inspiration in his work. This naturally raises the question of why Fassbinder has placed himself alongside these images of brutal, abusive men, both real and fictional, with one answer being that, in doing so, he is admitting to being dictatorial and sadistic to the audience.[25] It is quite an extraordinary self-assessment for any director to give, especially in a film born out of grief.

Another disputed element in the film among Fassbinder scholars is the motivation for Elvira's transition. Saitz, while engaging in a love affair with Zora, casually states he believes the impetus for Elvira's transition arose from his response to her declaration of love when they were colleagues, with Saitz saying, "only if you were a girl." This, however, only expresses Saitz's perspective, as a man who is as conceited as he is pathologically ruthless. Fassbinder's film treatment (a written summary that presents the essentials of a prospective film) acknowledges that Elvira knew her love for Saitz would never be consummated, and that her attraction to him was not physical — she needs him the way a masochist needs her sadist. Nonetheless, something does shift within Elvira on seeing Saitz with Zora — she reverts to men's clothes and cuts her hair. Yet Elvira is not switching back to Erwin. She looks dogged, beaten-down, and uncomfortable in the old clothes from her past, with makeup still smudged on her face. Elvira's complicated and shifting identity and needs, along with her conflicting desires and compromised relationships, help to show transness not as some idealized, static state of becoming achieved through transition, but instead as an ongoing fraught negation of the self and the world.

Another notable aspect of the film treatment for *In a Year of 13 Moons* is that Fassbinder has Elvira retain her name throughout the story, even as she is greeted as Erwin by other characters throughout.[26] As the coda states: "The next day, the poet finds Elvira in his cellar. She's already dead."[27] And in the film itself, Fassbinder credits Spengler only as Elvira.

It is only once Elvira takes her life that she is finally allowed to be heard. Tapes of interviews she did with a neighbor begin playing in her apartment. Her views of her relationships and the hope she felt in her transition are heard, yet the responses from all the characters run the gamut: apathy, mourning, stunned silence. When a trans person passes unexpectedly, suddenly the long trail of pain that they expressed takes shape for people, as though allowing them to hear and see it for the first time. Often, it's only in death that their personhood is finally embraced, but of course not always — many are never fully seen or heard.

Elvira Weishaupt is an unsettling trans film image — a truthful story of a doomed trans person whose fragile life cannot be saved by transition alone. *In a Year of 13 Moons* is a film that stemmed from grief, and so its melodrama and messiness is understandable. Elvira is not an uplifting trans film image and trans people may not universally embrace an image imbued with such tragedy, but *In a Year of 13 Moons* remains an audacious fictional narrative that places the viewer in the headspace of its trans lead and remains a significant, unflinching work of cinema.

New Pioneers, New Hostilities

Contemporary LGBTQ histories have worked to re-center important trans figures who had previously been written out. Two of the most important are Marsha P. Johnson and Sylvia Rivera, who are deservedly discussed primarily for their work in the 1970s with Street Transvestite Action Revolutionaries (STAR). But the activities of trans people in the 1970s were too diverse to distill into just one political trend. Trans people were not necessarily synonymous with activism, much less gay liberation, due to the many separate subsets active at this time.

In the 1970s, one of these subsets, trans masculinity, finally began to coalesce as a community. Regardless of the closing of the Erickson Education Foundation in 1977, Reed Erickson would remain trans medicine's most significant benefactor until his death in 1992. Despite his reputation as an eccentric — "the trans Howard Hughes," as he has been dubbed — Erickson was a patron of broader LGBTQ archives, such as what would later become the ONE Archives at the University of Southern California.[28] While there was no trans man who took on Erickson's role in the trans community in terms of largesse, what did emerge were newsletters and publications like *Gender Review* by Rupert Raj, who also oversaw the republishing of EEF materials. *Gender Review* would serve as a publication for Raj's organization Foundation for the Advancement of Canadian Transsexuals (FACT), and was a crucial precursor to his later 1980s publication *Metamorphosis Magazine*, which had an international subscription base of trans men and featured contributions from activists such as Lou Sullivan.

While "straight cross-dressers" did not necessarily get involved in liberation activism, a major event did occur in this decade. Similar to the Casa Susanna retreat in the Catskills in the 1960s, Fantasia Fair was created in Provincetown, Massachusetts, in 1975, and included many previous Casa Susanna patrons. The week-long fair still runs today, not only allowing cross-dressers and trans women to express themselves among a community, but also focusing on informational and harm-reduction sessions with medical professionals and for individuals and couples dealing with transitioning. In the 1970s, Fantasia Fair fostered many of the activists who gained prominence in the 1980s and 1990s. As it was then, it has largely remained a discreet affair which allows participants to maintain a level of privacy.

The difficulty in cataloging trans lives and representation is that many trans people often had no interest in revealing themselves to the world. This included straight cross-dressers who separated and compartmentalized their professional and personal lives to afford themselves privileges and privacy, or stealth trans women who never disclosed out of safety concerns and employment issues. This was exemplified by Aleshia Brevard — the model, actress, and Finocchio's performer — who first came out as a trans woman in old age, years after she had had several roles in film and television.

As well as Brevard, there were many trans people and cross-dressers living and working invisibly in the entertainment industry during this time, though increasingly, more successful people did begin coming out. These people were often married, had children, and were highly regarded in their field of work. The disclosures of writers and artists like Angela Morley, Jan Morris, and Wendy Carlos showed that there were many creative people of depth and substance who were trans — but the publication of Jan Morris' memoir *Conundrum* in 1974 showed that no matter how successful and intelligent you were, coming out as trans could still often be a spur to intense public hostility.

Morris was a prolific travel writer whose transition, including traveling to Casablanca for bottom surgery under Dr. Georges Burou, officially began in the 1960s. When Morris passed away in 2020 at the age of 94, modern sites and publications presented *Conundrum* as one of the great trans memoirs. They also noted that, when the book was published in 1974, even a figure of Morris's stature was not immune to transphobia.

The novelist Rebecca West showed no sympathy in her 1974 *New York Times* review of *Conundrum*, in which she repeatedly jumps between referring to Morris by her former name and as Jan. West, born in 1893 and from a much older generation, eschews empathy for Morris's explanation of her gender dysphoria, and simply considers Morris to be disturbed. "As for her psychology, Miss Jan Morri's self-portraits are chilling. She sounds not like a woman, but like a ma"'s idea of a woman," West declares.[29] Ultimately, she concludes in her "review" that, "I cannot accept *Conundrum* as the story of a true change of sex."[30] The most widely circulated review of *Conundrum* was by Nora Ephron in *Esquire Magazine*, later republished in a collection of Ephron's essays, *Crazy Salad*. In echoing West, Ephron writes, "Jan Morris is perfectly awful at being a woman," calling *Conundrum* a "mawkish and embarrassing book." Ephron trivializes Morris, joking that this "whole mess" could have been avoided if Morris had simply seen a good Freudian analyst. Ephron seems only sympathetic towards Morris's children and wife for having an "understanding that defies understanding" in accepting Morris. It then ends with this salvo:

> The truth, of course, is that Jan Morris does not know it is nonsense. She thinks that this is what it is about. And I wonder about all of this, wonder about how anyone in this day and age can think that this is what being a woman is about. And as I wonder, I find myself thinking a harsh feminist thought. It would be a man, I think. Well, it would, wouldn't it?[31]

It was clear that the public at large and those who held powerful positions in the media saw what they wanted to see: fools in dresses or something more sinister, even as published memoirs and interview subjects articulated their lived experiences of transness eloquently and plainly. Trans film images have long been warped and informed by prurience and sensationalism, but what was gaining momentum in the public imagination was a menacing, disturbed trans film image that had been percolating alongside a proliferation of real-life trans visibility. Even with potentially positive images like *The Rocky Horror Show* entering the cultural consciousness, trans film images in crossing the threshold of the mainstream often yielded a transphobic response.

The trans film image of a deeply disturbed, one-dimensional individual who embodied the unsympathetic villain was taking shape in this decade, often as threats to the typical white cis heterosexual heroes in mainstream cinema.

One such notorious example is Richard Rush's police drama *Freebie and the Bean* (1974), in which the trans film image is intentionally malignant and negative. The film is prominently featured in The *Celluloid Closet*,[32] as well as the documentary of the same name, and presents the infamous scene of a cross-dresser shot multiple times in a bathroom by good cop James Caan. The spray of bullets is so powerful that the cross-dresser (played by Christopher Morley in the role of "Transvestite") flails around with her torn dress revealing the bare chest of a man.

In the film, Morley functions as a near-perfect manifestation of the transphobic imagination, combining several myths and falsehoods that persist today for trans women and drag queens. Morley's character is picked up at a park by an older gentleman who happens to be under police surveillance for being a racketeer. Morley, however, is dressed to deceive — this cross-dresser is a criminal, which leads to her being followed, and a confrontation in a woman's bathroom ensues. During the shootout with Caan's Sgt. Freebie Walker, Morley takes a hostage, a young girl, who is held with a gun to her head. Caan frees the hostage and then, in combat, Morley rips off her wig and destroys her dress. Morley's character is far from a sissy; in fact, their demure disposition is just one of their many sets of tricks. They are an armed and dangerous criminal with unusually developed martial arts skills who, despite incapacitating Caan through sidekicks several times, seemingly never wants to escape the restroom. They return to the bathroom mirror to clean themselves up with a dead-eyed stare until they are shot to death, needing more than one bullet to be taken down.

The cross-dressing and trans publications that wrote about *Freebie and the Bean* at the time found it too ridiculous to be outright objectionable. A few even found Morley (a Marilyn Monroe-impersonator who was a major figure in the Los Angeles cross-dressing and drag scene) to be a "bewitching" screen presence.[33] Due to being a figure in Los Angeles queer circles, Morley interacted with many other performers and people who ran trans publications on the West Coast, so the reaction to seeing him on-screen is also colored by seeing a familiar face. Morley was not the only performer of a cross-dresser or trans background to partic-ipate in the creation of bad trans objects. These roles con-tinued to persist in film and television even without the participation of trans people, cross-dressers, or drag queens being cast in these roles. *Freebie and the Bean* is not regarded as great 1970s cinema, but its images of a negative trans object highlight the fear-mongering hostilities and images against trans people during the 1970s through the present day.

Alongside these negative trans film images, trans-ex-clusionary radical feminism began to take form in the late 1970s among some notably affronted second-wavers, and Ephron's "harsh feminist thought" in her *Conundrum* review gestures towards the existence of this brand of feminism. In 1979, Janice Raymond wrote her TERF manifesto, *The Transsexual Empire: The Making of the She-Man*, which argued that transsexuality should be mandated out of existence.[34]

In the immediate aftermath of *The Transsexual Empire*'s publication, there were smartly written criticisms in trans publications and by professional people who were friendly with the community, but nobody was given the same plat-form that Raymond and other pro-*Transsexual Empire* think-ers were afforded by the mainstream. There was not a robust community of trans people; there were splintered pockets of transsexuals, transvestites, female impersonators, and cross-dressers who rarely reached unanimity around polit-ical matters. The mainstream attention afforded to *The Transsexual Empire* was significant, despite how inflamma-tory Raymond was in the book, most notoriously writing, "All transsexuals rape women's bodies."[35]

A positive review of the book from the *New York Times*, written by the famous if controversial psychiatrist Thomas Szasz, begins by bemoaning the idea that rather than getting you locked up in a mental institution, as would have been the case previously, getting "bottom surgery" now warrants a cover of *Time Magazine*.[36] Virginia Prince published her separate review, but not so much to refute Szasz as to give voice to her own personal trepidations about surgeries, going so far as to declare it "a valuable contribution to the literature on this most controversial, little understood area."[37] Prince often ignored the fact that, while surgery did not have to be what defined her and her transness, that was not the case for others. Many trans people needed care from clinics and did not have the privileges Prince was afforded in life, such as generational wealth, to get around any bureaucratic roadblocks and receive that care. The following decade would see a shift in how gender clinics operated within the Standards of Care framework of the HBIGDA. But then, there were gender clinics that closed their doors due to the leaders of those institutions wanting nothing to do with trans surgeries. Few things were as symbolic of this shift as when, in 1979, surgeries came to a halt at the Johns Hopkins University Gender Clinic.

The end of the 1970s foreshadowed the incoming political and cultural backlash against the LGBTQ community. Gay men and women were the target of many discriminatory firings that made the news around this time. In 1976, physical education teacher Steve Dain made national news when he was fired from his position due to being a trans man. For years, Dain was the most visible trans man in the United States. He was blackballed from teaching for the rest of his life, despite having won his court case against the Northern California school district. The positive gains seen in the election of Harvey Milk for the San Francisco Board of Supervisors in 1978, and his role in leading the successful fight against the homophobic Briggs Initiative/ California Proposition 6 soon turned to tragedy when Milk and pro-gay rights San Francisco Mayor George Moscone were assassinated by disgruntled Supervisor Member Dan White. The subsequent 1979 White Night Riots in San Francisco, in reaction to White's light sentencing, showed widespread anger. These systems and institutions of authority had no interest in protecting queer and trans people. This would only get worse in the Reagan years of the 1980s.

CHAPTER 4
Weathering the Storm:
The 1980s

The New Fights

The end of the 1970s, with the publishing of and support for *The Transsexual Empire*, the Johns Hopkins University halting trans surgeries and the closure of many other gender clinics, in addition to the HIV/AIDS crisis, heralded a dreadful new decade for many trans people. Indeed, transness was further pathologized by the medical community. After years of research, the American Psychiatric Association's *DSM-III* (*The Diagnostic and Statistical Manual of Mental Disorders*) was finally published in 1980 and employed the term "gender identity disorder" (GID) to label those who were transsexual.

This would immediately have an impact, largely negative, and meet resistance. Much like homosexuals and their fight to have homosexuality removed from the *DSM* — a fight they ultimately won in 1973 — many trans people resented the pathologizing, medicalizing, and labeling entailed in having to be diagnosed with GID. The Standards of Care tied to being diagnosed with GID meant a long process full of contingencies and evaluation, often lasting years. For most people, even those with health insurance, this translates into being an incredibly expensive process. As Susan Stryker notes, "This was a truly inexcusable double bind — if GID was considered a real psychopathology, its treatment should have been insurable as a legitimate healthcare need; if treatment was not considered medically necessary, it should not have been listed as a disease."[1]

Trans medicine was entering a new era. Harry Benjamin would pass away in 1986, and while his reputation still made him a sort of Dean Emeritus figure in his final years, he was well into old age — 94 years old when Standards of Care was published by the HBIGDA. While there were new people who would assert themselves as the drivers of trans medicine, it would remain a predominantly cis male space.

More positively, this decade was also one in which a stronger apparatus for trans people to advocate for themselves was developed — the decline of gender clinics for those who sought trans surgeries and care serving to galvanize a generation of trans people into fighting back. Strong bonds were formed, and many new names rose to prominence in activist and leadership spaces.

Merissa Sherrill Lynn's work at both Fantasia Fair and later Tiffany Club in the 1970s helped her build networks and support in the New England area that ultimately led to the creation of the International Foundation for Gender Education (IFGE) in 1986. The IFGE ran annual conferences, phone lines and centers, and trans bookstores, and published magazines on community topics, all with the aim of combating transphobic ignorance within both the public and the medical communities. Crucially, the IFGE served as a bridge between transsexuals and transvestites who had for decades been separated by the medical community and by community members themselves. Although it became inactive by the late 1990s, and its magazine *Transgender Tapestry* would have its last issue in 2008, the IFGE was the necessary foundation for ensuring trans organizations were run by trans people. While this was one of some notable positive responses, activists faced an uphill battle as new images emerged on the big and small screens alike that in many ways stirred new forms of panic, ignorance, and misunderstanding.

Queer and Present Dangers: *Cruising*

Al Pacino continued to oscillate between criminal and cop for many years, and playing Sonny in *Dog Day Afternoon* would not be the last time he was tied to queerness or queer images. In 1979, he starred in the legal drama *...And Justice for All*, playing the lawyer of a vulnerable, doomed trans woman (Robert Christian). A year later, he starred in an even bolder, more provocative, and controversial film: William Friedkin's *Cruising*.

Much like *Dog Day Afternoon*, *Cruising* was linked to a real story, this time of convicted murderer Paul Bateson (who appeared as a hospital radiographer, his real-life job, in Friedkin's *The Exorcist*), whose alleged victims included gay film critic Addison Verrill, a friend of many people in the gay community and specifically Arthur Bell and Vito Russo, both of whom had been reporting on Verrill's murder, looking for answers.[2] This connection, in addition to the film being about a series of killings linked to the New York gay leather bars, caused controversy and led to protests during the film's release.

Cruising beguiled mainstream critics and alienated audiences. In truth, the film was never going to be a commercial hit in a country that would elect Ronald Reagan that same year, though it has earned contemporary reappraisals, especially among gay men, for being a snapshot of the period's leather scene pre-AIDS, when New York City felt a little more authentic and dangerous. But in a film about performance, roleplay, and leather as a costume to shift in and out of, the element that remained perhaps most fascinating is the trans film image of a character who is simply called DaVinci.

In the earliest moments of the film, DaVinci (played by Gene Davis, brother of Brad Davis) and her friend (played by Robert Pope in their only film credit) are a pair of trans leather dolls heading to one of the New York leather bars. They are detained by two cops who demand sexual favors in exchange for their freedom; Davis's resigned body language conveys that DaVinci has likely had to do this many times before.

Still presenting as a woman, DaVinci goes to a police precinct and straight into the office of Captain Edelson (Paul Sorvino). She tells him directly about her experience and names the cops who were involved; Edelson is dismissive. Later, however, DaVinci is approached by the NYPD to help them in their desperate search for the serial killer who is preying on BDSM leather bars across the Village, and she is willing to play informant in exchange for the department going after the cops that sexually coerced her. While an informant, she appears to be very effective in gathering valuable information. Unfortunately, her hope of taking down the cops who abused their power over her and her friend will never come to pass; she is simply being taken advantage of in a different way, in yet another bad transaction with the police.

Cruising expresses a deep ambiguity in the tension between the trans femininity of DaVinci and the traditional masculinity of the NYPD. She is marked as grotesque only to be desired, at once criminalized only to be fetishized, ignored only to be approached when she can be of use. For all the ways *Cruising*'s reception and reputation have shifted, DaVinci as a trans film image of her time captures some of the reality of those often put in the position of having to constantly negotiate out of sheer survival. In a film that operates as a commentary on the type of performances and costumes men put on to stand out or blend in, DaVinci is out of step; her female presentation is not a costume.

Karen Black Glows Bright in *Come Back to the 5 & Dime, Jimmy Dean, Jimmy Dean*

Throughout film history, there have been very few good performances from cisgender actors portraying trans characters, and even fewer great ones. The highpoint of such portrayals was not of a cis man playing a trans woman or a cis woman playing a trans man, but a cis woman as a trans woman: Karen Black as Joanne in Robert Altman's *Come Back to the 5 & Dime, Jimmy Dean, Jimmy Dean* (1982).

Black's work prior to portraying Joanne was varied and showed her range across genres. She was comfortable opposite Jack Nicholson's Bobby Dupea in *Five Easy Pieces* (1970), and alongside Peter Fonda and Dennis Hopper in *Easy Rider* (1969). She shined in ensemble pieces like Robert Altman's *Nashville* (1975), was embraced by the horror community for her turns in *Trilogy of Terror* (1975) and *Burnt Offerings* (1976), and became a camp icon in her role as the stewardess who lands the plane in the disaster film *Airport 1975* (1974). But it is as Joanne that she offers one of the most vulnerable and intelligent performances of her career.

Come Back to the 5 & Dime, Jimmy Dean, Jimmy Dean was a play by Ed Graczyk, directed on stage by Altman. Although it had a limited run to little acclaim, Altman was so taken with the text that he adapted it for film and featured the core ensemble of actors from the stage version.

In *5 & Dime*, a group of women who were once in a club called The Disciples of James Dean are reuniting 20 years after the death of the actor in their small town of McCarthy, Texas. There is something the other women do not know, however: their old friend Joe (Mark Patton) is now going by Joanne (Black), and her transformation puts into sharp contrast the ways in which these women have or have not evolved over the past two decades. This is a rare film from the 1980s that uses transness as a fulcrum for greater plot embellishment and drama, but does so in a way that allows its trans character to remain a fully realized person and not simply a narrative convenience. Joanne is neither a saint nor a deviant. She is a woman with baggage, just like all the other disciples.

Before Joanne arrives at the old five and dime storefront, where the reunion of The Disciples of James Dean is set to take place, her past is reflected upon by her friend

Mona (Sandy Dennis). Years ago, Joanne (then going by the name Joe and played by Mark Patton) stocked the shelves and mopped the floors and was treated like one of the girls. She gawked at James Dean with the others and, hoping to be cast as an extra, took a road-trip with Mona up to where they were filming *Giant* (1956, Dean's final role). In their free time, Joe, Mona and Sissy (Cher) liked to sing the songs of the McGuire Sisters and once dolled Joe up in a wig and a dress for a high school talent show. "He looks so good as a girl!" they remarked. But as a result, Joe is labeled a "sissy" and becomes a target of homophobic abuse. When Joanne inherited money from her mother, she used it to move away from west Texas and transform herself.

Karen Black plays her first scene with an anxious curiosity. She is quiet and careful with her words, because she knows that Joanne can only maintain anonymity for a short period of time. Her voice is thus a little uncertain, shaky, and skids along its tone, with wavering, purposefully faulty cadence, a little deeper than Black's typical register, but only slightly so. If Black were to have used a voice that was significantly deeper than her own, it would have made the character seem like a drag queen, but by only slightly lowering her voice, she embodies the mindset of a stealth trans woman. Even so, Mona still remarks that her voice is "peculiar" and "strange," which hints that her identity will be revealed, despite her best attempts at hiding it.

Joanne stops in her tracks at the makeshift shrine to James Dean; her shoulders fall ever so slightly, as if she can relax, because she has finally found something familiar from her past. It is an unconscious response that helps to make sense of the character. It is also mournful in some respects, because it is here where Joanne stops and stares the longest, expressing nostalgia with notes of tragedy. It is a quasi-religious moment, as if Mary Magdalene had come upon a stained-glass mosaic of Christ (the James Dean shrine features a cut-out promotional still from *Giant* where his arms are extended around a rifle, stretched out like an image of the crucified Christ). Joanne takes out a cigarette to calm herself in the routine of a comforting familiar habit, amid the turbulence of her emotions in being back home.

The beauty of this scene, and the performance in general, is in witnessing Black's control of technique. When trans characters re-enter a familiar cisgender space they inhabited before transition, it leads to a certain withholding and negotiation over when, if ever, to reveal themselves. The complexity of Black's performance is in how she manages the layers of artificiality in Joanne's gender expression. Black also emphasizes Joanne's weariness. She is hyper-aware of her surroundings and perceptions because she is a trans woman for whom passing and being stealth is necessary. She articulates her awareness of negative perceptions about trans people in a cutting remark. "Just tell them, I'm a freak! They'll know what that is!" she curtly responds to Stella May (Kathy Bates), another member of The Disciples of James Dean, after she asked if she is like the transsexuals on the television talk show circuit.

When Joanne mentions Mona's son "Jimmy Dean," whom Mona named after the actor, even claiming the child's father is James Dean, she cannot conceal her own sadness. Black's work as Joanne frequently represses emotion, brushing up against the jagged edges of the trauma of her character. Joanne will not allow herself to get too close to what hurts her, at least not while she is sober, so Black will often look away to compose herself and pull up a shield for the bigger emotions she wants to hide. In some ways, this is a type of closeting, because she is allowing Joanne to unconsciously work at lying to herself so that it does not hurt, but the acting is so careful that emotions slip to the surface and are only visible for the briefest of periods before they are tampered down again. It is complex in a way that cisgender actors almost never achieve when playing trans characters.

The real twist of the film is that Joanne is the one who impregnated Mona. When they were younger, she was

Mona's very own James Dean. In addition to being an icon of Old Hollywood and teenage rebellion, James Dean was also a queer figure, noted for an emotional expressiveness that broke with the leading men of the past. When Joanne hears about Jimmy Dean, she cannot help but feel regret for the child she left behind — a frequent complication for people who transition after their children are born. It all becomes too much to bear for Joanne. When she is asked later by Stella May if she regrets anything about her transition, the closest that Joanne comes to revealing how she really feels is when she says, "Only when I think about it." On the surface, it seems to say that she regrets her transition, but line-reading reveals the complexities of trans womanhood. Joanne gave up a lot to be the woman that she is, and that included her hometown, the son she "fathered," and the time she could have potentially spent with this friend group she grew up with who were so important to her. It is not the transition itself that is regretful, but the realities of trans femininity, which are tied to trade-offs, compromises, and losses.

Altman's use of a two-way mirror to shift from past to present also reflects a specificity about transness. When you are trans, you become painfully aware of the time lost in becoming yourself. Joanne is a woman stretching to reinforce her gender role in a pained, elaborate way among her friends, because she is trying to remove the past from her body. Through the two-way mirror, the audience can easily see the direct line between Mark Patton's Joe and Black's Joanne, and this allows for a continuity in mannerisms between the two actors. It is a testament to the work of both Black and Patton that there is minimal distance between the two performances.

Come Back to the 5 & Dime, Jimmy Dean, Jimmy Dean is one of the best films about transness, presenting a full picture of a trans person through a visual language of time and mirrors. Usually in movies about trans women, only a fraction of their life is shown, and it is rare to see a trans woman's life play out over decades and in a way that clearly suggests she has a life to live beyond the film's immediate narrative arc. In the movies, trans women are often like James Dean; beguiling, curious, temperamental, not meant to last, a flicker of a flame that quickly fades. Karen Black's Joanne is all those things too, perhaps the truest "disciple" of the friend group. But unlike James Dean, Joanne lives on.

City of Lost Souls: Found Queer Spaces as Cinematic Breeding Grounds

Rosa von Praunheim was a queer radical whose prolific film career often looked to the past to confront the present. Born in East Germany and raised in West Germany after his adopted family fled, he grew up with the name Holger Mischwitzky, but by the 1960s, he had adopted the *nom de plume* Rosa von Praunheim, with Rosa a reference to the pink triangle. He worked in America as an apprentice to avant-garde filmmakers and in Germany in close association with Werner Schroeter. He began making many diary films and scripted features about gay life in Germany, but also took great interest in the gay liberation movement in the United States.

Praunheim was not content strictly documenting the homophile movement that happened in the 1960s and 1970s. He sought to see the bigger picture of queer history and how queer lifestyles were multifaceted and, at times, conflicting. He proved to be a pivotal figure in subsequent decades, working in both the documentary form and feature films that were a genuinely radical hybrid of the scripted and the real, not dissimilar to *Funeral Parade of Roses*. Praunheim's focus and interest in the trans film image makes him one of the most forward-thinking filmmakers of the time, whether in queer filmmaking or otherwise.

Stadt der verlorenen Seelen (*City of Lost Souls*) (1983) is one of the most joyous films ever made about transness, a hybrid of documentary and musical that finds a group of misfits inhabiting and working at a fast-food joint called the Hamburger Queen. It stars Angie Stardust, Judith Flex, Joaquin La Habana, and Tara O'Hara as themselves, with punk-rocker Jayne County playing Lila, an exaggerated cis Southern Belle with dreams of Hollywood fame. The ensemble is wonderful, but *City of Lost Souls* is Angie Stardust's film. She was known as a singer, actress, and drag artist who broke barriers in the queer communities of New York City in the 1950s and 1960s and was considered the first black star of New York's Club 82. She caused controversy in the drag community when she began to take estrogen and relocated to Hamburg, West Germany, where she became friends with Praunheim.

Praunheim's model of queer cinema presents divisions between queer people as negligible, even if there are sometimes generational differences and disagreements in language and politics. He gives the performers space to work through their past via reenactment, and in *City of Lost Souls*, he ties together their histories with his own understanding of the remnants of German fascism still lingering in his homeland. His work is stridently political, while also a living, breathing document of queer persons and their experiences. His pictures do not have the stiffness that is typical of the documentary form, because his work is playful in its structuring, seeking to find new ways of expressing stories and open to discussion and testimony. As an example, the film includes a scene where Angie Stardust discusses her experiences with racism in Germany, such as being spat on on a boat by an older woman. This is not filmed in the manner of a conventional talking head, but given life through a dialogue scene between herself, Judith Flex, and Tron von Hollywood, and preceded by a re-enactment of a young white German boy using a slur toward her.

The way that Praunheim presents trans people, and queer people in general, is overflowing with admiration and joy for the full range of the queer experience, foreshadowing a more understanding and truthful depiction of the trans film image. One of the finest examples of this is a scene in *City of Souls* where Tara O'Hara and Angie Stardust have a conversation about the terms associated with transness, such as transsexual or transvestite. Tara believes that she and Angie are a "third sex," and Angie bristles at this distinction. They go on to talk about vaginoplasty, which Stardust expresses a desire for, because in her words, she does not want to die an "old man." Tara believes surgery is unnecessary, considering it "old school," and believes hormones and latent femininity should be enough. Angie takes exception to being called "old school" and stating it was women like her bearing the brunt of transphobia in the old days that made Tara's life possible. During this conversation, they are putting together outfits to wear that evening. The conversation is a real dialogue with no definitively right answer. This dialogic, rather than didactic, element of Praunheim's work has made it age remarkably well across the decades, presenting varied sides of queer experience without diluting any of the positions held by his participants.

Praunheim's camera is also very generous in shooting the nudity of his subjects, emphasizing the beauty in the way their bodies, while unique and separate from one another, are connected through queerness and desire. One of the finest examples involves Tara picking up a strange man, who perceives her as a cis woman. The film eschews the theatrics of a reveal or the mechanics of a "teachable moment." The man is unsure what to do with Tara's body, but because he is attracted to her, they still sleep together. No expression of queer desire is off-limits in this beautiful queer fantasia. Praunheim presents a queer cinema of possibilities, without rules.

Due to the chintzy sets and irreverent humor, *City of Lost Souls* is sometimes compared to the work of John Waters, but Waters' films were sardonic in a way that Praunheim's were not. Waters was at the vanguard of a transgressive queer cinema of bad taste, best embodied by drag queen superstar Divine. Praunheim's work aims for something different, presenting the very human wants, desires, and needs of its characters and personalities. The Berlin setting acts as a home away from home for these characters who have been pushed away by society, but the film never loses track of Berlin's flaws as a place either. Jayne County's Lila has numerous scene-stealing moments, through her mugging and hyper-expressiveness. Her most appealing scene in the film is a song about her crisis as a good, red-blooded Christian woman who has suddenly found herself in love with a Red Army soldier. Praunheim spoofs communism through this relationship, but so too does he spoof American ideas about communism. People ultimately find their home in each other and build real community in their relationships. This is expanded upon in the musical sections, where all the characters sing about the Hamburger Queen while slinging lettuce around and making a mess with ketchup and mustard. They are terrible at running a restaurant, but they would not have it any other way.

The entire ensemble is remarkably well assured, and the way they create absurd versions of themselves, while also honoring their actual histories, is a way of regaining control over the past and transforming it into comedy. The past can sometimes be a burden for queer people. But it does not feel that way when watching *City of Lost Souls,* which ends on a closing song-and-dance number about coming together in the face of annihilation. It is an ecstatic closing song that rivals any big-budget musical of that era, making the film a respite in a decade that often rendered queerness and transness a self-fulfilled prophecy of doom.

Rosa von Praunheim is one of the most vital queer artists of the trans film image. Usually in films about trans people, there is some palpable level of apprehension and discomfort on the part of the filmmaker's interacting with these subjects. Early films featuring trans subjects or characters can sometimes feel distant, or at a remove, even in their stronger depictions, due to this factor, and this prevents

both an understanding of the trans subject and the opportunity for viewers to learn and witness the depth of trans
experience. It is, after all, up to the filmmaker and editor
to choose what they want to show and what they wish to
present, and sometimes there is an agenda that is not completely invested in depicting a trans subject with honesty
— warts and all. Praunheim has his intentions, as any filmmaker would, but the way that he presents trans people,
and queer people in general, is overflowing with admiration
and joy for the full range of the queer experience and foreshadows a more understanding and truthful depiction of
the trans film image.

Gender-Play in the Mainstream

1980s mainstream gender-play came more from queer filmmakers and performers that did not strictly involve "reveals"
in their work or placate the puritanical sensibilities that
came to the fore during the Reagan era. John Waters' and
Divine's *Polyester* (1981) and *Hairspray* (1988) showed a
much more mature side of the performer, who would sadly
pass on shortly after *Hairspray* was released. While playing a
cis woman in prior Waters films, Divine's characters in this
period were more domestic, maternal figures, which created
a fascinating level of artifice and depth. But by and large,
these movies of gender-play primarily involved straight cis
filmmakers and performances.

Gender-play as embodied by the comic hero re-emerged
in the 1980s with Blake Edwards' celebrated remake of
Victor/Victoria (1982) as a musical and the commercial
and critical success of Sydney Pollack's *Tootsie* (1982), in
many ways an extension of *Some Like it Hot*, in which Jack
Lemmon and Tony Curtis pose as women in order to escape
the mob. The film's set up is that actor Michael Dorsey
(Dustin Hoffman) disguises himself as a woman called Dorothy in order to land a role in the daytime soap *Tootsie*. It
also functions as a spoof of soap opera tropes, particularly

the cross-dressing reveal in the film's farcical climax, when Dorsey takes off his wig and transforms from playing hospital administrator Emily Kimberly to her brother Edward, parodying the cross-dressing reveals that had been popping up within soap operas of the time. One of the most famous of these was *General Hospital* (1963–), on which *Southwest General*, the soap opera in *Tootsie*, was based.

The cross-dressing reveal arc that appeared in the fall episodes of *General Hospital* in 1980 was notable for just how long the plot device was sustained, running through several episodes. At the center of this controversy was Christopher Morley, the notorious "Transvestite" from *Freebie and the Bean*, in this instance playing a professional hitman posing as a woman. It was his most famous, longest-running television role. Morley carved out a niche for himself as a female impersonator willing to represent the trans trope of the "deceiver" and "the trap" in most of the parts he played, stretching from the 1970s to the 1990s — for example, on *Magnum P.I.* and *Too Close for Comfort*. Morley added nuance to often limited roles centered around a reveal, but often at the expense of circulating casual transphobia and harmful tropes. The plot line on *General Hospital* ended with Morley — once again — being shot, a violent death always looming over cross-dressing and trans characters.

Tootsie as "masquerade" is progressive in comparison to its inspiration. In *Tootsie*, the reveal is two-fold. Dorsey's character on *Southwest General*, Emily, becomes popular among viewers as a no-nonsense Southern Belle, and behind the scenes, his co-stars suspect nothing. Dorsey cannot keep up this masquerade, however. In Emily Kimberly's "reveal" as *really* being a man on *Southwest General*, we also find Dorsey revealing himself in an off-script moment to his co-stars. The sense of betrayal, shock, and confusion of his co-stars on the show also represents how Dorsey's colleagues, who had only known him as Dorothy, truly felt. This is best represented by Dorsey's castmate

Julie (Jessica Lange), who punches Dorsey in the stomach after the reveal.

Tootsie did not have the TERFs coming out of the woodwork pointing their fingers at the screen and declaring it as an example of how men dress as women to occupy women's spaces, but Hoffman dressed as Dorothy did become a cover for En Femme Publication's *The Crossdresser's Movie Guide*.[3] *Tootsie's* reputation in cross-dressing circles was not what its makers had in mind as their core audience, but that cross-dressers sought to claim the movie as their own is not at all surprising. *Tootsie* was a commercially and critically popular mainstream film that embraced the absurdity and comedic slapstick of a cis straight man in "gag drag." Nevertheless, cross-dressing communities at the time were beginning to wonder if this uptick in gender-play on-screen was becoming a little more than a trend, as other films emerged that made *Tootsie* and its success seem like even less of an aberration.

One of these is Barbra Streisand's *Yentl* (1983). Refusing to conform to the expectations of women at the turn of the twentieth century in her Polish *shtetl*, Streisand's Ashkenazi Jew Yentl Mendel poses as a man to study Talmudic law. Yentl, playing the male figure of Anshel, will not have to live as a man for the rest of her life, as the film ends with her emigrating to America with a clean slate of freedom and potential. As Stephen Whittle has noted, *Yentl* and other examples of female-to-male cross-dressing do ultimately serve a purpose for the characters:

> We see women who use male disguise in order to find a place in a man's world, and to learn and understand the world of men. Once accepted, they revert back to living as women, though it is accepted that they have some special knowledge and are as a result "better" women to the men they know.[4]

Yentl's adjacency to trans masculinity proved to be a guiding light for many trans men of this period — Lou Sullivan would list it as a notable film in his 1985 publication, *Information for the Male-to-Female Crossdresser and Transsexual*.[5] In *FTM International*, Jewish trans male activist Razi Zarchy would say at a Transgender Shabbat that "Yentl was my role model."[6] It showed that, with the paucity of mainstream trans masculine film images, even something that did not fully fit into the conventions of transness still went a long way for many.

When 1980s gender-play did involve specific transness, such as with British actress Vanessa Redgrave playing professional tennis player Renée Richards in the television movie adaptation of Richards' memoir, *Second Serve* (1986), it created a fascinating dynamic. According to the television film's producer Linda Yellen, she had been trying to get the film made since Richards made international news for trying to compete in the 1976 U.S. Open, but the topic was considered "too freaky" for the industry. It took nearly a decade for the film to get made and Yellen knew there would be a lot of people who would be "turned off" by the subject matter.[7] However, Yellen struck gold with Oscar-winning actress and activist Redgrave, herself no stranger to controversy due to her political activism.

For their time, Redgrave's comments about Richards read as especially progressive, particularly when compared to more contemporary actors like Eddie Redmayne and Hillary Swank, who would often use pre-transition names and incorrect pronouns when talking about the real-life subjects they were playing. Redgrave, by all accounts, had the typical mainstream prejudices when she started reading *Second Serve*, but soon grew to admire Richards' fight to be taken seriously. "Renée is a very courageous woman," she would say. "And this story is not about transsexualism but about all the social problems she had to face. The press witch-hunted her, but it only increased the admiration and warmth people had for her."[8]

Redgrave's gender-play was so effective that it impressed many in the trans community at the time, especially Lou

Sullivan, who stated in his *FTM Newsletter* that he believed Redgrave's role as "Richard" to be the best female-as-male performance he had ever seen.[9] Redgrave did not simply play Richards as a tennis player but played her before the transition — done up effectively with a buzzcut, believable masculine makeup, bound chest, and masculine postures that exude nervous energy and frustration. Redgrave also convincingly lowers her vocal register, which is impressive given that she is also trying to do an American accent.

Second Serve oscillates back and forth, undermining the typical transition narrative. As much as the film in many ways follows the tropes in building trans film images around transformation and surgery, Richards' story was a trans image that was an instant source of controversy and debate in the arenas of sports and civil liberty laws in its time, where her medical transition was an inescapable part of the story. The film, with cooperation from Richards, who had already written a second book on her misgivings in the spectacle surrounding her, is respectful in depicting her life struggles and successes. It portrays her as a deeply intelligent person who felt unfulfilled because she could not express this side of herself until she was in her forties. To be made at a time of so many negative trans images and an utterly dire political situation for trans people, *Second Serve* is an object worth revisiting even if it is tied to network television conventions and is dated in relation to trans medicine of that period.

Bauer: The Misunderstood Trans Martyr in *Vera*

Boys Don't Cry (1999) was not the first film to turn a real-life trans masculine figure into an on-screen martyr. That title goes to Sergio Toledo's *Vera* (1986), which requires reconsideration for its depiction of trans masculinity. While groundbreaking at the time, it has a complicated legacy. The film is a loose biopic of the short life of Brazilian poet Anderson Bigode Herzer, who in the film is referred to by the names of Bauer and Vera (and played by Ana Beatriz Nogueira who won Best Actress at Berlinale). The real-life Herzer was a trans male writer who became a celebrity in Brazil's cultural spaces for his poetry and was embraced by the left-wing for his class-conscious art. *Vera* opens with a text that states that this is a fictional story, and that any similarities to a real person or incident are purely coincidental. Except it could only be about Herzer, an orphan and product of Brazil's notorious FEBEM juvenile detention centers.

At FEBEM, in the brutal confines of the detention centers, Vera is a "tomboy" surrounded by tough girls, a few of whom are also gender-questioning. These early sections have the kitchen-sink realism and grit of Alan Clarke (a natural point of comparison would be Clarke's masterpieces *Scum* (1979) and *Made in Britain* (1982)), or one of the greatest films Brazil has ever produced, Héctor Babenco's *Pixote* (1980). There are also elements of the "women's prison" film genre, but undercutting the sense of matriarchal camaraderie and discord often central to those films is the fact that Bauer is coming to the realization that he identifies as male. This self-revelatory moment happens at a detention center party that mixes the genders. Bauer is drawn to a young man who takes a girl that Bauer fancies to dance and it becomes apparent that Bauer's attention is less focused on the girl and more on the young man, who shares similar physical features to Bauer. He begins to engage in sexual fantasies about being male that open up his consciousness to the drive to be male physically and socially.

When working as a civil servant as an adult and presenting as male, Bauer is consistently misgendered and at odds with his colleagues due to his trans identity. He pursues a romantic relationship with a coworker named Clara (Aida Leiner), a divorced young mother. Although aware of Bauer's trans identity from the outset, Clara stumbles in how to speak and express her feelings toward Bauer despite her attraction for him. Their relationship proves to be too fragile when their physical intimacy is undermined by his dysphoria.

Gender dysphoria is a major facet of Bauer's anxieties and his lack of access to care makes him an anxious, raw nerve. He expresses aspirations to get gender-affirming surgeries but is left to his own devices, which makes the moment of Bauer having his menstrual period become even more overwhelmed in self-loathing. Near the end of the film, there is a devastating scene of Bauer walking down the city streets at night only to stop at a store where he sees his own face on several television screens; a trans mirror scene now a kaleidoscopic, an inescapable, psychological prison. His suicide is not shown but implied.

In its initial release and bolstered profile through its success at Berlinale, *Vera* did reach some North American audiences and in the ensuing years played at trans film festivals through the 1990s. It had earned praise from trans activists like Rupert Raj, who reviewed the film in his *Gender Networker* publication.[10] *Vera* still remains one of the most notable films on trans masculinity and presents how often ignorance is society's reaction when directly presented with the struggles of a trans person.

What Sex Am I? and the Televisual Journalism of Transness

Television has its own history of trans film images and would be an undeniable inflection point in how trans film images would recirculate from the small to the big screen, and the trans community in the 1980s had understood there was some benefit in using television as a medium. Trade-offs were made and visibility was offered for the sake of educating others about trans people through daytime talk shows like *The Phil Donahue Show* (1970–1986). Although *The Phil Donahue Show* was a more progressive arena for trans guests, there was always a concern over their exploitation — something that later reached a nadir with programs like *The Jerry Springer Show* in the 1990s — but during the 1980s, these appearances were not exclusively sensationalist. Trans people in America who worked for the American Educational Gender Information Service (AEGIS), who assisted in organizing appearances on talk shows, tried to assess which of the shows would present trans guests in too salacious a manner, but too often the guests on these shows were never in contact with the AEGIS.

Still, television in this period was often more valuable in giving access to documentary features about trans people in ways that were not happening with most narrative films. In the United Kingdom, there was Kristiene Clarke, a trans filmmaker who made the documentary *Sex Change: Shock! Horror! Probe!* for Channel 4 in 1988. But Clarke was seen as an anomaly, with her documentary film career being extremely diverse and not exclusive to transition narratives. In the US, HBO's emergence as a pay-cable station offered another viewing avenue for non-fiction beyond network and public television. Oscar-winning actress and well-respected documentarian Lee Grant, while working on HBO's *American Undercover* series, made a handful of excellent documentaries in the 1980s that covered topics such as the housing crisis in the United States, domestic violence, small-town unions, and trans people. While she made better films than *What Sex Am I?* (1985), it remains a fascinating trans film image, because it is not only interested in trans women but also trans men and cross-dressers, which gave viewers a fuller scope of gender nonconformity at the time of its release.

What Sex Am I? explores multiple stories of trans people in America and starts with an interview with Christine Jorgensen. Jorgensen would die a few years later and had reached a stage where she appeared more reflective. She is a more seasoned interviewee than many of the participants, and her inclusion immediately gives the film a level of name recognition within the community and in the broader United States. There were also other trans people involved who had gained some level of notoriety due to heated, polit-icized discussions of their transness, such as Steve Dain, the gym teacher who was terminated from his position by his school district after he came out as a trans man and who then sued the school for wrongful termination. Dain's case was one the many firings of gay and lesbian school teach-ers in the 1970s based on their sexuality, part of the moral panic stirred up by Anita Bryant's "Save Our Children" cam-paign.

Through this legal battle, Dain became one of the most visible trans men of his era, and up until the Brandon Teena murder case, may have been the most visible avatar for trans masculinity in the mainstream. In *What Sex am I?*, Grant takes immediate interest in Dain's masculinity and athleticism — he is shown pumping iron, bare-chested by a pool, a genuine image of gender euphoria in an other-wise dispiriting tale of discrimination. Grant clearly empa-thized with and connected to Dain's struggles — Grant was famously blacklisted by Hollywood for a dozen years, a life-time for an actress, when she spoke out against the House of Un-American Activities Committee at the funeral of J. Edward Bromberg, her name subsequently appearing in the conservative dog-whistle magazine *Red Channels*.[11] Just as her career should have been blossoming, it was stripped away from her, and the same could have been said of Dain's teaching career.

Despite winning his legal case against the school district, Dain's life was disrupted and altered. Although he would use his increased public profile to offer counseling and mentor-ship to people within the trans masculine community, he could not go back to teaching. Employment discrimination is a running theme in Grant's documentary. *What Sex Am I?* is very clear-headed on the sacrifices that trans people make to transition. It is ironic that this act of becoming is also usually synonymous with the question of what will be lost. For some it is a job, or the level of income they were used to before they came out, and for others it is family, a wife, children, or parents, whose love came with limitations. In the documentary, these trade-offs are visible. Those who are medically transitioning, cross-dress, or are self-described "transvestites" rely on networks of other trans people who offer mutually assured discretion and support. Grant is straight-forward in her reporting, giving her subjects the chance to speak clearly about their experiences in the world and express their wants.

Grant's status as a cisgender person presents a real tension in her attempts at understanding the wants and desires of trans women, due to much of her documentary work being rooted in feminist journalism. She won an Oscar for *Down and Out in America* (1986), which focuses on the failing welfare system in the age of President Reagan. But equally as necessary are her films that focus exclusively on women, such as *The Willmar 8* (1981), which follows the strike of a small bankers union composed entirely of women, or *Battered* (1989), which focuses on spousal abuse and how women are failed by the criminal justice system. One of the more striking elements of watching *What Sex Am I?* is seeing how the problems experienced by cis women also emerge as problems experienced by trans women after medically transitioning. While some of Grant's questions and narration are often in dated language, the way in which she profiles trans women and gives them space is equivalent to her approach to cis women in her other documentaries. Beyond trans women and trans people of national notoriety, Grant speaks with numerous trans men, cross-dressers, and one person who has detransitioned. The fact Grant involves such a wider range of trans individuals demonstrates the importance of her having had trans people consulting on the film, such as photographer Mariette Pathy Allen.

Grant is primarily interested in answering the question of how transness happens. She is a talking-heads film-maker, an approach which can often be visually dull. But Grant makes the wise decision of beginning with the inter-view and then shifting to voice-over, while showing trans people going about their quotidian rituals. In her images, viewers see trans women in kitchens with other trans women, laughing amongst themselves while they prepare a meal for a visiting mother. She has a trans man out at a BBQ with his cisgender friends, a cross-dresser applying lipstick and laughing to themselves. Grant is a great documentarian, not because she answers all the questions she presents definitively. She has a genuine interest in demystifying her subjects, and with *What Sex Am I?*, she successfully gives trans people a level of humanity and space to showcase their lives and struggles.

The Rise of Home Video

VHS tapes emerged as a crucial tool for the trans community in the 1980s. For trans women and cross-dressers, how-to video tutorials became a major market for those who needed visual learning guidance in the privacy of their home. These forms of analogue media would give way to internet web tutorials, but the videos yielded trans film images that were made specifically for their market and promoted in trans publications and magazines focused primarily on helping other people just starting to explore their trans identities.

Many trans magazines also featured columns on older films, including *The Queen, She-Man: A Story of Fixation,* and *Funeral Parade of Roses.* These reviews were, admittedly, more amateur criticism than deep analytical readings, but they presented curious readers with trans film images of the past, allowing them to reemerge and be reassessed. Lou Sullivan's *FTM Newsletter* sold VHS tapes that were a mix of illegal re-recordings of newscasts, television talk shows on trans people, and television movie broadcasts like *Second Serve* and *What Sex Am I?*. In a time before DVR, streaming, or uploading, if you missed these telecasts, they were often gone forever, and so Sullivan was not so much engaging in media piracy, as he was creating and recirculating an archive of trans film images of both real and fictionalized people, which also fell into his interest as the founder of the GLBT Historical Society in San Francisco. Sullivan, a major cinephile, also recommended a list of films he perceived as trans masculine film images and examples of cross-dressing in his *Information of the Female-to-Male Crossdresser and Transsexual.*[93]

Sullivan himself would also become a trans film image for the purposes of education and advocacy. Sullivan was a gay trans man from San Francisco who had Steve Dain as a mentor. He spent several years writing and corresponding with medical professionals across the country, whose aim was to shut out gay trans men of phalloplasties and other techniques of bottom surgery, denying them proper recognition by the medical community. As a gay trans man, he was told in no unsubtle terms that people like him did not exist, but there were doctors who were prepared to listen and found him to be compelling. Sullivan collaborated with former HBIGDA president and psychiatrist Dr. Ira B. Pauly in a series of filmed interviews and conversations via the University of Nevada Medical School, where Dr. Pauly served as the school's chair. The resulting videos, called *Female-to-Gay Male Transsexualism*, were broken up into four parts and released from 1988 through 1990.[12]

Sullivan would die of AIDS complications in 1991. Even with his physical decline evident in each subsequent video with Dr. Pauly, and with AIDS itself becoming a central topic, Sullivan's bravery showed the power of the trans film image. His trans image survived him as a force for change, ensuring those like him could receive necessary and affirming care.

CHAPTER 5
Trans Grotesquerie:
From Post-*Psycho* Slashers to
The Silence of the Lambs

I. Killers with a Twist

The ending of Alfred Hitchcock's *Psycho* (1960) had a prolonged negative effect on the perception of transness in North America. Hitchcock's filmography contains many films with queer coding and subtext that evaded the censors, such as *Rebecca* (1940), *Rope* (1948), and *Strangers on a Train* (1951). Much of this was due to queer source material from Daphne du Maurier and Patricia Highsmith, along with working with gay writers like Arthur Laurents, who wrote the screenplay for *Rope*. But something about murderers "not being what they seem" clearly appealed to Hitchcock. His 1930 film *Murder!* precedes Norman Bates in *Psycho* with a cross-dressing killer. But *Psycho*'s immediate and long-standing cultural legacy created a new subgenre of slasher horror in which questions of a character's gender identity and warped self-perception would be interwoven with an insatiable urge to kill.

Killer Norman Bates (Anthony Perkins, whose queerness was a guarded secret to the public and an open secret in private through much of his life) is loosely based on the real-life serial killer Ed Gein. Gein terrorized Plainfield, Wisconsin, in the 1950s, and gained widespread notoriety when authorities discovered that he was sewing together a "woman suit" made of flesh he had stripped from corpses in the hopes of transforming himself into his mother.[1] Norman Bates became intertwined with the neurotic, trans-feminine serial killer that became commonplace in horror films and erotic thrillers, and it caused the viewing public to sometimes merge transness with evil.

The ending of *Psycho* was unusual for Hitchcock, because he felt the need to explain what the audience had just seen. Typically for Hitchcock, it would have ended with the arrest of Norman at the last second before he killed again, but the film drags along for another ten minutes. At the police station where Norman is being held, a psychiatrist (played by Simon Oakland) is introduced, and his role is not unlike that of the white-jacket figures of trans exploitation pictures from the period. He goes on to explain that Norman is no longer present in his own mind, and his mother has taken over his personality. He explains that he had been dangerously ill since his father had died, and that when he killed his mother, it tipped him over the edge. One of the cops suggests that Norman was a "transvestite," and while *Psycho* tries to explain away Norman's actions while sheepishly denying the transvestite suggestion, the mention of the word tied Norman to its context. While *Psycho* is not explicitly a film about a trans person, it was and has been confused as such. Furthermore, the *Psycho*-like films that came after it immediately leaned into this idea of the secret trans killer; as a result, *Psycho* is a testament to how a work of fiction can spill out into the public ecosystem and affect the trajectory of how cross-dressing and transness are perceived in film.

For example, William Castle's early *Psycho* rip-off *Homicidal* (1961) has an exposition-laden monologue from the authorities about the killer Warren/Emily taking a "trip to Copenhagen, Denmark" — an allusion to Christine Jorgensen and sex change operations. However, the most popular of these knock-off characters came in Tobe Hooper's *The Texas Chainsaw Massacre* (1974). The film's masked killer,

Leatherface, is positioned as the feminine Gein stand-in, complete with smeared eyeliner and lipstick, and as the films in the series progressed, Leatherface's feminine characteristics were increasingly emphasized, peaking with *The Return of the Texas Chainsaw Massacre* in 1994. This incarnation of Leatherface was inspired by John Waters' regular Divine, now sporting a pair of breasts, low-cut dresses that accentuate their cleavage, a voluminous wig, and lipstick on their mask. The film also features Leatherface undertaking a makeup routine while listening to old jazz standards in a sequence both so ridiculous and oddly sincere that it becomes camp.

William Lustig's *Maniac* (1980) also sought to give the trope of the neurotic trans feminine killer new legs, and garnered controversy upon release when Gene Siskel called the film out, not for transmisogyny, but for run-of-the-mill hatred towards women. Both *The Texas Chainsaw Massacre* and *Maniac* gained a reputation for being notorious, raw horror films, but neither were as dangerous or as cruel as Brian De Palma's *Dressed to Kill* (1980). De Palma's film is the only one that uses real-life terminology and the medical information associated with gender transition to define its killer, ripping from the headlines and real-life trans images to create the narrative.

II. *Dressed to Kill*'s Calamitous Homage

Dressed to Kill relies heavily upon the reveal of a character whose gender is not what it seems. In an interview with *Rolling Stone* in 1980, De Palma stated that he got the idea for his transsexual serial killer while watching Nancy Hunt — a real transsexual — on an episode of *The Phil Donahue Show* dedicated to transsexuality. De Palma subsequently became fascinated by transsexuality and began reading up on it.[2] Despite this research, De Palma remained unenlightened about the concept: "They have a wonderful word for it — Gender discomfort! Gender discomfort... Can you imagine?"[3] The *Rolling Stone* piece notes that De Palma states this all while barely suppressing a laugh, even joking about showing up in women's clothing at a dinner party to get reactions.

De Palma bristled at the notion that *Dressed to Kill* was a rip-off of *Psycho*, but objectively the film does follow the same structural pattern by killing off the assumed main character (Angie Dickinson as Kate Miller) in the first act, and then introducing us to new characters who investigate the murder, a climactic reveal, and a concluding exposition-heavy scene with a psychiatrist. Norman Bates was never written as a real transvestite, but Dr. Robert Elliott (Michael Caine), the murderer in *Dressed to Kill*, is canonically a trans woman. He is given the character detail of a split personality (one male, one female) fighting for dominance, and whenever he is aroused the "female" part of his brain takes over, believing it must kill whichever woman has given his body a male erotic response. De Palma had this character see a psychiatrist for gender dysphoria, gives him the wish of having vaginoplasty surgery, and finally upon arrest, gives them the label of "transsexual."

Robert Elliott is a model of what not to do when writing trans characters, and De Palma used his newfound fascination with transness to dive into some of his predilections: castration anxiety, fear of power in female sexuality, and the submissive male. Transsexuality literalizes all these topics for De Palma, such as when Keith Gordon's character Peter learns about gender transition and says with unease on his face: "This gives me an idea for a new science experiment. I'll make a woman... out of me."

For a character so central to the film's machinations, there has not been a De Palma lead character as thinly defined as Robert Elliott. Little is learned about him other than his wishes for surgery and his sexual desires for his patients. There is a vacancy in Caine's performance and the taped recordings of Bobbi, one of Elliott's transgender patients, still feel disparate even with these revelations. De

Palma regular Nancy Allen plays Liz Blake, an escort who is stalked by Bobbi, who is following her and leaving voice messages about killing women. Liz is positioned as a contrasting point to the neurosis of Bobbi, meant to further highlight the differences between trans feminine people and cis women.

De Palma is a director of unusual visual gifts, as seen in films like *Blow Out* (1981) and *Femme Fatale* (2002), but *Dressed to Kill* is left wanting. His trademark split-screens and split-diopter shots are used in a blunt manner to evince the split personality of the trans character, and they have no other thematic visual component. He creates his most regressive and harmful sequence in a split-screen where Liz is on one side of the frame discussing rates for her sex work, while Dr. Elliott is on the other side watching a special edition of *The Phil Donahue Show* centered around trans guests. A voiceover track of the killer cuts in while the face of Nancy Hunt, a real-life trans woman and guest on *The Phil Donahue Show*, is in close-up, and he talks about wanting to murder women to let out his "little girl inside," associating the actions of this character with real-life trans people. De Palma frequently layers images, sound clips, and eroticism on top of one another to create a total visual and aural experience. That is the intention of this scene, but the implications of these combined elements create a portrait of transness that does not broaden the character in the film, but instead impinges on the humanity of a real-life trans woman.

Nancy Hunt did not deserve what De Palma did to her image and likeness. Hunt rejected linking transness to trauma and did not believe that transness needed to be pathologized by psychiatrists. She was a war correspondent and a respected journalist, and was a guest on Donahue's show to promote her book, *Mirror Image: The Odyssey of a Male-to-Female Transsexual*, which became a mainstay on trans reading lists through the entire decade. There have been people on record who have said that after that appearance on television, Hunt assisted other trans women who reached out to her seeking help in navigating transition.[4] But De Palma placed her image alongside the voiceover of a trans serial killer. Hunt had difficulties in being accepted by her colleagues and family members, like numerous other trans people from this era often did, but having judgment about her life amplified in such a way by De Palma went beyond cheapness and bad taste. De Palma mentioned Hunt by name in the press-cycle for the film because it was with her image that he began to consider the film.[5] It is not a coincidence that they made Bobbi Elliott up to look like her in the final product. The way that De Palma used Hunt's image is one of the more deplorable things a director has ever done with a trans person in film.

In the reveal, "Bobbi" (Elliott's female persona) tries to kill Liz, but is stopped dead in her tracks by a female police officer. Bobbi is arrested and is sent off to Bellevue; back at the police station, a psychiatrist is summoned to remind the audience that all of this is a mirror to *Psycho*. The difference, however, is that *Psycho*'s rendering of psychiatric elements attempted to create distance between the killer and the lives of trans people. It failed to do so, but it is at least notable that there was a cushioning blow of "Not really!" when the psychiatrist was asked if Norman was a transvestite. In *Dressed to Kill*, the psychiatrist begins by saying that Bobbi was a transsexual. De Palma creates no flexibility for the audience to see this murderer in any other way. The psychiatrist then goes on to explain that Bobbi was driven insane because she was on the cusp of having sex reassignment surgery, but could not decide if she wanted to kill her male self. In the following scene, Liz explains to her investigative partner Peter how a man can become a woman through hormone injections, and her information is medically accurate. Peter is unsettled by this information, even though he cracks a joke, and in the background, a woman overhearing their conversation can be seen growing faint. Are the effects of transition so shocking that they warrant this type of seedy black comedy? It is all a laugh for De Palma. By using the real images of trans people, De Palma makes a mockery of transness and treats it as just another cheap plot device to pull from.

III. *Sleepaway Camp*: Worse Than Murder

In Robert Hiltzik's cult slasher *Sleepaway Camp* (1983), transness is treated with revulsion. *Sleepaway Camp* runs in an extensive line of films that treat the reveal of transness as a moment of abject horror.

In the early 1980s, the slasher film was all the rage after the wild success of John Carpenter's *Halloween* (1978) and Paramount's knock-off *Friday the 13th* (1980). It was cheap entertainment that usually made a profit due to the popularity of these films with teenagers and with the blossoming home-video market making horror an easily relied upon commodity for independent studios, who could churn out sequels to the more popular titles. *Sleepaway Camp* came to life in 1983 because of these factors, and would be nothing more than a dime-a-dozen slasher film, if it were not for its twist ending, which remains one of the genre's most notorious.

Sleepaway Camp relies upon the audience understanding the structural model of the slasher film, which follows a routine of teenagers being stalked by an unknown killer, who are murdered one by one after having sex, concluding with the heroism of a chaste final girl defeating the murder until the next film is produced. *Sleepaway Camp*, however, complicates this model, with the final girl and killer combined into a Chimeric image that relies upon transness as an outlet of disgust.

Angela (Felissa Rose) is a selective mute who is off to camp with her cousin Ricky (Jonathan Tiersten). At camp, Angela is ostracized by the other more sexually forward girls and is treated as a whipping post to garner sympathy from the audience, because she has no ability to fight back, verbally or physically. She is introverted to a point of solitude, regarded and dismissed as "strange" in the eyes of everyone around her. At the camp, the slasher element kicks in, with kids and adults alike dropping like flies. Hiltzik has none of the visual intelligence required to make any of it captivating. It is soon apparent that Angela is not who she appears to be. She is revealed as the killer, but that is not what has prolonged the life of this film. Angela has a penis, much to the shock of camp counselors Ronnie (Paul DeAngelo) and Susie (Susan Glaze). It is simply treated as the most horrifying thing imaginable. They say aloud, "How can it be? She's a boy."

The real-life implications of creating a scene where a woman is shown to have a penis to the disgust of others cosigns the idea that trans bodies are monstrous, unnatural, and repulsive. Ronnie and Susie find Angela naked, cradling the head of Paul (Christopher Collet), the boy she had a crush on throughout her time at camp. She gently strokes his head and hums to herself. Before Angela's genitals are revealed, a flashback sequence is used to show the audience that Angela had died in a boating accident along with her father and his secret boyfriend. Angela is, in fact, her brother, Peter. Her caretaker Aunt Martha (Desiree Gould) decided to raise her as a girl. As a result, Peter has gone completely insane by being forced to present a gender identity other than his own. Here lies a potentially captivating idea about being forced to express gender in a way that is not aligned with who the person is, but *Sleepaway Camp* does not do anything with it. At the conclusion of the flashback scene, the film returns to Angela for the reveal. A drum roll begins to play, which transitions into a blaring horn when Angela quickly whips her head around, displaying a malicious grin. With her teeth bared and her eyes wide open — unblinking — Paul's head rolls off Angela's lap.

However, this image alone was not enough for the filmmakers of *Sleepaway Camp*. To drive home the disgust, Angela begins to hiss and grunt like an animal. The final image of the film is a close-up of Angela's frenzied face, and the color turns a sickly green, reminiscent of vomit, to further emphasize a feeling of nausea. *Sleepaway Camp's* legacy in the horror genre resides in this twist and these final images. The film has retained its status as a cult classic with this twist ending being acclaimed as part of the pantheon of great shocker endings in the league of Hitchcock's *Psycho*. This reveals an inherent problem with films that treat trans bodies as twists. It creates the assumption that a normative body is cisgender and anything outside of that realm is then subject for questioning, scrutiny, and disposability.

Sleepaway Camp is a "reveal narrative" that echoes real-world consequences of the discovery of and reaction to the reveal of trans bodies. Through these two counselors, Angela's violence is not the focus, but her body is made a subject of judgment. Hitzlik used a model of a cis male body underneath the head of actress Felissa Rose, and he created a false concept of what a trans body looked like. Horror movies, at their best, bring about empathy for those who suffer under the actions of violence, or ask tough questions about human behavior. *Sleepaway Camp* does none of these things and has somehow retained its status as an object of fascination among horror fans — not because it is a well-made film or that it managed to have anything of import to say through genre conventions, but that it functions like a carnival sideshow act. In the sequel films, Angela is free and kills again. She has adapted to her gender identity, and has even undergone sex reassignment surgery, but these films struggle to elaborate on anything particularly interesting arising from this idea and settle for rote slasher narrative structures.

The fear of the trans feminine body is recurring in post-*Psycho* slasher horror. *Dressed to Kill* and *Sleepaway Camp* are fueled by an emasculation complex and cisgender anxieties rather than the real-life anxieties and experiences by trans people. These are otherwise redundant motion pictures that repeat the same narratives of inevitable reveals and outings. *The Silence of the Lambs* (1991) also taps into these fears but became a transcendent film that broke through from being a genre film into an Oscar-winning juggernaut. It is more complicated than either of these pictures, and finds empathy where other horror films project scorn, but it also reaches back to Ed Gein to construct a trans woman through the character of Buffalo Bill.

IV. Buffalo Bill: The Power in Suggestion

The character of Buffalo Bill in *The Silence of the Lambs* is the single most culturally influential and dominant trans film image to date, and the lingering effects of his characterization have only recently begun to dissipate. On the night of the 64th Academy Awards, *The Silence of the Lambs* was nominated for seven Oscars, and took home five of them, including Best Adapted Screenplay, Best Director, Best Actor, Best Actress, and Best Picture. It was a full sweep in the most important categories. This was unprecedented for a horror film, especially one that was released in February — American films released early in the calendar year are rarely up for awards by the year's end — but its cultural impact was immediate. It was the talk of the town at the 63rd Academy Awards, broadcast in March 1991, and would end up being a top-five domestic grosser at the box office. But during the 64th Academy Awards in March 1992, across the street from the Dorothy Chandler Pavilion in Los Angeles, several hundred protesters organized by the queer rights group Queer Nation marched and chanted behind a police barricade — their primary target was *The Silence of the Lambs*.[6]

The early 1990s were a desolate period for Hollywood interest in queer stories. Mainstream pictures actively ignored the AIDS epidemic and societal homophobia was still present, manifesting in everything from hate crimes to employee discrimination. Mainstream movies could have taken a stand, but queer erasure and negligence predominated. It was visible in many critically acclaimed films from

1991, with the "straight-washing" of adapted stories like *Fried Green Tomatoes*, Oliver Stone's *JFK* suggesting that the president's assassination involved a gay cabal of conspirators, and *Prince of Tides* featuring a character who is traumatized after he is raped by a homosexual as a child.

Buffalo Bill was the last straw. The LAPD arrested numerous Queer Nation protesters that evening. In a Q&A held after the Awards, *Silence of the Lambs* director Jonathan Demme said, "There is great cause for anger from the gay population of this country," expressing genuine empathy for queer people when he went on to say, "It's the responsibility of filmmakers to have a much broader range of characters."[7] Demme would apologize numerous times over the years for Buffalo Bill, and followed up *The Silence of the Lambs* with the well-intentioned, Oscar-winning AIDS discrimination legal drama *Philadelphia* (1993), whose reputation today is as weepy, well-intentioned, liberal pablum.

Demme and screenwriter Ted Tally tried to distance Buffalo Bill from transness by suggesting he was not a "real transsexual." But in the court of public opinion, the perception was that Buffalo Bill was trans, something that has had harmful and insidious ramifications for trans women in relation to the film's legacy. There are many anecdotes in the aftermath of trans women being unwittingly associated with the character. Jen Richards, a trans actress and creator of the award-winning web series *Her Story* (2016), recalled that when she disclosed to a friend about being trans, the friend earnestly remarked, "You mean like Buffalo Bill?"[8] Jame Gumb (Buffalo Bill's real name) has for many remained a constant and unforgiving signifier of transness in the decades since the release of the film. *The Silence of the Lambs* was a larger puzzle-piece of the cultural appetite for comedic and humiliating transphobia in the 1990s that began with this film and concluded with the popularity of the low-brow *The Jerry Springer Show* and middle-brow network television where transness was a regular punchline in sitcoms.

Despite all the harmful effects of the character, there is nonetheless a complexity to what is objectively a deeply negative trans film image. In the depths of his depraved actions, inspired by real-life serial killers, there are some authentic reflections on a trans person put into a state of total crisis — though these were not the explicit aims of Thomas Harris when he wrote the book, nor the screenwriter Ted Tally when he adapted it.

When Harris began to write *The Silence of the Lambs* in the 1980s, his sequel to the best-seller *Red Dragon*, he researched real serial killers and had conversations with investigators in the behavioral science unit of the FBI. Harris has rarely given interviews to assist journalists, critics, and readers in understanding where his influences were drawn from, but the resemblance between Buffalo Bill and the crimes of Ed Gein is clear, with Bill's "Woman Suit" being the most obvious inclusion from Gein's history. The novel follows FBI trainee Clarice Starling, and she is written with some depth — a plucky, intuitive figure with good instincts for sussing out abhorrent behavioral tendencies. She ends up investigating the Buffalo Bill case after impressing her bosses in the FBI and making a connection with the incarcerated serial killer and cannibal Hannibal Lecter.

Clarice Starling as played by Jodie Foster embodies the character as conceived by Harris. Gumb/Buffalo Bill (Ted Levine), however, was a more cumbersome adaptation. In the novel, Gumb's relationship to his own body is foregrounded. He spends his time repeatedly shaving and obsessively rewatching a VHS tape of a beauty pageant featuring his departed mother. In the novel, he is on black-market female hormones, which have changed his body in minor ways. He has had numerous run-ins with medical professionals who have stalled his progress in transitioning because they do not believe him to be a "true transsexual." This is also the way the film tries to distance Gumb from trans people. But in suggesting that there were rules and expectations of what constituted a genuine trans person, the film and the novel highlight, and in some ways co-sign, the realities of trans medical gatekeeping and the sabotage of trans healthcare in the time leading up to the 1990s.

When Starling is on the case, she asks Hannibal Lecter, former psychiatrist of Jame Gumb, whether he is a real transsexual. Lecter insists that he is not, but it is merely an identity he has latched onto out of a denial and self-hatred of his own identity. Starling responds that she believes that transsexuals are naturally very passive. This is meant to keep the film safe from criticism. Instead, such suggestions summoned ideas and images associated with transness in the minds of audiences who were led there by the film and novel.

Gumb's trans adjacency is tied into the character being denied care at the Johns Hopkins University Gender Identity Clinic. It is a crucial element of his origin story, with Harris's novel going into more depth on how the clinic saw Gumb and how the FBI seeks to use what information the clinic holds on him to help in his capture. In her conversations with the lead investigator of the Buffalo Bill case, FBI Agent Jack Crawford, Harris presents Clarice Starling as far more curious about the red flags associated with Gumb going to such a clinic. Crawford even reveals what to look for in a trans criminal record, such as if the crimes were non-violent, in relation to the "gender identity problem," namely "cross-dressing in public." The film version of this discussion focuses more on the personality issues, with gender identity not uttered once — an attempt by the screenwriter to elide the question of Jame Gumb being linked to transness. Real gender clinics at the University of Minnesota and Columbus Medical Center are also referenced as potential places where Gumb could have sought care. But JHU became the most suitable setting, with its proximity to the FBI headquarters, even though the real-life institution had not been performing trans-related surgeries for years.

The Johns Hopkins University had one of the most well-known gender clinics in the United States. Beginning operations in 1966, its history in relation to *The Silence of the Lambs* book and subsequent film is fascinating for a number of reasons. The connection to Gumb puts the gender clinic in an unsavory position, even in their denial of Gumb's claimed transsexualism, because they would still have files of Gumb's application. Those files become the necessary information to help assist the FBI in their search. Even as Ted Tally's screenplay makes efforts to smooth over and not delve too deeply into the matters of gender identity and transness that the novel explores, he chose not to remove the Johns Hopkins University as the holders of the applicant file. There is a confrontation between Jack Crawford and Dr. Danielson, head of the gender clinic, in which Crawford threatens to leak the Gumb-JHU connection to the press unless Danielson provides the FBI with the application files.

The film's version of the confrontation is quick and blunt — Danielson, the nebbish, well-meaning doctor and bureaucrat, buckles under square-jawed tough guy Crawford's pressure. The book's exchanges between these two characters are incremental, with them sharing multiple conversations that are longer and more drawn out. Dr. Danielson is less of a pushover and is given more commanding lines, which Crawford allows because he is granted the applicant file from Johns Hopkins: "If anything comes of it, I want you to make it clear to the public that he [Jame Gumb]'s not a transsexual, he had nothing to do with this institution."[9] It is a more calculated, less bleeding-heart statement than Danielson's introduction in the film, in which he characterizes the FBI's interest in talking to the gender clinic as a "witch hunt": "Our patients are decent, non-violent people with a *real* problem." Harris's Danielson is high-status and ambivalent, a man obsessed with optics, while Demme and Tally try to show a decent man forced to compromise.

The real JHU gender clinic was the bellwether of gender clinics in the 1960s and 1970s. Prior to *The Silence of the Lambs*, the most notable on-screen reference to the institution came from native Baltimore filmmaker John Waters' *Desperate Living* (1977), with trans masculine character Mole McHenry (Susan Lowe) stating he got his phalloplasty procedure performed at "Hopkins." But by 1979, something shocking had happened. The clinic abruptly closed and trans surgeries were effectively, indefinitely halted. This happened the same year a study titled "Sexual Reassignment Follow-up" was put out by a JHU psychiatrist, Dr. Jon K. Meyer (with his secretary Donna Reter as a co-author), which argued that there was little benefit to sexual reassignment surgery, thereby raising the question of whether medical institutions should engage in it at all.[10] Under the leadership of Dr. Paul McHugh as the head of the Psychiatry Department, JHU would not perform any trans-related surgeries again until 2016, when he left the clinic (trans surgeries became available at the university shortly after).[11] This detail is missed by both Harris and Tally.

The Meyer-Reter study was published in the medical journal *Archives of General Psychiatry*, with it being tied to one of the premiere medical institutions in the world. Nonetheless, the fact that a non-mental-health professional was also the study's co-author, that it contradicted studies from other reputable gender clinics, and its being promoted via a press conference, all caused the trans community and those who worked in the field to view it skeptically.[12] "Much publicized and often quoted, the Meyer-Reter study was the turning point, despite critical reviews and a general lack of acceptance within the professional community. The study has, however, been a rallying point for private individuals, bureaucrats, and government entities seeking to end or severely limit sexual reassignment surgery in the United States," *The TV-TS Tapestry* would publish seven years later, in the wake of many gender clinics shutting down.[13]

There was a sharp increase in closures of gender clinics in North America in the aftermath of the study. In 2002, *Transgender Tapestry* estimated the number of gender clinics in the United States dropped from 40 to four within a few years of the study and the JHU shutting down surgeries.[14] It was also widely understood that Dr. McHugh had intended to close the gender clinic down the moment he was in a position to do so, because he did not want the Johns Hopkins University associated with sexual reassignment.[15] Medical gatekeeping and stonewalling very much defined the 1980s for American trans people.

The JHU's history still casts a dark shadow on its reputation among trans people to this day. There were many trans people who suffered due to being denied care and who did not fulfill the narrow definition of a "true transsexual." This is why the book version of Dr. Danielson feels like a more accurate portrayal of the 1980s trans medical gatekeeper, whereas, in trying to maintain distance from the topic, the film whitewashes the critical issues surrounding gender clinics of the period. Transsexuality is spoken about in *The Silence of the Lambs* as an abstract concept, which does not include Jame Gumb, because the movie defers to such narrow definitions set by real-life gender clinics and medical institutions. But then, if Jame Gumb is not trans, are they merely a destructive monster?

Gumb's significance within the text beyond villainy is still important. The character was conceived of as a counterpoint to Clarice Starling. To understand Gumb, one must also understand Starling and the trajectory of her role as a feminist creation in relation to Gumb's monstrosity. In an interview with the British Film Institute from 2018,[16] Jodie Foster would say that the novel *The Silence of the Lambs* was very appealing to her, because she looked at Starling and saw someone who was a hero and a victim at the same time. She was taken with Starling's general curiosity and empathy for the women who were murdered. Foster also saw the novel in fairytale-like terms, with Buffalo Bill being a monstrous figure to be defeated and Catherine Martin (Brooke Smith) being the damsel in distress to be saved, with the chivalric knight being her character. But where Clarice's androgyny and masculine traits make her an appealing, uncommon film hero, the non-conforming nature of Gumb/Buffalo Bill makes him a non-human monstrosity. Despite this characterization, Demme was a director whose gift for empathy meant that he could not help but find moments and images that allowed Gumb to be complex in his pain. In an interview for the DVD release of *The Silence of the Lambs*, Demme, when talking about Gumb, stated, "You have to understand humanity in order to heal it... in order to forgive it.[17]" In the film, he and actor Ted Levine try to find out who Gumb is and why he is so tortured, but Demme also plays into the horror conventions of the character.

When shooting the film, Demme and cinematographer Tak Fujimoto took every opportunity to emphasize Starling's size and stature, which only further highlighted the differences between herself and Gumb. They wanted the audience to walk in her shoes and accomplished this by shooting many scenes at eye-level with Foster, while also taking a direct camera approach, which had many of the actors performing directly to the lens in extreme close-up. In the beginning of the movie, Starling is training at FBI headquarters in Quantico. In one scene, she boards an elevator and is surrounded by men, all of whom seem like giants compared to her. To illustrate her singularity even further, the men are all wearing red shirts, compared to Starling's gray sweatshirt. She is fundamentally at odds with what is expected of an FBI agent in every way. Later, Starling and a friend of hers, Ardelia (Kasi Lemmons), are running together and having a conversation, but the camera drifts just enough to let the women fall out of frame and show that male FBI students are gawking at them. Their gaze is on Starling, but she is used to it and trained to accept their gaze as a woman.

At its heart, *The Silence of the Lambs* is a movie about the way men look at women, but curiously the techniques used to signify Starling's point of view are not transplanted to the way that Gumb looks at women. The way he looks is tortured and carnal but riddled with shame, not at all how other men look at women in the film, which is either with generic dismissal or lust. Hannibal Lecter (Anthony Hopkins) is right in his estimation that Gumb covets what he cannot have. Demme and Tally emphasize the taboo in Gumb's longing through the character's slip-ups in revealing his interest in "big, fat" women when speaking to Starling near the end of the film, and the way he is seen sewing the skinsuit methodically, without any sense of transgressing norms, in order to make what he wants for himself. There is another scene where he cuts the unconscious Catherine Martin's blouse open from the backside. Shot from his point-of-view, he stares in admiration over her back, caressing it, and emotionally says aloud to himself, "Good. Good..." He has found his perfect body. This scene is not meant to evoke a sexual need, but to admire a body he wishes were his, with the point-of-view shot placing the viewer inside Gumb's perspective. It is chilling, because viewers understand that his actions are wrong, but can also glean the underlying motivations behind them. It deepens the complexity of a horrible character who the audience is meant to both fear and empathize with in some small way.

Roger Ebert's famous quote that movies are the most powerful empathy machines has a flipside in that they can also be used to create negative feelings and spread hate. Demme's film was not intended to be hateful, but the public transformed it into a vessel for wrongheaded ideas about transness. Scenes of Gumb expressing himself were instantly and endlessly lampooned in films like *Scary Movie* (2000) and the animated sitcom *Family Guy* (1999–), which alluded to Buffalo Bill not as an unstable, dangerous killer, but a grotesque fool. But Gumb was never meant to be seen as a joke. He was meant to be seen as someone who is in pain and inflicts that pain on others. The tragedy of Gumb is that he had sought help for something he thought was the root of his troubles in his gender identity, but he was denied care and not taken seriously.

The sustained reaction of discomfort to Gumb's character can be traced back to anxiety about castration. This is most prominently realized in the scene where Gumb is in makeup, tucks his genitals between his legs and dances in the nude to "Goodbye Horses" by Q Lazzarus. It enters the realm of sideshows for the cisgender audience. These same viewers were somehow able to understand Hannibal Lecter even though he was cannibal, primarily because he is a character in such control that he is captivating like some suave, debonair Count Dracula. It was more difficult for audiences to understand the desire for a sex change, and Gumb was not given "heroic" or aspirational qualities, like in the way Hannibal was given his intellect in the Thomas Harris novels and film adaptations. Whereas the novel ties Gumb's femininity to the grieving of his dead mother, Demme gives the character a sexually forward exhibitionism that made the character forever notorious.

Gumb is naked and self-possessed when he exposes himself through dance. This was a scene not in the script of the film nor the book. It should be no coincidence that this off-script moment of tucking and drag-like performance gestures most overtly towards why Gumb is perceived as a trans woman, whereas the script actively sought to avoid any such connection. Gumb's dancing and "femme" look are on full display in this private, personal moment, but through the cisgender gaze, it becomes a sleazy, perverted homemade peepshow with the onus on Gumb and not the viewer, who become involuntary voyeurs. In the tucking scene, Gumb attempts to create a feminine self, but it is poisoned because the viewer is already aware of the woman suit he is sewing together. That image takes on a Janice Raymond-style transmisogyny in how it considers the trans feminine to be synonymous with men violating women's spaces and bodies. It is both telling and curious that the prevailing cultural image of horror in this scene has nothing to do with violence enacted upon women, but that of a character tucking his genitals between his legs and posing in a feminine manner.

Gumb is complicated further by some curiously placed bits of dialogue and Levine's agonizingly painful rendering of a character so completely torn up inside by who and what he has become. The most astonishing of these is when he yells back at Catherine Martin, who is trapped in the bottom of a well with Gumb's dog, "You don't know what pain is!" Levine delivers the line with spittle and barks out each word, dropping all pretense of feminine vocal presentation, which he had previously been trying to adhere to. It reveals something true about the character: a deeply damaged person beyond repair.

When Gumb is killed by Starling in the climax of the film, it is not played as a note of triumph or treated as an act of heroism, but of relief. Gumb's death, which comes from a gunshot wound, is like that of a horse with a broken leg being put out of its misery. Demme tries to give Gumb a moment of grace with the humane gesture of cutting to a twisting butterfly model as he is lying dead on the floor. The cut is significant, suggesting a transformation has occurred, and while it is not one of beauty, it is one of release. It is something akin to peace for this character whose violence was all-consuming. But the real tragedy of *The Silence of the Lambs* is that few read the film this way, simply seeing it as a work about a feminist hero saving the damsel in distress from a monster, who is commonly perceived as trans. Jame Gumb's sins and violence are inarguable, but the character's depth and complexity also exist within the frame.

In the years since *The Silence of the Lambs*, there have been some trans women who have reclaimed Jame Gumb as a punk image. Laura Jane Grace of Against Me! put the image of Gumb from the "Goodbye Horses" scene, with his satin wings pose, on the front cover of the band's *True Trans* EP (2013). Others see the character as a victim, whose monstrosity was the product of society. While Jos Truitt criticizes the film and novel in an article for *Feministing*, she positions Gumb as an inescapable image of transmisogyny that must be empathized with based on its creation, because it was how trans people were seen for decades as the worst lies were spread about transness.[18]

If Jame Gumb is to be widely reclaimed by trans people, it would be as a provocation that acknowledges the cis transphobia tied to Buffalo Bill. It would be reminiscent of the way that groups like "Transexual Menace" wore their name like a badge of honor. The character is among an extensive line of monstrous figures given trans shading. Susan Stryker's reclamation of the "transsexual monstrosity" shows how the power of darkness and rage in being labeled a monster is a struggle that can also nourish and empower trans people to act rather than live in self-loathing and despair. *The Silence of the Lambs* unwittingly circulated cultural transphobia to new levels all while being an expertly acted, directed, and memorable film. It cannot be taken lightly as both great and harmful cinema. Its legacy with trans viewers is complicated at best. But when the trans viewer regularly faces being called a monstrosity, encompassing all things evil, perverted, and unholy from religious figures, politicians, family members, and total strangers, trans film images like Buffalo Bill take on a different meaning for the trans viewer. They begin to feel like kin.

CHAPTER 6
To Be Real:
Documentary Depictions of
Transness

Non-fiction filmmaking has been a substantial driver in the trans film image, mainly because the images were less compromised and problematized compared to the fictional trans film images out there. Documentary can have its own formal tics and ingenuity. There are hundreds of documentaries about trans people, and more are released with each given year, but Jennie Livingston's *Paris Is Burning* (1990) has, since its release, been the consensus great documentary work that heavily features transness. It is a film that is not only canonized among queer pictures, but also the non-fiction film canon and the New York film canon, and presents a densely layered snapshot of queer history in New York during the specific period of the late 1980s.

While *Paris Is Burning* is an astonishing, important work, it has also overshadowed other documentaries about transness, and its reputation as a kind of *Citizen Kane* (1941) of the trans film image has given viewers the false sense that it is the only film worth seeking out. Due to various issues of availability, many of the other documentaries about transness are hard to come by and are, as a result, not as widely seen. But by looking at these films in a broader framework of trans non-fiction, with *Paris Is Burning* being the peak, trans people can more easily see themselves across generations than in the narrative framework of dramatization in a diverse array of trans film images.

When diving into trans non-fiction and looking back at so many of these films, there is a certain level of nuance that one must bring, especially in terms of language. The terms in which transness has been described and continues to be described has always been in a state of constant evolution, and the will for trans people to define themselves however they see fit means that language will continue to evolve. Nuance is key when looking into past histories of transness on-screen, and while it can be uncomfortable to be made to stare into the transphobic past, it is a necessary tool in understanding trans histories and the transphobia of the present. This also concerns the understanding needed in looking at trans life in general. One must reckon with what was expected, or wanted, among these trans individuals with gender roles, presentation, and their embodiment in the past. Not everything can be modern, up-to-date or correct in the context in which someone is engaging with a work of the past.

Non-fiction documentary filmmaking is not without its redundancies in form and formulaic styles. The best trans documentaries function as a window into their era of time, with a visual language and command of form that is in a dialogue with its subjects. There are countless televisual documentaries that cover transness, which do not function in this manner, but instead as an informational delivery system that often appeared on "educational" cable channels and carried blunt titles like *My Body, My Choice* or *Male to Female*. At the time, these were valuable based on them being widely available through basic television packages, but the information that they held was basic and dated, with these works vacant of any artistic quality. Much of trans non-fiction can be tied back to educational and medical films that were rarely screened for public viewing. Mondo films also brought an exploitation streak to real trans film images. But with the advent of public and cable television, there were ways in which informational works about transness recirculated for the broader public.

The common modes of presentation used in trans non-fiction have usually been traditional, even if the subjects themselves were radical. The rare times these films were intended to be widely seen, whether at film festivals or theatrically, such as Frank Simon's *The Queen*, it was largely because the film's producers had major Hollywood ties. Then there is Doris Wishman's *Let Me Die a Woman* (1978), a film that defies categorization and was by no means a traditional rendering of the trans film image, but a singular viewing experience where exploitation collides with reality. *Let Me Die a Woman* is one of the most distinctive works of the trans film image — the only comparable film is Ed Wood's *Glen or Glenda*.

A Fine Line Between Exploitation and Truth: *Let Me Die a Woman*

Doris Wishman was the queen of American exploitation. She made numerous nudist and sexploitation pictures, including *Behind the Nudist Curtain* (1964) and *Bad Girls Go to Hell* (1965). Initially, Wishman was only interested in directing as a hobbyist, but she became a legend in her own right. She stood out for her willingness to highlight exhibitionists, which gave us new types of bodies on-screen, and this may have been a factor that sparked an interest for her in making a film about trans people.

How Wishman got into making a documentary about trans people and trans medicine specifically has long beguiled many. In her audio commentary on Wishman's *Diary of a Nudist* (1961), trans archivist and programmer Elizabeth Purchell persuasively makes the case that it was Wishman's relationship with Zelda Suplee that likely led to this project coming to fruition.[1] Suplee's nudist camp was featured in Wishman's *Diary of a Nudist*, but she was not just an exhibitionist; Suplee was also an editor of magazines, a researcher, and a sexologist. She was approached by trans medicine benefactor Reed Erickson to run his foundation the EEF and did so until its closure in 1977, passing its work and archives to future HBIGDA President Dr. Paul Walker and the Janus Informational Facility thereafter. It is quite plausible that, before the EEF closed, it was seeking to make a new medical film. It had made medical films before, such as 1972's *I Am Not This Body*, which featured Suplee and Dr. Leo Wollman, who is also featured in *Let Me Die a Woman*.[2]

Dr. Wollman was a significant figure in the field of trans medicine, and he is the dominant voice in the white-jacket segments of *Let Me Die a Woman*. In the 1970s, he appeared on television to speak about transsexualism and served as one of the founding members of HBIGDA. When he passed away in 1998, his archives went to Dr. Rusty Mae Moore, head of the New York City trans shelter Transy House.[3] The sequences involving Wollman feel like classroom lectures on the subject, but their hybridization with Wishman's exploitation sensibilities means the film functions almost as a *détournement* of the typical clinical presentation of transness on screen.

Let Me Die a Woman is unclassifiable and has some strange hallmarks, such as being screened at porn theaters, but was also given a published novelization. It is never quite sure what to make of itself and contains so many broad elements, like moody re-enactments of suicide attempts, botched self-surgeries, and group therapy meetings involving Dr. Wollman that contains noticeable dubbing. These therapy meetings play out like most stilted educational films of the time, except the entire group of subjects are trans people. The concept of "womanhood" suggested as a goal by Wollman during these sessions is difficult and built upon conservative ideals of the post-atomic age, and it is both dated and illuminating what these trans women are expected to go through to re-enact a pre-feminist version of womanhood. The trans men in these same meetings are not given quite the same screen time, but their presence is extremely notable. There are also numerous incidents of racism by the medical staff that blend into the picture and are not called out due to the ingrained bigotry of the time. One scene where a black trans woman is made to strip and her body is inspected piece by piece by Wollman is particularly uncomfortable, especially in how he compares her to her white counterparts.

C. Davis Smith is listed as the sole cinematographer of *Let Me Die a Woman*, but it is widely known among trans elders that Andrea Susan Malick shot a substantial amount of the film.[4] Malick, who cross-dressed and outed herself later in life as one of the photographers of the Casa Susanna photos that reemerged in the 2000s, shot a lot of the interviews, testimonials, and the scenes of Wollman interacting with patients who present their naked bodies for the camera. The seams of these two different methods of storytelling ("authentic" but clinical and salaciously exploitative) are visible in a way that perfectly surmises the sensibility of Stryker's "My Letter to Victor Frankenstein": of seeing a patchwork of ideas sewn together. These elements are not smoothly integrated but collide against one another, as if they belonged to separate films. This is apparently due to the disjointed shooting schedule that spanned several years. The film was initially going to be called *Adam or Eve*, and the white-jacket segments were more in line with the EEF. Given that the organization had ceased to exist by the time of release, it stands to reason that Wishman's exploitation elements became more prominent as a result.

Let Me Die a Woman has a salacious reputation, which largely stems from the decision to include live footage of a vaginoplasty. In the past, it was slotted alongside films like *Cannibal Holocaust* (1980) and *Faces of Death* (1978) as a film for cult audiences looking for something more gnarly. *Let Me Die a Woman* surely dissatisfied those looking to satiate their bloodlust as the surgical sequence takes up little of the film. The inclusion of this material, however, is greatly of note for trans film imagery, particularly in the documentary vein, because it is possible to see how surgery has evolved since, when compared with other films, like

Transexual Menace, made decades later, which also discusses surgery in detailed terms. For Wishman, the inclusion of the surgery is a transgressive image, amplified by the over-wrought score of the film, a signifier that gender-affirming surgeries are too much of a taboo. To her credit, Wishman does not flinch, and presents vaginoplasty in a matter-of-fact, scientific manner. Because of this, it is a powerful image of medical transness on-screen and is normalized in the context of this film.

For as negative as *Let Me Die a Woman* can sometimes be, in the way that it lingers on transphobia, there is also an argument to be made that there is power in presenting transphobia and trans suicide as it was. In the modern climate of more "positive" representation, which often sands down identities, there is less interest in acknowledging the existence of these negative forces still permeating in trans spaces. But these negative forces are necessary inclusions in projecting a full picture of such experiences, because very few trans people live without having been touched by their effects.

Dr. Wollman speaks clearly and plainly about the process of medical transition, along with interviews of numerous trans subjects from the period. Some of these interviewees are otherwise stealth and have made their transness as invisible as possible in the public eye — something expected of trans people at the time. Wollman says it is the "final part of transition," in voiceover. This film wonders aloud: If you were given the chance to blend into society as a cis person, would you? This complicated element of "living stealth" is still something that certain trans people grapple with and is a contributing factor to why trans history can sometimes be difficult to parse. Transness was seen as a medical concern with an end goal in mind, and once the end goal was reached there was an assumption by many that the trans element of a person could disappear by blending in. Numerous trans people lived that way in the past and continue to do so in the present.

There is a scene in the 1971 documentary *The Transsexuals* — a film collectively made by then film students Susan Milano, Shridhar Bapat, Daniel Landau, Elyshia Pass, and Garret Ormiston, with EEF funding — that features a trans woman dropping her skirt to show off the results of her bottom surgery that she got from "that surgeon in Casablanca" (Dr. Georges Burou, who is also mentioned in *Let Me Die a Woman*). This is an educational image, and trans men and women would sometimes do this very thing in close company, in a pre-internet world where they would find each other in support groups or in zine publications. There would be this evolution where educational films on transness were made less for the medical community and more so for trans people who would buy them on VHS and Betamax tapes with the knowledge that they were often made by those in the community, including Andrea Susan Malick, who had a reputable filmography working in Hollywood beyond *Let Me Die a Woman*, although under her birth name.

Wishman's film remains complicated, as it is no doubt worthwhile in the history of the trans film image, but it is also a carnival sideshow in some of its more salacious aspects of lifting the lid on transition for its audience. Through its twin identities as an exploitation picture and a medical documentary, the film creates a contradictory mode of presenting the trans film image that is discursive, albeit truthful.

Dressed in Blue: "A Perversity of the Earth"

Antonio Giménez-Rico's recently rediscovered *Vestida de azul* (*Dressed in Blue*) (1983) proves that the trans film image is an evolving documentation of history beyond the borders of North America. *Dressed in Blue* follows the lives of six transsexual women (Eva, Nacha, Loren, Josette, Rene, and Tamra) in post-Franco Spain. The access that Gimenez-Rico was given to his trans subjects is more expansive and intimate than is usually afforded in trans documentaries and is reminiscent of the open quality felt in the work of Rosa von Praunheim. *Dressed in Blue* broadens and subverts trans narratives in a multitude of ways, while also being clear-eyed and blunt about presenting a tapestry of trans feminine experiences in a country that has a fascinating relationship with transness.

The film is shot with the framing device of these women partaking together in a luxurious gathering space for afternoon tea, talking openly about their lives, experiences, gender, and labor. It contrasts the beginning of the film, shot at night with a street-level view of a police raid against trans sex workers, trying to pick up johns on the street. The scene ends with an arrest and a still frame telling the audience that all the characters in the film are real and all the stories are true. This opener sets a precedent for how much access Gimenez-Rico was given to his trans subjects, particularly through the lens of sex work. Usually in trans documentaries, sex work is discussed but rarely presented this directly. *Dressed in Blue* even goes beyond the streets and into the bedroom in one scene. Some of the trans women featured in the film like doing sex work, while others find it agonizing. Neither viewpoint is given more influence than another, and each woman is allowed to have her preferences. In general, this is a film that gives a great deal of space for diverse opinions and experiences for its trans subjects, which makes it such a valuable discovery.

Dressed in Blue was shot in 16mm, and great care and consideration was taken in how each of the women were presented. Gimenez-Rico has a great feel for the nude human body, and none of the nudity ever feels exploitative. Instead, there is real beauty to be found in how each woman carries herself on the streets and in the comfort of her own home, further emphasizing the differences in lifestyles and personalities. The sequences in club settings also feel intimate, with Eva's striptease being particularly evocative. Gimenez-Rico cuts to the crowd, who are not gazing at her with lust or hatred but seem simply immersed in the spectacle. There are even kids sitting up front, witnessing her disrobe, and the film finds nothing morally question-able about this. Sequences like this sometimes occurred in narrative-driven films about trans people from the region, like *Cambio de Sexo* (*Change of Sex*) (1977), *Mi Querida Senorita* (*My Dearest Senorita*) (1972), and *El Transexual* (*The Transexual*) (1977). But these films were more violent than *Dressed in Blue*, foregrounding transmisogyny and the trauma in transition. Instead, *Dressed in Blue's* narrative highlights the presence of numerous trans characters who often helped one another.

The anxiety of violence and the exhaustion that can come from being queer in public exists in *Dressed in Blue*, but it does not overpower the film and its subjects. The negative social aspects of transness are instead felt in an ambient way that is appropriate to how the subjects would have felt their transness was viewed in the public sphere, but rarely becomes explicit. Although Spain had nowhere near the medical gatekeeping and level of pathology placed on transsexuals as in North America, there was still the Catholic church, along with a right-wing government and cultural institutions, not to mention the ingrained socie-tal machismo, which were all heavily transphobic. Some of these trans women have been rejected by their families and some have not. Some want vaginoplasty surgery and some do not. They have all had their bumps along the way towards their trans embodiment, but none of those struggles dom-inate the film, which is usually the case in documentaries about trans people.

Trans documentaries usually latch onto one theme or one question they interrogate and eventually answer, but *Dressed in Blue* operates differently. This is a film that lives and breathes with its trans subjects, and the camera follows alongside as if it were a friend for them to confide in, and the openness that all these women have to the camera gives the film an authenticity that few documentaries about trans people manage to accomplish. These women never feel as though they are at the mercy of the filmmaker or the final edit, but are free, as if they were guiding the film, not the director. It is a testament to Gimenez-Rico that he manages to come at this project without pretension, filming these women with grace and dignity, unconcerned with political signaling but instead threading together a rich trans tapestry of film images.

Dressed in Blue risked falling completely through the cracks, as it was unknown to most English-speaking audiences and critics. The catalyst for its return to public consciousness was its appearance within the celebrated Spanish-language television series *Veneno* (2020), about the life of Spanish tabloid media sensation, singer, actress, and sex worker Cristina Ortiz Rodriguez, better known as "La Veneno" ("The Poison"). In the series, a VHS copy of *Dressed in Blue* is discussed by the elderly La Veneno (Isabel Torres) and her friend Paca La Pirana (playing herself) when talking to a newly out trans woman, Valeria Vegas (Lola Rodriguez), with both telling her of the film's significance for them and the Spanish trans community. This moment of passed-down cultural ephemera is marvelous, reintroducing older cultural objects that feature older trans film images not just to Valeria, but the entire viewership of *Veneno*.

Paris Is Burning and How to Be Seen

The House of LaBeija stretches across generations in trans documentaries, dating back to Crystal LaBeija's appearance in *The Queen* and continuing through their prominence in *Paris Is Burning*. However, *Paris Is Burning* was not the first documentary film to cover the ballroom scene. There was also *T.V. Transvestite* from 1982, which shared many notable names and faces, in addition to other performers who were legends of the ballroom scene.

T.V. Transvestite is not as audacious in form or as beautifully photographed as *Paris Is Burning*, but the ball scene remains intoxicating, and the early influence of MTV-style music video editing is present in some of the choices made by directors Michele Capozzi and Simone de Bagno. There are also some intertitles that feel like less developed versions of those that Livingston employs in *Paris Is Burning*. It also suffers from datedness — one of these intertitles reads in delicate cursive, "None of these performers you are about to see are women," before showing us a cavalcade of some of the most beautiful women you could imagine.

T.V. Transvestite is largely a snapshot of this period and eschews complex themes, but there are a few select scripted moments and more formulaic documentary set-ups that are not without interest. A young trans woman (whose name we are never told) speaks eloquently about her history of family rejection and going on hormones at the age of 15, interwoven with some inter-cutting of the ball scene and a montage of images of makeup being applied. In a later scene, this same woman is seen in front of the Twin Towers dressed as Marilyn Monroe, lip-synching a song of hers. Monroe can also be seen in Natcha's bedroom in *Dressed in Blue* and in the bedroom of Eva Love in *Transexual Menace*. These trans women never seemed to want to conjure the image of Audrey Hepburn — the other Hollywood personification of womanhood from the era of their childhood — perhaps because she was too lithe to realistically approach, but Monroe seemed like an open image for trans women to claim as their own, and thus Monroe was a guardian angel of potential feminine beauty for many trans women of this era. Like *Paris Is Burning*, *T.V. Transvestite* does present a wider story of trans people, and while there are also notably more visible plays on trans masculine and butch presentations compared to *Paris Is Burning*, *T.V. Transvestite* functions as a worthwhile supplemental work to the former.

Paris Is Burning has a wider canvas and has become a totemic film in queer cinema because it expresses the trajectory of queerness and transness at the intersection of race, poverty, and artistic expression. As we have seen throughout history, there has been infighting and separation within the LGBTQ community, but *Paris Is Burning* is a near utopia of queer people of color coming together for the sake of each other. It is a political film, because transness and blackness are inherently political, and it is very smart about how these factors intersect and communicate with one another.

Paris Is Burning captures the late 1980s ballroom scene in a version of New York City that existed in between the bankrupt sleaze of the 1970s and the Giuliani clean-up era of the 1990s. It begins with the retelling of a streetwise lesson of prejudices intersecting:

> You have three strikes against you in this world. Every black man has two, but if you're black and a male and you're gay... You're going to have a hard fucking time. If you're gonna do this, you're going to have to be stronger than you've ever imagined.

This is the context in which *Paris Is Burning* needs to be understood. The director, Jennie Livingston, makes the smart choice of prefacing this story with shots of a near-bankrupt New York, where a lit billboard can be seen broadcasting the following words: "White Supremacist Church Begins National Conference." This is the world these queer people inhabit, and that is why they had to build their own — the world of the ballroom.

Livingston came to this film through happenstance. She moved to New York in 1985 after graduating from Yale, wanting to be a still photographer, and took a film class at NYU with the idea of potentially getting into filmmaking as well. One afternoon, while she was "people watching" in Washington Park, she met some young men who were dancing. She asked if she could photograph them, and they excitedly agreed. She asked what those moves were, and they said "voguing." As a result of this conversation, Livingston went to a ball with a camera and was astounded by what she saw.

Livingston evokes that initial feeling of awe when introducing viewers to the ball scene in *Paris Is Burning*. She uses a tracking shot to follow Pepper LaBeija from the dark dingy street into the center of the ball's glamor. LaBeija is dressed head to toe in gold, her outfit reminiscent of something Elizabeth Taylor might wear in *Cleopatra*. The ball space is just a small gathering hall, but it feels like a palace ballroom due to the way LaBeija is dressed and the way her audience responds to her. Livingston shot the film on 16mm, which she said "has a nice, human scale",[5] and due to the grain of the film stock, everything has both a timeless quality and a texture that embodies realism. This shot of LaBeija is one of the most stunning introductory images in all of filmmaking, setting the tone for the viewer, making clear what the ball is, and what it means for those who participate.

The ball is more than a contest, and more than a gathering in a safe space. The beauty in the ball scene is in participation and expression, with all its undertones and complexities. The ball is a fantasy of personal embodiment where a participant can transform, become what they deeply wish to be, and have that transformation cheered, instead of scorned, as would be the typical response of the straight world to queer bodies in the 1980s. There are "shades" and "reads," playful jabs at one another that manifest into vogue-offs that function like fights, but it is inherently non-violent. The criticisms thrown around are playful and endearing, functioning as a form of mentorship in better attaining your look.

Paris Is Burning articulates some of the deepest desires of queer people. Livingston expresses this most clearly in the language of a shot/reverse/shot as ball participants and trans women Octavia St. Laurent and Venus Xtravaganza talk openly in their bedrooms about what they want out of life. They are both giddy when thinking about who they might become in the future, but they are also honest about the limitations they have experienced due to economics, race, or their gender identity. Venus is quite talkative about why she wants sex reassignment surgery and her dreams alongside surgery are modest. She wants to get married, she wants others to think she is pretty, and she wants to be treated like a woman. Venus has no shame about her desires, and she is confident in her belief that one day it will happen for her.

Octavia's dreams are of a career that gives her freedom. She wants to be a model. She has magazine centerfold photos plastered with scotch tape on her bedroom walls. She looks up at her ceiling while talking, as if to God, and she smiles, because she can envision a future, and a future is not something all trans people are guaranteed. When Octavia St. Laurent goes to a Ford model search, Livingston finds her in crowded spaces, blending into the fashion world seamlessly, and there is a moment where model executive Eileen Ford can be seen talking about womanhood and attempting to reconcile modeling with feminism, with Octavia in the periphery of the frame. This framing captures the multitude of ways transness intersects with mainstream beauty standards, how passing can afford a level of invisibility that still only goes so far and how feminist concerns of the period were often incompatible with trans feminine desires. It is a complicated, daring image of difference, but one which expresses that trans femininity has its place in spaces usually confined to cis women. In the ball scene, this is called being "real," but the film also reinforces that realness only goes so far — something the later murder of Venus Xtravaganza makes plain. Until transness becomes liberated from the violence of the reveal, passing is only in the eye of the beholder, and its privileges are not sustainable.

Some of *Paris Is Burning*'s affective qualities are driven by how the subjects carry themselves in day-to-day life. Livingston's choice to shoot many of her exterior interviews at magic hour certainly helps, but the ball and the structure of walking in it only required Livingston to capture what was already there. Ball legend Dorian Corey is also interviewed, and her segments have some of the most incisive

CHAPTER 6: TO BE REAL

and wise anecdotes. She speaks of the history of the drag ball, and how back when she was starting everyone wanted to look like Marlene Dietrich, how that evolved into Marilyn Monroe, and that in the 1980s queer people had moved away from cinema and were focused on fashion models like Iman, or primetime soap operas like *Dynasty*. Meanwhile, pictures of Corey over the years in drag balls are shown, and she concludes that she should not have been following white standards of beauty, and then speaks fondly of African American screen star Lena Horne. Throughout, she is preparing her makeup — the talking head segments often involve a personality involved in another activity, which livens up the frame and tells us more about the person being interviewed. Pepper LaBeija smokes and is lit with a small bedside lamp. To the right of her is a statue of the head of a Pharaoh. LaBeija's moments in the film are opulent and full of humor. All the subjects interviewed seem to understand their angles, where the lighting is best, and how to perform for the camera, and this allows the viewer to be seduced by the subjects with relative ease. The star-power of all involved is certainly one reason why mainstream culture was drawn to this documentary and why it was a financial success, grossing $4 million at the box office. This did cause some rift and controversy between the subjects and the filmmakers about proper compensation, later rectified in a lump-sum payment to the performers that, nevertheless, still sparks dialogues surrounding the question of what is and is not exploitative labor in non-fiction film practice.[6]

These matriarchal Houses, of performers, artists, and models, additionally serve as support systems, in roles as elders, friends, brothers, sisters, teachers, and students of the scene. It is beautiful and affords many of these queer people a new lease of life. But the reality of violence is always lingering. Angie Xtravaganza, the Mother of the House of Xtravaganza, reflects on Venus's murder (she had to identify her corpse). She speaks eloquently about Venus, understanding the risks that she and others like her take.

Being trans is a game of survival, and the deck is stacked against trans people who are not white. Not everyone who left the ballroom was a breakout star like Willi Ninja, who found work in the music industry and helped bring voguing to the mainstream, and even his success did not preclude him from suffering. Ninja passed away in 2006 from AIDS complications, like many of the performers and figures featured in *Paris Is Burning*. Or they suffered a fate of violence like Venus. While watching *Paris Is Burning*, it is necessary to remember that death was in the air, and everyone involved knew it. Perhaps this is why they all fought so clearly to create a world in the ballroom where they could express themselves as they wished.

Paris Is Burning is one of the most lauded and significant instances of the trans film image. The language, the aesthetic of the ball scene, and voguing were all incorporated into the broader spectrum of pop culture. Madonna topped the US Billboard Hot 100 chart in 1990 with her single "Vogue," drawn from the ball culture her dancers had ties with. Terms featured in the film recirculate on *RuPaul's Drag Race* and the internet, becoming common slang used by everyone. The film's popularity and its language being appropriated by the cisgender mainstream has unfortunately obscured the larger intersecting questions of queerness, race, and poverty that make *Paris Is Burning* what it is. Despite this, *Paris Is Burning* remains a time capsule and memorial for an extinct New York City and the diverse set of larger-than-life personalities that commanded the screen with aplomb and innate charisma. Such a moment in time can recirculate, but it can never be recreated.

The Salt Mines and *The Transformation*: Homelessness and the Specter of Detransition

There are sometimes gaps in presentation in trans documentary filmmaking from this era due to its focus on successful medicalized transition. What is sometimes lost, therefore, are documents of those who were trans and denied health-care for arbitrary and restrictive reasons by the increasingly discriminating medical field. Additionally, as many of those denied healthcare were the most marginalized — including trans people of color, unhoused trans people, and sex work-ers — they are often excluded from this era's documenta-ries.

Paris Is Burning tackled these subjects with its focus on the intersection between transness and race, but it was not the only film from this era to do so. *The Salt Mines* (1990) and its follow-up *The Transformation* (1995), directed by Susana Aikin and Carlos Aparicio, also cover similar terrain, but do so without the celebratory dynamics of the ball scene that gave *Paris Is Burning* its glamor and respite.

These films are direct, with a fly-on-the-wall approach, and are some of the most illuminating in the documentary field on how transition often intersects with homelessness and HIV/AIDS. These films also convey how joblessness and capitalism's lack of interest in the queer body render trans people as disposable if they are not exceptional or do not conform to society's standards of beauty, which is to say, white beauty. They are important films and historical docu-ments of their period, and the financial duress and immedi-ate economic difficulty that the subjects in these films face is still a relevant concern for the average trans person in the twenty-first century.

Like *Paris Is Burning*, *The Salt Mines* came into existence through happenstance. Aikin met the subjects of the film in the late 1980s when she ran into a man named Bobby, who was getting water from a fire hydrant for himself and the girls "living in trucks" in a disposal area called "The Salt Mines." Aikin came from a television news background, and Aparicio was a freelance cameraman who primarily made documentary featurettes for news organizations, and their working together forged a portrait of trans people hustling to not only stay alive but also to transition.

The film focuses primarily on three trans women —

Sara, Gigi, and Giovanna — all of whom come from various parts of Latin America. Sara is from Cuba and has been living in America since the Carter administration; Gigi is from Puerto Rico and her husband is imprisoned at Rikers Island, which has left her homeless; Giovanna is from the Dominican Republic. In talking head segments, they discuss the difficulties associated with their transition. The recurring theme is family rejection, which has contributed to their lack of an economic and social safety net and made them more susceptible to homelessness. It is not all tragic, however, because Gigi speaks with immense pride about how she managed to graduate from school despite the deck being stacked against her — a small victory in an otherwise devastating film. In these early segments, where they speak with Aikin, the women seem comfortable, and in her self-published book, *Digging Up the Salt Mines: A Film Memoir*, the director speaks of how she bonded with them early on because she spoke Spanish and they were interested in her job as a newscaster.[7]

The Salt Mines presents sex work as an act of survival, showing the women turn tricks in Manhattan's Meatpacking District. In these scenes, the talking head dynamic is abandoned and the visual language becomes more voyeuristic, with Aikan shooting from a van to create the client's point of view. As a result, these are some of the most honest depictions of sex work in a trans documentary, as viewers brush up against the edges of the work without getting in the way of it. The Canadian sex worker documentary *Hookers... on Davie* (1984) employs a similar dynamic by placing the camera at street level and manages to get into the reality of the nightly enterprise. This method of observation is a good one for trans documentaries, allowing the films to take on a *verité*, downplaying the tendency for trans film images to accentuate the stylized and flamboyant.

The failure of the New York City government in handling the problems that stem from homelessness, drug abuse, and sex work is at the forefront of *The Salt Mines*. The system's putative solution is to destroy the encampments of broken-down sanitation trucks where these trans women and others live, without offering them any visible assistance or shelter. Instead, the government is simply "cleaning up" — removing the eyesores and undesirables. This means that the only offers of "help" come from Christian charities. This "help," however, involves a considerable trade-off: that trans women must detransition and undergo conversion therapy in exchange for housing. Gigi and Giovanna are steadfast and say no multiple times, but Sara agrees. She has been put in an even more vulnerable position due to an HIV/AIDS diagnosis and is coping with the recent death of their mother. She was in too vulnerable a position to say no.

In the follow-up film, *The Transformation*, viewers now see Sara living as a man named Ricardo. Ricardo is now strictly adhering to the church's conversion program of living "straight," including being married to a female churchgoer. They have rebuked their queerness, calling it a "phase," and now work as a prop for the church to promote their conversation therapy service — all while dying from AIDS. These are tough but necessary scenes that show how the failures of government institutions allow transphobia to manifest in different ways. In one scene, Sara/Ricardo goes back to the Meatpacking District, doing the bidding of the religious organization that took them in, and attempts, along with the same church figures who were featured in *The Salt Mines,* to get Gigi and Giovanna to detransition. These are scenes of emotional annihilation, and it cuts deep, because we know the circumstances of Sara/Ricardo's decision. The relative fragility of transness as a livable, social, or medical concern is on full display.

The Transformation concludes with a final scene of Sara/Ricardo wheelchair-bound and in extremely poor health from AIDS. They are considering their life, and they tell the filmmakers that they wish they still lived as a woman. The film ends. This is followed by a closing text that tells us Sara/Ricardo died of AIDS-related complications. *The Salt*

Mines and *The Transformation* are mournful reminders that there are many trans people whose stories are seldom told. These were people who slipped through the cracks and could never live out their lives without the risk of homelessness or death, due to the reality of institutional failure and the influence of faith-based charities and organizations.

Two by Rosa von Praunheim: *I Am My Own Woman* and *Transsexual Menace*

Rosa von Praunheim was drawn to the early years of sexology in its relation to cross-dressing and transness, especially due to its ties to his native Germany, later directing a biopic of Dr. Magnus Hirschfeld called *The Einstein of Sex* (1999). Another figure he found compelling was a trans woman called Charlotte von Mahlsdorf, a curator at the Gründerzeit Museum who had lived openly as a trans woman since the 1940s and had been a target of both neo-Nazis and the police. Praunheim would adapt her memoir, *Ich bin meine eigene Frau* (*I Am My Own Woman*) (1992) into a film of the same name.

I Am My Own Woman (1993) is the most experimental of all Praunheim's films covered in this book — a frequent fourth-wall-breaking dramatization of Mahlsdorf's life where the subject is an active co-author of the film, giving direct input and notes to Praunheim and the actors on-camera. It is transparent in its collaborative process and shows that the film's provocative look at Mahlsdorf's sexuality is a feature she wants shown, actively encouraging its portrayal as a key part of her existence. The mark some people have against Rosa von Praunheim's work is often the prominence of nudity and hyper-sexuality in his subjects, both scripted and in documentary. But queer cinema finds its specificity and true nature in these modes.

Mahlsdorf grew up in privilege with an abusive fascist father. A major turning point in the self-realization of her trans identity came when she read Dr. Hirschfeld's books on sexology and transvestism in the family library (they had belonged to another family member who also expressed a trans identity). She discovered and read these books right as World War II was underway. In a heroic act, she killed her abusive father and was incarcerated, but freed after the Allied victory. She then explored her queer sexuality and gender identity and lived as a woman under her new name, working in professional spaces as a restorer and domestic worker and expressing herself sexually by cruising the bathhouses of East Berlin.

Mahlsdorf had a sexual relationship with her employer, engaged in years of no-strings-attached cruising in male restrooms, had a BDSM relationship with a longtime lover, and self-identified as a trans woman — all of which could have had her labeled as a criminal. Mahlsdorf was a "Gender Outlaw" and proud of it. The fact that she was so open about this side of her life, whilst being a successful figure both in East Berlin's queer community and in her work in historical curation, demystifies the taboos tied not just to trans identity but also kink identity. Mahlsdorf finds that her womanhood does not need to be defined by biology, and this is partly why she never felt that she had to undergo surgery to live the life she wanted. She tells Praunheim ever so matter-of-factly: "I am my own woman."

Mahlsdorf would live to see the reunification of Germany and was optimistic about the future, particularly for the LGBTQ community. But she was also the target of neo-Nazis and decided to live the rest of her life in Sweden for her own safety (Praunheim and her would reunite for the 2003 short, *Charlotte in Sweden*). Mahlsdorf's work with the Gründerzeit Museum and her preservation of queer history and ephemera in East Germany made her a deeply consequential figure. In collaboration with Praunheim, Mahlsdorf occupied the rarefied space of a trans memoir in which the living author and subject has a direct role in the retelling and dramatization of that trans life. As trans filmmaker Jessica Dunn Rovinelli (*So Pretty*, 2019) wrote of the film, "The transgender body, as it so often does in film, becomes the figure of fascination, but here it is also a locus through which history passes: in the clothes she wears, the people she brings together and the history of her life."[8] *I Am My Own Woman* remains a singular work of hybrid non-fiction filmmaking in service to the trans film image.

Praunheim's interest in the United States and LGBTQ rights would continue from the late 1970s through the 1980s and into the 1990s. He had covered everyone from Fred Halsted to David Wojnarowicz to Tally Brown. The 1990s saw trans activism becoming increasingly assertive, such as the response to trans exclusionary incidents at Mich-Fest (Michigan Womyn's Music Festival) that led groups like Transexual Menace to create the counter-protest event Camp Trans. In addition to fighting exclusion, the fight for trans inclusion in spaces occupied primarily by gay, lesbian, and bisexual rights activists was growing. The LGBT community was coalescing, although it was still a restless set of bedfellows who had varied approaches to advocacy and activism. Praunheim's *Transexual Menace* (1995) is a tapestry of various trans lives under the emerging umbrella of the term "transgender," which at the time was beginning to catch on as the common, more inclusive term.

Language is a crucial element of *Transexual Menace*. It dates the film, but also gives an important snapshot of the period. At this time, terms like "tranny" were used liberally and not derisively. Prior to "cisgender" being used today as the popular term to describe a non-trans woman or non-trans man, people said "biological male" or "biological female." "Pre-operative," "post-operative," and "non-operative" were used to describe those who were seeking surgeries. These terms, and their evolving states, represented the community's attempt to define themselves in this era, rather than be defined by the medical establishment. By the 1990s, the International Foundation for Gender Education (IFGE) and the American Educational Gender Information Service (AEGIS) were making concerted efforts in advocacy and education to modernize the Standards of Care. This coincided with the modernization of language used to describe what was reframed as the "gender community" and the transgender community. The name "Transexual Menace" itself derives from the fact that the activist group wanted to de-pathologize trans identity by removing the second "s" to make "transexual" a more *en vogue* term.

Although the titular activist group bookend the film, with its iconic scare font t-shirts popping up intermittently in other segments, they are not the sole focus. The Southern Comfort Conference, Fantasia Fair, the band "Transisters," models, old-school cross-dressers, sex workers, individual activists, and the Transgender Lobby Day legislative activists are all featured and given equal time. It is a deeply egalitarian film, not unlike Praunheim's *Armee der Liebenden oder Aufstand der Perversen* (*Army of Lovers or Revolt of the Perverts*) (1979), which showed the various spectrums of anti-heteronormative queer sexual expressions in the 1970s. In *Transexual Menace*, it is quite apparent that Praunheim's curiosity draws him in several directions with a lot of optimism and empathy.

The most crucial interaction that Praunheim has is with Leslie Feinberg, the transgender activist and author of the groundbreaking work *Transgender Warriors* (1996), which is credited with mainstreaming the term "transgender." Feinberg's testimonials anticipate many of today's ongoing conversations around gender. Feinberg outlines the institutional issues — such as obtaining a passport — where people are boxed in by the gender binary. Additional discussion points include pronouns, gender-markers, and the ways in which identities were broadening. Feinberg also frequented the talk show circuit, with their passion and intelligence not reduced to simplistic soundbites, especially when recalling life in blue-collar Buffalo, New York.

The film also presents the economic realities of trans medicine and how trans surgeries, regularly presented in the film as costing five figures, are simply unaffordable for most American trans people, who, due to their transness, are often excluded from stable, well-paying jobs. Beyond the more privileged settings like Fantasia Fair and some individual success stories like Phyllis Frye (a Texas-based judge, attorney, and activist), most of the people interviewed are working-class and well aware of the risks of losing their livelihoods if their trans status were to be revealed. Riki Wilchins, then head of Transexual Menace, speaks to how that lack of a safety net in and of itself can lead to a cycle of violence, exploitation, and harm against trans people.

Praunheim does not go too deep into the political machinations of trans advocacy through Transgender Lobby Day. He does, however, show the simple act of these trans people being visible and walking through the halls of Congress as a necessary and crucial step forward. But beyond the film, there is a more complicated legacy tied to Transgender Lobby Day and legislative advocacy.

In the United States in the 1990s, in the aftermath of the height of HIV/AIDS activism, there was a lot of momentum in wanting to combat years of homophobia, targeted violence, and hate crimes against the LGBT community. At the same time, legislative activists also sought to combat discrimination in hiring and firing in the workplace based on sexual orientation, pushing for the passage of the Employee Non-Discrimination Act (ENDA) in 1994 (although, to this day, it is still not signed into law). The trans activists protesting as part of the Transgender Lobby Days on Capitol Hill captured in *Transexual Menace* were largely there to push for trans people to be included in the protected groups under ENDA, along with gay and lesbian people. The exclusion of trans people as a protected class in the various attempts to pass ENDA in the 1990s and 2000s resulted in a lot of finger-pointing among trans activists, and questions arose if Lobby Days and Political Action Committees (PACs) were really the political fight they should continue.[9] Some trans groups, like It's Time, America! (ITA), decided to focus instead on state and local levels of government to get anti-discrimination and hate crime legislation passed, in which they had some success. But nationally, it was events like the murder of gay student Matthew Shepard in 1998 that launched a national dialogue about hate crime legislation in ways that the murders of trans man Brandon Teena in 1993, or trans woman of color Tyra Hunter in 1995, whose death is addressed in *Transexual Menace*, did not.

One of the more understated moments in *Transexual Menace* is the brief clip of Sylvia Rivera towards the end of the film, who was facing hardships due to housing and financial insecurity, looking out at the Christopher Street Pier in silence, deeply pensive. By this point, she has survived for decades, from pre-Stonewall and through the height of the AIDS crisis, while many of her fellow compatriots had not (Marsha P. Johnson's body was recovered from the Hudson River in 1992 near that same pier, and her death is still widely believed to be the result of foul play). Rivera's fighting and activism could easily have worn her down, and yet she still has this spirit to her that carried her through life. She would not die homeless; instead, she lived within her community at Transy House in New York City (a project inspired by the house Rivera's old group STAR created in the 1970s) until her death in 2002.[10] Rivera would be one of the most visible activists of her time, but in this moment in *Transexual Menace*, she is shown in quotidian terms, with little fanfare and reaction around her. At the time, Praunheim knew of her importance and significance to his own rights and those of other queer people's fight for liberation. Later, the rest of the world would come to rightly acknowledge Rivera and her involvement in post-Stonewall liberation activism in New York, although much of this acclaim happened after she had passed.

Southern Comfort: A Portrait of Dignity and the Lack Thereof

Trans masculine film images were emerging in non-fiction during the 1990s and into the 2000s at a much greater pace than in fiction. There was *Shinjuku Boys* (Jano Williams and Kim Longinotto, 1995), *You Don't Know Dick: Courageous Hearts of Transsexual Men* (Bestor Cram and Candace Schemerhorn, 1997), and the films of Monika Treut, including *Gendernauts – eine Reise durch das Land der Neuen Geschlechter* (*Gendernauts: A Journey Through Shifting Identities*) (1999) and her short film *Max* (1992), about trans activist Max Wolf Valerio. But one of the strongest films of this era that explored the nuances and intricacies of trans masculinity in the United States was Kate Davis's *Southern Comfort* (2001).

Southern Comfort came about when filmmaker Kate Davis reached out to famous trans photographer Mariette Pathy Allen through a mutual friend, due to her interest in creating a documentary about trans subject matter.[11] Allen saw a willingness from Davis to learn more about the trans community and encouraged her to make a film that was political and not just about transition. This was in contrast to the trans documentaries on television and those which made it to theaters at the time, which were primarily styled as a series of vignettes and included personal stories about being out and coming out of the closet. Allen encouraged Davis and her small crew to go to the True Spirit Conference, a trans conference that took place in Atlanta, Georgia, in 1998. It was there that Davis met Robert Eads, a trans man from rural Toccoa, Georgia, and his close-knit group of friends. She had her film.

The story of Robert Eads is at its essence about cruelty and ignorance on both a personal and broader cultural scale. Eads was a trans man dying from ovarian cancer. Doctors turned him away when he was seeking a hysterectomy and he was routinely denied care. Eads is introduced through a shot of him looking out at the horizon, framed like a hero in a Western, his image reminiscent of Henry Fonda in John Ford films like *My Darling Clementine* (1946). He speaks with clarity about the discrimination he has experienced in not being treated, but he does not hate these people. He does not seem to have hate in his heart. Eads is from the conservative Deep South, but he is ever the optimist, seeing the good in everyone, even as he is near the end of life. He is looking forward to the Southern Comfort Conference that he knows will be his last.

In the film, Eads talks about his chosen family, which includes not just other trans men, but also a trans woman lover named Lola. Robert's trans masculine identity is presented alongside other expressions of masculinity that are typical, such as his father and son, and his numerous trans masculine friends, all of whom have distinct personalities and interests. Davis films each of these men with an emphasis on their relationships and their home life and touches on minor details, which tell the viewer a lot about the relationships they have with one another. She also forgoes the traditional straight-forward talking head device in favor of more adventurous framing choices, like that of Robert and Lola at a coffee table flirting with one another in a shot/reverse/shot. This allows for greater intimacy both between her subjects and the audience. Robert's relationship with Lola is central and she is also allowed room to express her personality and the various complexities of her life. Lola still must present as male in her profession and is less able to pass and present as stealth in her everyday life. To have this relationship — a "t4t" relationship before the term was coined in the internet age — presented in such a multidimensional way in 2001 makes *Southern Comfort* a radical film for its time.

Robert's two trans male friends, Cas Piotrowski and Dr. Maxwell S. Anderson (both of whom appeared in Rosa von Praunheim's *Transexual Menace* in the trans conference portion of the documentary), testify to their own experiences of the discrimination they face from the medical field and speak of the enormous costs of surgeries like phalloplasty. At the heart of the documentary is the anger and frustration of trans men, who vocalize their rage at the exclusionary and discriminatory medical practices they have experienced. It is not only that these men feel neglected, but that modern medicine is reticent in evolving and improving the caliber of trans masculine-related surgeries. These discussions are still relevant in trans masculine circles today.

Notably, Eads never got bottom surgery, and despite the nature of his cancer diagnosis, he is secure in his masculinity. He wants young transitioners to know that getting bottom surgery does not have to define their trans masculinity. Eads is not just positioned as a trans man in a small-town, but as an outspoken trans elder and mentor to others. His discussions about bottom surgeries not having to be a prerequisite also shows the shift in conversations within the trans community. The film also wisely allows Robert's point of view to exist without undercutting the frustrations expressed by Maxwell and Cas. How they all define their gender-affirming care varies, but they are bonded in solidarity in their horrific experiences with the medical field.

The film equally does not shy away from the complexities of being a man who, prior to transition, had married and had a child. Multiple generations of his family are present, and the audience sees the negotiations of those relationships through Robert's graceful point of view. Robert mentions his attraction to women being consistent, noting that, even though he entered the lesbian community first before transitioning in the 1980s, the only time he felt "gay" was when he was married to his husband. When talking about parenting, he reveals the trauma of giving birth to a son, and that he never wanted to do that to his body ever again, even though he clearly loves his child. His son struggles with Robert's pronouns but is clearly trying and still has Robert involved in his life, and he is raising his own child whom Robert dotes on. He encourages the young grandson to call him Papaw, and he does. With the innocence of a child, he sees Robert exactly how he wishes to be seen. Robert's parents are more cumbersome. His father still holds onto remembering Robert as a little girl. Robert leans into those small victories of still being able to interact with his family, but his recollections of childhood show how his parents' image of him at that time is at odds with his image of himself.

There is a scene of Robert and Lola going through his childhood photos and Robert repeatedly referring to himself in a dress as his "drag." In every picture, he states that he wishes he were wearing his baseball cap instead. This is often how trans people see their earlier lives, in passable but miserable drag, with each person eventually deciding that cis heteronormativity is an unsustainable life. Robert came out at a time when being a lesbian was considered a radical life change from the nuclear family, and it took him by surprise how well his mother received the news. But he also remembers how much of a shock it was for his family when he finally came out as trans. Yet, there is something so innately masculine to Robert as a trans film image that it is impossible to imagine him feigning any traditional feminine role. The same can be said for Maxwell and Cas. Cas runs into passing so well that he feels like he cannot be perceived as trans at the Southern Comfort Conference, whereas Maxwell's energetic, extroverted, activist streak makes him instantly a central character in those settings.

Even during the film's pre-production, due to Robert's deteriorating health, it was a deep worry among Robert's family and friends that he might not make it to Southern Comfort to be one of its keynote speakers. The conference serves as the emotional heart of the story, and it took a lot of negotiating to film there, with many attendees not wanting to be on camera. According to Allen, the conference's steering committee could only offer them the compromise of 15 minutes to shoot Robert with Lola and the rest of them for "The Prom That Never Was" sequence of the film.

It is pulled off beautifully and sensitively, and the rest of the night is filmed with discretion, blurring out faces of the other people at the conference.

Robert Eads would die in 1999, leaving behind a community in mourning that was angry at the circumstances of his death. When the film made the rounds at festivals, it received major plaudits, including the Grand Jury Prize at the Sundance Film Festival and a Special Audience Award at the Berlin International Film Festival. Today, it lacks the public interest and cultural foothold that a film like *Boys Don't Cry* received, partly perhaps due to the fact that dramatized versions of real events, even when a documentary pre-exists them, receive more critical and viewer engagement. When considering the idea of a narrative based on *Southern Comfort*, Mariette Pathy Allen would remark in 2003, "What actors could possibly do as good a job in the Hollywood version we [the documentary's director and crew] fantasized?"[12] Robert Eads was too guileless to be anybody's martyr, and yet his story remains incredibly relevant. The trans film image in *Southern Comfort* memorializes not just Eads, but the many trans people who were not allowed the basic human right of healthcare.

CHAPTER 7
David Cronenberg, Body Horror, and Empathizing with the Artificial Other

"Body Beautiful": Cronenberg's Predilections

The taste of trans cinephiles reveals an unconscious pull towards certain themes and images. The idea of trans-coded or trans allegorical images has emerged as trans viewers have taken modes of storytelling, certain aesthetic textures, and metaphorical readings to invent a cinematic language of their own to balance the scales of history and representation. One such emerging pattern centers around horror films that focus on the monstrous transformation of the body as a means of metaphorizing the experience and process of gender dysphoria.

Dysphoria is a symptom that often necessitates medical intervention via hormone replacement therapy or corrective surgery but is often glossed over onscreen and subordinated to the narrative structure of the typical transition narrative. With its outward expression of internalized feelings of displacement, body horror is the most significant image-making canon that trans people have access to which evokes a central feeling of transness. In this subgenre, the human body can become abstract and mutable, employed for the purposes of surrealism, philosophical interrogation, or probing the depths of new genders and sexualities. This allows trans people to reclaim the notion of monstrosity and re-cast it as a vector of potentiality and newness rather than something which must be destroyed for the status quo of gender binaries to be reinforced. Through this idea, body horror has started to become a prominent mode of expression for modern trans horror filmmakers such as Louise Weard, Jane Schoenbrun, and Alice Maio Mackay, all of whom have been influenced by the godfather of the subgenre: David Cronenberg.

This notion that Cronenberg's work is an attempt to forge a new aesthetic sensibility and a positive libidinal monstrosity is emphasized by Cronenberg himself — he is not fond of the term "Body Horror", but prefers "Body Beautiful."[1] His career-long interest in the body and how it has evolved with the introduction of new technologies and changing concepts of gender and sex has also given his work a socio-political valve that has meant it has remained relevant across decades, right up to his 2022 feature *Crimes of the Future*. Asked about the relevance of the film, Cronenberg stated that it was about questions of bodily agency:

Who controls the bodies of citizens... who controls women's bodies... and who controls the bodies of transgender people. Can the government actually tell you what to do with your body even if it affects nobody else?[2]

Cronenberg has never been shy about potential queer readings of his work, and queer themes have been present in his films from the earliest stages of his career. *Stereo* (1969) is presented as if it were a pseudo-medical documentary, not unlike some of the white-jacket segments added to the earliest trans films. What follows is a series of medical experiments where the subjects attempt to learn telepathy by neglecting their other senses during a period of intense isolation. In one scene, two men and a woman sit at a table performing tarot, touching each other, and flirting without speaking. This suggests the telepathy that bolsters the medical aspect of the film, and then, in voice-over, these characters communicate, attempting to suss out the gender identity and sexuality at play.

The effect of this successful telepathy introduces a tantalizing idea: suddenly someone who thinks of himself as a man can hear a woman's voice in his own head. Cronenberg is interested in how this would force an identity to evolve and charts this through visual cues. A pseudo gender transition occurs when the male student from that telepathic scene who wore a magician's cloak no longer needs it, and it is now given to the woman he was communicating with telepathically. Is she now he? Have they switched identities? *Stereo* posits that both are realistic possibilities. Sexuality is also considered in how it may evolve under these circumstances when it is proposed in voice-over that, if a man found himself living alone with another man for a sustained, uninterrupted period, would he then become a homosexual out of necessity? Cronenberg is not visually competent enough at this stage in his career to make his provocative combination of science-fiction, eroticism, and philosophy into a coherent visual tapestry, but the ideas that are suggested in voice-over introduce the core elements of his philosophy as an artist.

These early themes are more fully expressed in *Shivers* (1975), in which Lynn Lowery's Nurse Forsythe, one of several characters who has been possessed by a parasite that has turned the residents of a high-rise apartment block into sex-obsessed predators, delivers a monologue to the camera:

I had a very disturbing dream last night. In this dream, I found myself making love to a strange man. Only I'm having trouble, you see, because he's old... and dying... and he smells bad, and I find him repulsive. But then he tells me that everything is erotic, that everything is sexual. You know what I mean? He tells me that even old flesh is erotic flesh. That disease is the love of two alien kinds of creatures for each other. That even dying is an act of eroticism. That talking is sexual. That breathing is sexual. That even to physically exist is sexual. And I believe him, and we make love beautifully.

Trans film critic Christianne Benedict argues that this operates as a manifesto for the films of Cronenberg and that the embodiment of his images interrogates notions of sex and gender.[3] Cronenberg's cinema is open to new forms of libidinal investment where what constitutes a desirable body can be reinvented. These explorations push into the abject space of disgust and exhilaration, which allows for transness to feel representative through conflicts of ecstasy and dysphoria, feelings which frequently collapse on one another when living in a transgender body. The nature of body horror itself is one of constant potential for evolution, as the body is put under a microscope of change as it passes from one form into the next, and the core function of that idea is not unlike the ambient liminal feeling of transness.

In *Shivers*, sex is not used for procreation, which evokes a queer sexuality. These parasites put humanity on the course of extinction by turning the reproductive act into a necrotic one of modified bodies, behavior, and function, to spread the parasite, which feeds on the host from the inside out.

Cronenberg's follow-up *Rabid* (1977) expands the themes of *Shivers* but narrows the focus down to a single character, Rose (Marilyn Chambers), and her experiences of bodily change when she is given a skin-graft after a motorcycle accident. She develops a phallic spike under her armpit that she uses during sex to satisfy her newly acquired thirst for blood. The introduction of a new phallic body part destabilizes her identity as a sexual being and her understanding of herself as a woman, queering her in a way that alludes to trans feminine dynamics. Cronenberg uses Montreal as a near void-space, wintery and cold to the touch, and films Rose alone in quiet bedrooms and lonely kitchens, where she sits with her urges and what her body now requires of her. Chambers gives the character a depth of frustration and disappointment in a life now dominated by new habits and behavior, and the character often disassociates whenever she is left in solitude. This is not unlike the emotional texture of a forced puberty and trying, and failing, to get used to the dominant hormone coursing through the body. There have been scientific studies which suggest the brain sends a signal that the body is injured at the onset of the subjective experience of gender dysphoric feelings.[4] *Rabid* finds familiar ground in the way that Rose shuts down when she is dealing with the full scope of her new body.

The Brood (1979) presents a further image of internalized bodily dysphoria becoming external, this time through the new psychiatric technique of "psychoplasmics," triggering bodily transformations in patients when they make a breakthrough in their therapy, created by Dr. Hal Raglan (Oliver Reed). The first time the effect of this new therapy is shown, Raglan is talking to a patient whose trauma is rooted in gender and who reveals he was never comfortable with what was expected of him as a man. Raglan takes on the role of the patient's father and brutalizes him with insults like "Daddy's girl": the boils that erupt all over his body as a result are one of the more direct instances of body horror being used to capture the experience of gender dysphoria.

Perhaps of all Cronenberg's films, *Videodrome* (1983) is the most reckless in its pursuit of a new definition of self and new bodies. Through the characters of late-night TV exec Max Renn (James Woods) and radio personality Nikki Brand (Debbie Harry), Cronenberg charts an erotic journey that causes bodily and political transformations, set against a backdrop of the popularization of television satellite broadcasts and the arrival of home video as a recording device. Renn is looking for something "tough" for his television station and finds it in the snuff broadcasts of "Videodrome," which feature masked men whipping nude volunteers and mirrors real-world Canadian Television station CityTV, which was known for broadcasting pornographic content and violent films on its "The Baby Blue

Movie" programming block in the early 1980s.[5] Renn and Brand are unsure whether the violence and sexual stimulation is real or staged, and that excites them. Brand likes rough sex and has masochistic tendencies. She invokes her own name during acts of foreplay by "nicking" herself with a razor and "branding" herself with a cigarette, elucidating the possibility that her name might be a chosen one — another externalization of internal states — rather than something given. Brand even goes as far as to tell Renn that she is going to volunteer for "Videodrome."

"Videodrome" proves to be more than just a subversive television series when Renn, after regularly viewing the program, begins to hallucinate that his body is transforming. He sits alone in his living room with nothing but the hum of static from his television to accompany him and begins scratching at his stomach. Cronenberg uses numerous close-up shots to enliven the physical qualities of the practical effects work and the beginning of an indention can be seen. He continues picking at himself until he finds that his stomach now has an opening in the shape of a vulva, and he has the sudden urge to impregnate himself by inserting a Betamax tape. This perverse incarnation of Cronenberg's thesis on the human body evolving with the introduction of new technologies is made even more surreal by giving Renn qualities that are more commonly associated with women. Now with a vulva of his own, he begins to hallucinate that his changes are not complete, and his hand begins transforming into a weapon that is reminiscent of a Glock pistol.

Those in charge of "Videodrome" are not merely television executives, but political terrorists who have goals of their own, and Renn's hand becomes a literal weapon they can use. *Videodrome* concludes with Renn escaping to a derelict ship after assassinating a political figure who was responsible for the "Videodrome" broadcast. He hallucinates an old box television, and Brand, who is believed to have been murdered, is seen on the television beckoning him to join her in eternity by killing himself and becoming another violent image incorporated into the "Videodrome" signal. She urges him to experience a "total transformation," telling him that to become the new flesh he must kill the old flesh, and he does so by taking his pistol-hand and pulling the trigger, declaring "Long Live the New Flesh."

The original ending, which Cronenberg details on the commentary track, would have then followed Renn after his suicide into the arena of "Videodrome" where an orgy would have taken place. Characters of all genders would grow new sexual organs, like Renn's chest vulva, and have sex with one another in an "afterlife." Cronenberg changed his mind during the shoot, because he did not want to suggest any religious connotation with his ending — the orgy itself was not the issue, and neither was the idea of Brand growing a penis. This potential ending never became reality, but it would have made the language of transsexuality bubbling under the surface in Cronenberg's oeuvre explicit. "Long Live the New Flesh" and all that it implies evokes a very specific trans feeling of rebirth, and the belief in a newer, purer realization of personhood.

When *The Fly* was released in 1986, it was believed to be a metaphor about the AIDS pandemic — a reading Cronenberg does not reject, while also arguing it could be about any disease. In *The Fly*, brilliant scientist Seth Brundle (Jeff Goldblum) has invented a successful teleportation machine in the form of two connected pods. Brundle uses himself as the first human teleportation subject. The initial moment of triumph becomes one of concern when he realizes something has gone wrong with his otherwise successful test — when re-assembling his DNA, the computer has fused it with a fly that flew into the pod. What follows is a genuine tragedy of unstoppable transformation, with Brundle experiencing a loss of bodily agency. His lover Veronica (Geena Davis) is also drawn into the horror — learning she is pregnant and worried that she may now give birth to the world's first human/fly baby.

Cronenberg has also had a few explicitly queer pictures

in his career: the William S. Burroughs adaptation *Naked Lunch* (1991) and *M. Butterfly* (1991). *M. Butterfly* remains a curious affair — it is the only film to directly feature a potential trans character, but relies so heavily on the trope of a gender reveal that trans people had little emotional access to the film, and it has not proved to be a point of inspiration for modern trans filmmakers. Cronenberg never lost track of the body throughout the 1990s and 2000s, however, and *Naked Lunch* presents a hallucinogenic travelog of shape-shifting bodies and sexualities. There are arachnid typewriters, adolescent sexual escapades, and Roy Scheider playing a hairy-chested, cigar-chomping man living inside the body of a buxom woman — a throwaway image, but one that speaks to the way that transness is endemic to the metamorphosing worlds that Cronenberg creates. *eXistenZ* (1999) also further explores the ways technology infiltrates and estranges its users, but his most theoretically sophisticated film of the decade is his J.G. Ballard adaptation, *Crash* (1996).

Crash tells the story of Bob Vaughn (Elias Koteas), a cult leader by way of Frankenstein's monster. He finds eroticism in car crashes and is interested in the "reshaping of the human body through modern technology," a quote that also acts as a thesis statement for a central strand of Cronenberg's oeuvre. *Crash* has a cold medical rhythm where the fallout of car crashes is meant to evoke the combination of the clinical and visceral found in pornography.

In *Crash*, Cronenberg fixates on images which elaborate Vaughn's thesis — a passenger-side door dented in the shape of a vaginal opening, the wayward picking of a fingernail on the scab-like warranty sticker of a used car. With these images, he suggests that vehicles are undergoing a transformation and taking on human characteristics. The sleek appearance of a brand-new car is a dead image, a mere object, but a vehicle that has been damaged becomes more alive, imprinted with identity through collisions and wear and tear.

As Donna Haraway writes in "A Cyborg Manifesto": "Our machines are disturbingly lively, and we ourselves frighteningly inert."[6] The characters who take part in Vaughan's erotic vehicular cult begin to take on the characteristics of the motor-vehicle after they experience the bodily trauma of the car crash. Cronenberg lingers on one of Vaughan's disciples, Gabrielle (Rosanna Arquette), whose metal leg braces are encased in squeaky leather pants — she is given a close-up when she bends over the hood of a car in a dealership while the protagonist James looks on, knowing his time in the dealership, the car wash, or on the highway is all a game of sexual foreplay. When Gabrielle wants to climb into the driver's seat, she does so with difficulty. Her act of situating her body as the leather squeaks and the metal braces lurch is its own act of erotic insertion. Her chest presses against the driver's side steering column in another close-up shot meant to tease the greater collision to come.

The eroticism that is inherent in Vaughan's philosophy is rooted in the conjoining of man and car through the sexualized situation of the vehicular collision — conjoining the two through action. When this does happen, the vehicle becomes something new, as though imprinted with the DNA of the drivers.

Vaughan's quest to combine his sexuality with cars is an erotic forebearer of orgasm and a genuine desire to reshape his body in an image that he prefers. Vaughan has received numerous tattoos on his body to outline the scar-tissue he has received whenever he has crashed his vehicle. His goal is one of both transcendence through orgasm, and transformation by collision. In Ballard's book, the character of James remarks to his wife Catherine that Vaughan's vehicle has the strange effect of appearing as though it is transforming into its owner with each recurring crash and modification. Vaughan has a death drive that contrasts with his wish to be reborn in the arms of his new sexuality and body. It is no coincidence that the paint scheme of his car carries the same hue as his faded leather jacket. It is touches like these that endear Cronenberg to trans viewers, because if one thinks about the broader notion of transformation in film, it opens potential images of transness to other textures and modes of expression. This is Cronenberg's "Body Beautiful" in action.

The interrogation of the evolving human body is clinical and austere in *Crash*, compared to Cronenberg's visceral early work, but *Crimes of the Future* (2022) was promoted as a late return to body horror with a trailer in which Kristen Stewart's character Timlin whispers the phrase, "Surgery is the new sex." This provocative phrase naturally led trans audiences to wonder where the director was headed, and if he was going to make the allegorical transness that courses through his work explicit.

The answer proved to be complicated. The film's overarching thesis is that the human body is evolving under the pressure of the environmental effects of an event like the climate crisis. In the director's notes for the film, given to critics ahead of release, Cronenberg wondered aloud about how the body was evolving to cope with what humankind has done to the environment, referencing the fact that microplastics are now commonly found in everything, including humans. He posits, optimistically, that evolution is possible, and presents this optimism through characters who can grow new organ systems and digest plastic more easily than traditional food sources.

In *Crimes of the Future*, Cronenberg once again positions his art alongside those whose bodies are modified. In earlier films, there have been modifications that characters had little to no choice in undertaking, but this time around his characters radically alter themselves on a whim, expressing a desire to do whatever they please with their bodies, and the government wants to precisely know every situation in which this is happening. The film's central character Saul Tenser (Viggo Mortensen) is a performance artist who has "Accelerated Evolution Syndrome," and his body is growing new internal organs at a rapid rate. His artistic and romantic partner Caprice (Lea Seydoux) operates on Tenser in an autopsy machine called a Sarc-Unit. She tattoos his new organs, and then they are removed as an artistic statement. Those in the National Organ Registry like Timlin and Wippet (Don McKeller) take great interest in Tenser and others like him, who perform live surgeries and mutilations for a paying audience. In this reality, the evolutionary state of humans has caused their pain receptors to have diminished, and it has made the human body its own palette for modification. Even with the radical possibilities inherent in such idealism, Cronenberg grounds it in a real danger. He understands that any modification of the status quo will be fought, sometimes violently, by those who wish to organize and control what can be expressed. In an edition of *Body Talk for Reverse Shot*, trans film critic Sam Bodrojan focused on Cronenberg's interest in bureaucracy and institutions:

> So much of *Crimes'* world-building is fixated on the mundanities of health care — upkeep on AIDS, registration, legislative violence. To Cronenberg, non-normative bodies are a material concern, and the film's villains are just as much those who wish to exterminate them as much as those who wish to allegorize them.[7]

The film hinges on a child named Brecken. He has a new system of organs inside of his body that would give humanity the possibility of a sustainable future, because he can safely consume plastic and other forms of waste. However, Brecken's mother kills him because he is different. His father, Lang (Scott Speedman), a revolutionary with a swath of other like-minded people on his side who choose to only consume plastic-like candy bars, is haunted by the knowledge that his son could have been the messiah for a new age. Lang proposes that Tenser and Caprice perform a live autopsy on Brecken to show the world the future, but when he is opened, his body has been defiled by the National Organ Registry, and instead of a new universe of organs, there is only a system of inserted organs placed there by the registry.

Crimes of the Future's nocturnal aesthetic and narrative qualities built on secret societies is reminiscent of film noir: both because there is an undercurrent that someone is out to get these characters due to their artistic practices, their bodies, and philosophies, and also in that it gestures to the post-World War II atomic age, where the black market and underground flourished in the crosscurrents of diminished production and rapid modernization. The black market has often been the outlet and resort for many trans people who cannot get the care they need, whether due to socio-economics, geography, or outright exclusion from institutions. Brecken's father Lang is portrayed as a black-market hero whose altruism is not tied up in prospering from tragedy, but seeing the lies of the government and the cruelty of the modern world, including that of his former spouse. But Lang's reputation makes him a target, and he is assassinated by agents who see his plastic-like candy bars as a threat to their corporate order, as they work for the company that manufactures medical chairs and furniture for those with Tenser's digestive condition. The film presents how the status quo is often reinforced by those who operate as the agents of change or help enact it in the form of private enterprise, and government bureaucrats.

Tenser also replicates the attitude found in hard-boiled and noir protagonists, expressing coolness and ambivalence towards the authority figures he meets. Tenser can interact with these authorities due to his unique status as an artist of influence, but the paranoia of the situation is innate. It feels as though there is no freedom in the supposed liberation of the body as an artistic palette for Tenser and others as they are being closely watched by authority figures. Trans critic Mackenzie Lukenbill wrote of *Crimes of the Future* in the same *Body Talk* conversation for *Reverse Shot* that

Cronenberg's movies are rarely about the horror of the self, rarely about masochism, disgust or self-hatred. His films are so pertinent and enjoyable because they take great pleasure in imagining a governmental response to bodily development. The spectacle of *Crimes of the Future* is not so much that Viggo Mortensen has a zipper installed in his abdomen, but because of the legislative and bureaucratic fuss that ensues as a result of that act.[8]

Lukenbill's points reach further than personal identification in the work and trace a through-line between "othered" bodies and the capitalist response to the desires of these bodies — the reaction to those who upset the status quo is one element, central to the likes of *eXistenZ* and *Videodrome*, that drives Cronenberg's work

Tenser is perhaps an avatar for Cronenberg in his old age, and one gets the feeling that this is a personal film. Aging is its own transformation. Tenser spends a great deal of the picture twisting in his Orchibed, an invention that predicts pain in the human body when it is at rest and minimizes it. Additionally, Tenser must eat in a technologically advanced chair that resembles the Mugwump from Cronenberg's *Naked Lunch*, otherwise he cannot digest food. Timlin says of Tenser's art, "His work has meaning. He is rebelling against his body and creating it on his own terms." But Tenser does not want to be a revolutionary artist. Tenser has been cooperating with the Organ Registry and acting as a spy, but instead of cutting out what is growing inside of him, what if he let it grow? What if he allowed himself to become what his body wished itself to be? Mortensen's performance is wonderfully evocative, discomforted, and sarcastic. When "Surgery is the new sex" is spoken in the film, he takes on a tone of ambivalence and replies, "Another epiphany." All these prickly undertones present a film that conflicts with itself, and is restless when trying to produce answers, because Tenser has none. There are only more questions, and the film concludes on an image replete with contradictory meanings. It is a close-up of Tenser finally eating a plastic candy bar with a complex look of ecstasy and anguish on his face. It is a shot that recalls Maria Falconetti from *The Passion of Joan of Arc* (1928), due to the silver color-grading of the cinematography and the glint of a complex tear resting in the eye of Tenser, whose emotions are difficult to parse. Cronenberg has spent his career telling interviewers that he is an existentialist, and many of his films conclude in images of death, but *Crimes of the Future* offers an ellipsis, and in doing so finds something generative in contradiction.

Cronenberg, whether he wants the mantle or not, has been the guiding force for body horror, and as a result has influenced the trajectory of trans film images, but there are body horror images that preceded him and also influenced the trans film image in a way that is evocative of Susan Stryker's "relatable monstrosities."

A Friend of Darkness: On *Cat People*

The Jacques Tourneur–Val Lewton classic *Cat People* (1942) is one of the earliest, most refined and elemental examples of transness as metaphor captured onscreen. The film, written by DeWitt Bodeen, a gay man, and equally influenced by European immigrants Tourneur and Lewton, presents a mysterious, exotic "other" in the form of Irena Dubrovna (Simone Simon). Irena believes in an old family legend that whenever she becomes sexually aroused, she will transform into a black panther and kill her lover. It is a film that understands the unconscious ways that women who are different are made to feel inferior to those perceived as "normal," and how jealousy can stem from coveting those qualities. Irena is positioned in contrast to Alice (Jane Randolph) and their differences in personality, looks, and sexuality are heightened when Irena's husband Oliver (Kent Smith), tired of her loneliness, starts to fall for Alice.

In reacting to this revelation of Oliver and Alice, Irena's

psychology — one where she compares herself to Alice's more conventional beauty and emotional stability — is like a trans feminine emotional spiral. She can never feel she is good enough. Lewton's films had a poetic quality that followed characters into darkness, rather than fleeing from it, and Irena claims that darkness is "friendly." This is evoked through Nicholas Musuraca's cinematography, which is dripping with shadows and curved light sources that only reveal the most necessary information. This is a nocturnal film, because Irena cannot bear to be seen in the light — touching on a common trans experience of caution or outright avoidance of being in public out of concerns for safety.

Simon's physicality emphasizes the way Irena emotionally distances herself from others. She frequently slouches her shoulders, casting her eyes downward as if she has too much shame to look at her husband. Her reading of, "I envy every woman I see on the street. They lead normal, happy lives. They are free," is saddled with so much regret, resigned frustration, and jealousy that it casts a pall of deep pain across the film. Trans women can have a particularly potent response to the longing Irena expresses here in wanting to be normal. It is easy to get a sense that Irena has struggled with these feelings of inadequacy her entire life. The faintest blow to her confidence could destroy her self-image forever. For many trans people, that consciousness and anxiety over their difference and how they are perceived is an everyday burden.

The tension that Irena feels is in what constitutes a "normal" womanhood, and what is seen as separate fuels the specificity of the trans feminine reading. When you have absorbed all the way that trans people are separated from others in society and called "monstrosities," then films like *Cat People*, *Frankenstein* (1931) and *The Wolf-Man* (1941) become relatable. The beauty of *Cat People* is in its empathy for those who have experienced this societal "othering" by foregrounding Irena's point of view. In one of the most captivating images in the film, she slinks into a bathtub after reassuring her husband she is fine, and weeps continuously. Viewers are asked to observe her distress for a long time. Her sense of her own monstrosity is one she has been taught and has absorbed.

Lycanthropy as Trans Feminine Puberty: On *Ginger Snaps*

Another film that deals directly with the idea of femininity being corrupted by monstrous transformation is the teen werewolf movie *Ginger Snaps* (2000). Lycanthropy, where characters find themselves in a state of transformative crisis, is a deep tradition in fiction. It was most famously imagined in *The Wolf Man*, with Lon Chaney Jr.'s tortured face captured in a time-lapse shot as he slowly became a monster. The slow dissolve of his transformation is one of the great images of shock in all of horror, but the frozen state in which the actor creates a portrait of fright at what he is becoming has some uncomfortable relevancy to trans people who have experienced unwanted physical changes. Puberty is not an instantaneous transformation, but a prolonged one, and many of the relevant body horror films that evoke gender dysphoria are situated around that period of change.

In *Ginger Snaps*, Brigitte (Emily Perkins) and Ginger Fitzgerald (Katharine Isabelle) are sisters and unlike other girls, or that is at least how they think of themselves. They are overpowered by teen angst and disaffected Gen-X nihilism. They dress in nothing but black and never brush their hair. They are obsessed with death, and the opening montage consists of violent mock photographs of impalement or severed arteries in which they imagine their demise. They treat these mock suicide attempts like their very own art installations, with Polaroids of their beautiful deaths plastered all over their bedroom walls. The girls see these mock-suicides as preparation for the day they finally kill themselves for real because "the world sucks." Ginger likes to play with a real knife the way other teenage girls use a nail file, and she and Brigitte have made a suicide pact with one another: "Out by sixteen or dead in this scene." Ginger is 15 years old and has not yet had her period. She hates the idea of her body changing, as many teenage girls do, but she knows it is inevitable. She expects her changes to be like those of any other girl, but after she is bitten by a rabid dog at the onset of her menstrual cycle, her changes do not go as planned.

Screenwriter Karen Walton wanted to make a movie about werewolves and menstruation as a ritualized full-body process of female maturity, an unexplored topic in horror — which can perhaps be attributed to the horror genre's gender gap in writing and directing — and one ripe for exploration.[9] Prior to *Ginger Snaps*, the only horror film that tied menstruation into werewolf conventions was Jacqueline Garry's *The Curse* (1999). However, Garry's characters were not adolescents, and it is this difference that gives *Ginger Snaps* more power as a film about transformation. Previous popular werewolf movies like *An American Werewolf in London* (1981) and *The Howling* (1982) do not dwell on the personal catastrophe of the shifting identity that comes with lycanthropy, making them uninteresting as trans metaphors. Karen Walton achieved her goal in making *Ginger Snaps* a parable of menstruation-as-horror, but what she did not anticipate was the appeal that her movie also had for trans girls, whose bodies were developing in ways analogous to Ginger's transformation.

Ginger does not become a werewolf overnight, and her change mirrors the process of puberty. Slowly, her body starts growing hair in unusual places and she also sprouts a fleshy phallic tail. She screams at her sister, "I'm not supposed to have a hairy chest. That's FUCKED!!" after a close-up reveals hair sprouting all over her torso. Ginger tries to shave her legs, but it is futile, with a shot of a Venus razor so clogged it has been rendered useless. If someone were to make a straight-forward film about a young trans girl dealing with problems related to the blooming of secondary sex characteristics because of testosterone, it would include a scene like the one with Ginger and her clogged Venus razor. Ginger's resistance to these changes is tied into what she expects of her gender identity, and how her transformation is not in alignment with how she perceives herself.

The strongest of *Ginger Snaps'* trans feminine pubescent images is Ginger's tail. Her tail has made it impossible for her to wear feminine clothing in a comfortable manner and Brigitte helps by giving her a tuck job. She takes some black masking tape and, in a medium shot, can be seen wrapping the tail around Ginger and taping it in place, not unlike how some trans women and drag queens use a gaff to hide their genitals. But this method is not a long-term solution. This tail damages Ginger's sense of self so severely that she can be seen trying to cut it off with a knife later that evening. Brigitte stops her mid-severing and ensures her that they will seek out a different solution to "cure" this desperate condition.

This moment bears a resemblance to other instances of "self-surgery" in films like *I Want What I Want*, but does not carry the same assaultive impact. The elasticity of metaphorical images in genre filmmaking allows Ginger's moment of weakness to represent more than one endpoint with her body, while still upholding the emotional weight of her experience. It resonates with trans viewers as an honest emotional climax about a phallic body part as opposed to an image of literal castration.

When there is a real tension between what the character wants their body to be versus what it is, trans viewers find relevant images. Ginger does not have much control over what is happening to her body, and this parallels the concerns of young trans people, whose identities are withheld due to lack of access to puberty blockers, hormone replacement therapy, and the freedom of expressing themselves socially. Ginger's potential as a trans film image is that she acts as a mirror for trans girls — puberty is hell on Earth when you are becoming something you do not want to be, and *Ginger Snaps* is one of the very few films to address that idea with the appropriate amount of horror in the loss of identity and bodily definition.

Human Embodiment: *Under the Skin*

Of all the monstrous films that comment obliquely on the nature of transness, Jonathan Glazer's *Under the Skin* (2013) is the darkest, and perhaps the most powerful. Released when trans visibility was beginning to become a topic of discussion in the mainstream, it polarized critics at the Venice Film Festival and later the Toronto International Film Festival. Cisgender critics often said it was a "black widow" fable about the nature of female sexuality,[10] while other critics found it to be a cruel misogynist exercise.[11] Trans critics experienced something different. They saw themselves in this story of a nameless alien who begins the film pretending to be human (Scarlett Johannson) who then develops a newfound identity as a woman.

The alien is introduced in a blinding white room as she changes into the clothing of a woman she has trapped. In her mission, she is tasked with seducing men into a void where they are eaten alive for reasons that are never specified. *Under the Skin*'s greatest asset is not in the seduction scenes it repeats several times over, but rather in the subtle examination of learned behavior. The film elaborates the distance between being mentored and trained in a socialized gender role and showing all its traditions, and learning it yourself through observation. In the first scene of the film, the alien learns gender presentation through clothing and looks from a woman who has been abducted, then goes to a mall and buys makeup, boots, a fur-lined coat and a basic pink top. This section is shot in a *verité* style that is in stark contrast to the more expressive sci-fi elements used throughout. There is a montage of women applying makeup, and they are seen talking with one another in a matter-of-fact way. Viewers are placed in the alien's point of view, observing humanity and the nuances of gender through her eyes. She is fundamentally at odds with these other women, as she knows she is different, which is why it feels like she is purchasing camouflage. The film drives this home by ending the montage with a cut to the alien applying her makeup in solitude in the car park of the mall, instead of trying it on in the makeup store. She does not linger; instead, her first impulse is to retreat into isolation. Her sense of femininity is internal and external, but stripped of the communion other women have with one another.

Much of the alien's understanding of gender is through trial and error — like trans people — and whatever notions she had about the power she would glean from being a seductive bombshell of a woman are disrupted with the reality of how male characters treat her. She roams Scotland in a van — a gender-flipping of conventional images of a predator and not unlike Buffalo Bill in *The Silence of the Lambs* — and manages to seduce several men, but she is also sometimes met with harassment when she finds herself in the wrong place at the wrong time. Initially, the alien does not seem to understand the power dynamics inherent in the way her identity is assessed by others, and moves through the world without concern for her safety, but as the film moves along, she becomes vulnerable and aware of the way her body operates in the real world. In one scene, a gang of drunken men try to pick her up and she retreats towards a crowd of women at the bar, having understood that women are safer in numbers. The alien's experience is not dissimilar from that of trans women re-learning how to move through society, adopting survival mechanisms that cis women acquired while they were growing up.

While the first half of the film is dominated by the alien's pick-up and seduction scenes, *Under the Skin* changes direction when the alien encounters a man (Adam Pearson) with a skin condition that causes him to grow benign tumors on his face. Their conversation is not transactional in the way that the alien's previous conversations with men have been. They relate to one another, and she finds friendship. She is curious and interested in why he only goes out at night, and why he separates himself from others. There is reciprocal flirting between these two characters, which is a new experience for both. The man hides from other people because they "rile him up," and under the cover of darkness he goes about his daily life, much like the alien, who prefers to operate in the dim hours after midnight. With this character, she finds a like-minded soul and begins to question the validity of the seduction mission that she has undertaken. Pearson's "Deformed Man," as he is billed, is the only character the alien has second thoughts about sending to an inky doom. The relationship between the two characters recalls the empathetic encounter between Frankenstein's Monster and the blind old man in *Bride of Frankenstein* (1935), who cannot see Frankenstein's monstrosity and so treats him companionably.

The alien starts off as a blank non-human, but she slowly comes to terms with human responses and her evolving femininity. She learns, but she is also hit with realizations of the limitations of her alien body — she cannot have sex in the conventional manner that a cis woman might. She falls for the seductions of a nameless man in the countryside, and during the only sex scene in the film, realizes he cannot penetrate her. There is no further information as to why this happens, and the alien is shocked by this denial of pleasure. She affixes a bedside lamp alongside her genitalia and then throws it on the floor, frustrated. In the close-up shot that follows, the alien's response feels achingly close to gender dysphoria; she appears distraught that all her efforts to be the woman she appears to be are for nothing. It is made more painful by a contrasting scene of euphoria that occurred moments earlier, in which the alien luxuriates in the shape of her body in the same mirror, lit by a golden light.

After this moment of sexual crisis, she flees to the woods

and isolates herself in a rarely used public cabin. She is later found by a trucker, who tries to rape her, and in their violent confrontation, she is set ablaze due to the trucker's horror that what he perceived as a woman was "not what she seemed." It is a brutal ending and dramatizes a particular type of transmisogynistic violence rooted in genital fright and panic. It is the body that limits her but also what makes her who she is that ends in ruination. *Under the Skin* is a bleak, disturbing film that twists the traditions of the monster movie to uncover new forms of empathy for new kinds of gendered expression.

A.I. and Robots: A Connection in "Othered" Non-Human Bodies

Similarly to the empathetic monster in horror films, there are relevant trans textures and emotional embodiment of relatable experiences in narratives about artificial lifeforms who are aware of their difference. By tapping into science fiction's probing, speculative questions regarding the human body and gender, trans viewers can find another gateway through to complex trans images rooted in metaphor.

In *Blade Runner* (1982), "replicants" are artificial lifeforms that resemble humans, developed to work on space colonies as slave labor. They are built to expire after five years have passed, but a group of rogue replicants return to Earth to find their maker and have him reprogram them with a life expectancy equivalent to their human counterparts. They are then hunted by a special police force known as "blade runners." This is a film of uprising and questions of personhood, but is most captivating on a granular level through the figure of the replicant Rachel (Sean Young), who was programmed with memories and believes she is human. With Rachel, the film twists notions of memory and family, and ties them into questions of how they relate to the maintenance of a stable identity. When she learns she is a replicant, the revelation fractures her psyche, and her character is given space to meditate on who she is and what she wants out of life now that she must remake herself with a new self-understanding.

Blade Runner was part of an emerging wave of sci-fi films that foregrounded how computers and artificial intelligence would interact with humans to create a new "other," and with it a certain type of trans-adjacent image was born. Steven Spielberg's *A.I. Artificial Intelligence* (2001) became a favorite among trans cinephiles during the 2010s. It is not especially difficult to understand why, with its story of an artificial boy looking to become "real" so he can be loved by his mother. David (Haley Joel Osment) is a creation for a grieving family, made by a grieving scientist (William Hurt), who made the robot in the image of his dead son. With David, the family and creator of this human-like innovation are hoping to hold onto something that was lost. David is considered a breakthrough, the first robot capable of complex emotions.

A.I. is set in a future that is not dissimilar from the one that climate scientists have predicted will become our reality. Major cities have been rendered uninhabitable by flooding, large swaths of the population are unable to be fed due to agricultural catastrophe, and ruling governments have mandated that childbirth be limited to stave off further global apocalypse. David is seen as a solution to the childbirth problem, and is introduced with a shot that immediately distances him from his human family: in silhouette, the image warped to make it appear as though David's body is normal, but his neck unnaturally elongated and his head too round to be human. He most resembles an alien in this image, but then the camera refocuses, and he appears like any other boy his age. He embodies the promises of a future where the image of humans can live on in something non-human, but he is quickly cast as the "other" by his family. This sets the stage for a futuristic update on *Pinocchio*, with David yearning to be human

A.I. started as an idea of Stanley Kubrick's. He read

Brian Aldiss's 1969 short story "Supertoys Last All Summer Long" and began crafting ideas for what his adaptation would entail in the late 1970s. His dissatisfaction with what was then available as visual effects technology left the film in limbo for several years until Kubrick, in a rare gesture, offered to give the film to Spielberg in the belief that he was a better fit for the material.[12] Kubrick would pass away before *A.I.* became a film, but his fingerprints are all over its concepts. If David is an amalgam of the divine and the artificial, the film itself is an amalgam of Kubrick and Spielberg. There is a Kubrickian cold and hollow quality to the world that these characters inhabit — and this, combined with Spielberg's inherent belief in possibility, makes for complicated, rich emotional terrain.

Despite the inherent limitations of this robotic child, it is David's emotions that are the most complex, because it is in interaction with the difficulties and failures of the humans around him — most notably those of his mother Monica (Frances O'Conner). Monica spends most of her days at a local medical facility reading to her comatose natal child Martin (Jake Thomas). She is characterized as someone whose identity as a parent is so essential to who she is that her life all but stopped when her child became sick. Her husband Henry (Sam Robards) works for the tech company who are inventing an emotionally complex robotic child, and he is chosen to adopt David because his family meets the necessary criteria. Monica despises Henry for what he has done, interpreting it as pushing her to move on from Martin, and even though David appears human, she can never share the same connection with him that she did with her first-born son.

The first hour of *A.I.* is a melodrama interrogating the effect that a new child can have on the family, and speculatively explores themes of adoption, autism, transness, and divergence from the expected behavior and development of a child. David is different by nature because his technological state is so advanced, while his cognitive and emotional skills are those of a child. Eventually, the family begins to find comfort and familiarity in the new dynamics of their home with David, but then a miracle happens. Martin wakes up. He comes home and is convinced that his parents tried to replace him with David, and proceeds to sabotage David's relationship with his parents. Martin does not refer to his brother as a sibling, but as a toy, and it feels like a slur. David does not really understand the intent. It unearths a feeling of disposability for the artificial child The Pinocchio-isms of the character are not rooted in the central desire of bodily dysphoria, but one where he wants to change so that he can be loved.

Monica makes the choice to abandon David alone in a forest after an incident involving Martin that nearly caused him to drown. In the Aldiss short story, David is eventually brought back to the tech company and put down like an animal as he wonders when his mother will come pick him up. But in the film, he is left to wander in the dystopian cities, looking for an answer to an impossible question about the limits of his body.

David cannot move forward without the love of his mother, but it is not something he can bring into existence either. The tragedy of David's love for Monica is that he cannot see that she failed him and that he can choose others to love and be loved by. His opportunity to feel her love and experience an ideal boyhood is, however, afforded to him in a bittersweet ending.

2000 years later, David is found at the bottom of the sea, his body left in remarkable condition. Along with Teddy, a toy bear, he is resurrected by an advanced form of the Mecha prototypes that David sprang from. The mechs find David's memories of humans to be of anthropological interest and they have the technology to make those memories physical and modify them to David's wishes, not unlike a holo-suite program from *Star Trek* (1966–). His dream life where Monica treats him like her son is granted through this technology, but the technology is only advanced enough to allow David to physically experience his mother for one day. David gets his wish, but it is compromised. Despite Spielberg's reputation for being saccharine, this ending is devastating. David survives and persists through centuries, still holding out the hope that he can be seen and perceived as a real boy that had a mother who loved him. Plenty of trans people are still waiting for the approval of their parents and have been put into the position of building replacements out of other mother and father figures. In *A.I.*, that reality can be felt through the coding of David's story.

Films like *A.I.* have an unconscious relation to the trans film image and open up possibilities for trans filmmakers going forward. One example of this fruitful exchange of trans-coded images is Mamoru Oshii's adaptation of *Ghost in the Shell* (1995) — a film that, in its prescient story about identity in the internet age, went on to influence perhaps the most famous trans film in existence, *The Matrix*.

Ghost in the Shell follows Major Motoko Kusanagi as she investigates a sentient hacker program called "The Puppet Master." In the movie's dystopian vision, the human body can be "enhanced" through cybernetic implants and machinery, and the definition of what constitutes a human has evolved. Oshii is a filmmaker who luxuriates in presenting the solitude of his characters as they consider the themes at hand, and he does so frequently with Kusanagi. In one scene, she talks to her partner Batou on the docks, with a beautiful backdrop of a painted midnight sky. He asks her what defines humanity. She considers the question deeply before giving her answer. She believes that to be human is to have a consciousness, memories of childhood, and a belief in the future — all things that the replicant Rachel is given to create the illusion that she is human in *Blade Runner*. As a cybernetic being whose only human characteristics are her brain and her memories, which could be implanted in any artificial shell, Kusanagi states that being human also resides in all the unconscious things that people take for granted, such as their voice or the way their hands look, and perceives a kind of comfort in the limitations of humans and the way their consciousness is permanently tied to a single body. For Kusanagi, her body does not feel real, but her mind does.

Following her conversation with Batou, Kusanagi walks through the city and spends her afternoon watching people. She sees a woman who looks exactly like herself, but who is human. She longs for the ambivalent way this other woman seems to treat her latent femininity. For her, it does not appear to be a question left unanswered in her soul. It is reminiscent of the way *Cat People*'s Irena looks at women who have something that she does not. Kusanagi and the woman share a glance with one another, but no words are spoken, and Oshii conveys how Kusanagi feels in a following close-up shot of mannequins in a department store.

This image of mannequins is one of the finer trans-coded images in all of science fiction and anime. It represents the way that people whose bodies are outside of the social norm can sometimes feel less than complete. Kusanagi is on the outside looking in, but affixed in her identity as a woman, because she looks at other women and is confounded by what they possess that she does not. Their lives and what they may entail is a fantasy that she has resigned herself never to attain, along with all her further contemplations of identity.

The Puppet Master is also plagued by these questions after they become sentient and begin considering the differences between human and cybernetic life. Those in the tactical force of Section 9, whom Kusanagi works for, refer to the program as "he," yet the Puppet Master has chosen a female cybernetic life form as a host. The plot follows the Puppet Master in their long quest to experience the human qualities of reproduction and death, both of which are not feasible for a program. Section 9 seeks to destroy the Puppet Master, but Kusanagi is fascinated by their quandary and finds it related to her own. In the closing stretch of the film, the Puppet Master, whose female body has been destroyed, is connected to Kusanagi with a USB-like device and finally confesses to their desires to unite with her. In doing so, the Puppet Master would experience death, losing their old identity, before taking on a new one by being reborn in Kusanagi's body. Batou, who accompanies Kusanagi on their mission to stop the Puppet Master, tries to prevent this from happening, but Kusanagi and the Puppet Master find common ground and become one. In doing so, the identities of both characters are modified, and they become something new. Section 9 destroys Kusanagi's body and places her brain in the black-market shell of a pre-adolescent girl, another image meant to convey that Kusanagi's identity is forever shifting, evolving, and changing under the weight of this new future and its technologies.

In these films, and many more, there is a potential evolving trans cinema that is built upon gesture and theory as much as direct representation, and through this, patterns of a potential visual language of transness on-screen are beginning to coalesce. More recent films like James Cameron's *Avatar* franchise (2009–)[13] and *Alita: Battle Angel* (2019), which Cameron produced, have garnered critical attention for their possibility as trans allegories,[14] and it is likely that trans people will continue rummaging through cinema for trans film images until an overt representation of transness with depth, dimension, and nuance becomes the norm.

Whether direct and original trans representations proliferate or not, viewers and artists will still be drawn to creating a trans cinema and trans film image through re-modification, forcing texts to undergo a transition of a sort. Take, for example, Vera Drew's trans take on Batman for her film *The People's Joker* (2022), which became a festival sensation and turned Drew into a *cause célèbre* when Warner Bros.–Discovery sent a cease-and-desist after the film's debut in the Midnight Madness Program at the 2022 Toronto International Film Festival. With the tagline, "An illegal queer coming of age comic-book movie," Batman's Gotham

City, built from hyper-stylised DIY animation and wall-to-wall green screens, becomes the background for Drew to tell her story of transition. Her Joker confronts gender identity in a world of chaos, pursues a career in comedy, and details how her trans identity was unlocked by seeing her own trans-coded image in Nicole Kidman in *Batman Forever* (1995). This remixing, parodying, and modifying, along with mining trans-coded images and textures, show that with guile and imagination trans filmmakers will mold new flesh out of old skin. "Long live the new flesh" may very well be how transness defines itself in genre cinema in the twenty-first century.

CHAPTER 8
Subversion of Fate:
The Matrix Series and
the Wachowski Sisters

The films directed by Lana and Lilly Wachowski are driven by the pivotal choices of characters who seek to take control of their own destiny, lending their most famous films, *The Matrix* series, to trans readings that preceded the filmmakers coming out as trans women. In the years since the original franchise trilogy (1999–2003), Lilly Wachowski has gone on to say that *The Matrix* (1999) was always a film about being transgender, but that the world was not ready for it.[1] In 1999, few filmgoers were thinking about transness, much less about transness as a metaphor in a cyberpunk science-fiction film. But through such trans coding, the Wachowskis presented characters altering time, form, and their own destiny. What started as an oblique, closeted coding of transness as allegory has developed into a more direct allegory built upon lived experiences in the most recent entry in the series, *The Matrix Resurrections* (2021). The original *Matrix* could have simply existed as another film claimed by trans filmgoers as part of an unofficial canon, alongside the films discussed in the previous chapter. But the trans authorship of the film series, with both filmmakers explicitly stating the initial trans allegory was intentional, has foregrounded *The Matrix* in trans film history.

Some scholars argue that *The Matrix* is a film that ushered in "trans cinematics." Wachowski scholar Cáel Keegan surmises that *The Matrix* is significant "not simply because it relates a recognizable trans identity narrative, or because it is authored by trans creators, but because its aesthetics emblematize the multiplication of temporalities, realities and embodiments induced by gender transition."[2] *The Matrix* has characters who exist in a transitory state, which imposes ideas, textures, and possibilities of transformation and change. The trans allegory functions through these modes. Beyond the theoretical ideas and political discourses that have emerged from this film, the Wachowskis' oeuvre presents a journey of how these filmmakers, through trans coding, were able to articulate their desires, anxieties, and latent humanism as artists. These elements have since all become explicit with their coming out, and they have been open about their intentions as artists in the years since.

The Wachowskis came from the comic book world, before entering the film industry as screenwriters and later directors. Their directorial debut, *Bound* (1996), still stands out in their filmography. Upon release, it was hailed as a queer film that injected a modern, open sexuality into the mode of classical Hollywood film noir. In addition to *Bound* being about two women who fall in love within a taut crime plot, it also contains the ideas of destiny and opportunity that would later characterize their filmography.

Two Girls in a Closet: On *Bound*

The relationship that I have with the story [of Bound*] really begins with me struggling with the depiction of people like me in media. I watched* Psycho. *I watched* Dressed to Kill..., Sleepaway Camp, *and just the endless films that are trans people as psycho killers, and chopping people up. And it really hit me the hardest with* Silence of the Lambs... *and* Silence of the Lambs *is made by an amazing, brilliant filmmaker [Jonathan Demme] and it has Jodie Foster and I love her so much, but the film just made me feel physically sick. I couldn't even sit in the theater and I ran outside* *and I went to the bathroom. I'm crying in the bathroom, and I just sat there and I was trying to think of like one film that was set inside of a genre world where an LGBT character won and went off and lived happily ever after. And I'm sitting there racking my brain and I can't think of one and then I was like... in this tiny, icky sticky bathroom I thought... I'll make it.*

Lana Wachowski, 2019[3]

In *Bound*, the Wachowskis uncorked a bottle of vintage film noir eroticism that felt both modern through its queerness and also a throwback to Old Hollywood through its film-making. It existed as a hybrid of two of the hippest trends in 1990s American independent filmmaking: Quentin Tarantino's slick, post-modern crime films and New Queer Cinema. But *Bound* still felt novel.

The first shot of the film is, cheekily, a tracking shot through a closet, which concludes on an image of Corky (Gina Gershon) tied up. Viewers can hear her heart beating and her lover, Violet (Jennifer Tilly), is heard in voice-over saying, "I had this image of you, inside of me... Like a part of me." It is quite a tone-setter for not only the film, but for their filmography.

Corky is a butch handywoman who has just gotten out of jail. Her queerness is expressed through her clothing — a white tank-top and dark jeans, covered top to bottom in paint stains. She has her eyes on her neighbor, Violet, who is by contrast very femme, with perfectly applied makeup and a slinky black dress revealing deep cleavage. When they see each other for the first time in an elevator, it is reminiscent of the explosive implied sexuality between Humphrey Bogart and Martha Vickers in *The Big Sleep* (1946) — they devour one another with their gaze, in homage to the language of studio production code flirtation. There is, however, one big problem: Violet is the trophy wife of a mob lackey named Caesar (Joe Pantoliano) and he believes his wife to be a doting, heterosexual ditz. Around Caesar, Violet is purposefully passive, suppressing both her queer sexu-

ality and intelligence while presenting a traditional femininity that is in deference to what her man wants, such as
how she dresses. Through Corky, Violet finds herself and a
reason to break free. They formulate a grand plan of robbing
Caesar of all his dirty mob money and running off together.

While the sensuality between Corky and Violet is rooted
in film noir pairings of the past, it also owes a great debt to
the erotic lesbian film images that, while not mainstream,
had an audience through the VHS tape home video market.
The Wachowskis sought out Susie Bright, a bisexual journalist and erotica author, to guide them through the ins and
outs of lesbian sexuality on-screen by being a sex coordinator for the lesbian love scenes. Bright patterned the sex
scenes on her own experiences of love-making with women
and storyboarded the intimate scenes with input from
the Wachowskis. Bright also acknowledges that, while her
instincts were based on her experiences, she also looked
to pornography as a visual inspiration, and singled out the
hardcore film *3AM* (1975) by Robert McCallum (the pseudonym of Gary Graver), which featured real-life lovers performing lesbian sex.[4]

The first scene where Corky and Violet meet alone has
numerous lesbian signposts, the most significant of which
is a shot of Corky's hands, which are paired with Violet
speaking in voice-over about her father's hands. This introduction kickstarts a visual motif of hands being sexualized
that the film returns to numerous times. On the commentary track for the film, the Wachowskis stated that these
signifiers were only noticed by audiences when it played
at the San Francisco Gay and Lesbian Film Festival. Susie
Bright would remark, "The hands are the cock and every lesbian who saw that movie understood."[5]

Bound's usage of hands shares a lineage with other queer
films, namely those of lesbian experimental filmmaker
Barbara Hammer, whose works of sapphic love and sexual
pleasure were often foregrounded in the avant-garde film
space. *Bound* could never become equivalently explicit with-

out being awarded an NC-17, but that explicit form of lesbian pleasure is implied in the following scene where Corky retrieves an earring for Violet out of a broken sink. *Bound* also uses a signifier of wetness to express female sexuality, and Corky's job as a handywoman gives her great excuses to use her hands. When she is retrieving the earring for Violet, the framing is very precise, and in a split diopter, Violet's hosed legs are visible alongside Corky's hands twisting at the pipes. Intercut are close-ups of her hands and moisture is visible on her skin. The sexual tension between the two continues after the earring is retrieved. The two settle on the couch and their intimate feelings for one another take over. There is a close-up of Corky's hand on Violet's heavy left breast and Violet takes that hand and begins sucking on Corky's fingers. Their foreplay is interrupted when Caesar catches them on the couch, but this disruption makes the eventual sex scene between the characters explosive, because viewers have been forced to wait for the payoff. In this queering of film noir, *Bound* manages to achieve the wonderful effect of making its audience long for queer sex with great intensity.

When they do eventually have sex, it is wonderfully erotic, and devoid of the male gaze that most erotic thrillers of the 1990s contained. The Wachowskis were guided by Bright's experiences and their own instincts of how these characters would behave in the bedroom, prioritizing a romantic shared orgasm instead of a quick release of sexual tension. Their post-coital moments together share a key image of an overhead shot of them in bed with one another. A closet door can be seen with a sunbeam coming out through the cracks. This is signaling that there is freedom waiting on the other end of their queer identities and foreshadows that *Bound* will have a happy ending.

What starts out as a thrilling fling quickly turns to love for Violet and Corky, and with it comes a plan. Violet needs to untangle herself from a marriage to the mob, but Corky has past demons of her own, including a five-year prison sentence for robbery. What unspools from this narrative yarn is an exercise in the genre of noir being built on tightly woven stories of bad men and worse women, which are then subverted through overt queerness. With her sarcastic drawl, constant raised eyebrow, and laconic demeanor, Gershon evokes a role associated more commonly with the male lead in noir films, such as Robert Mitchum or Humphrey Bogart. Gershon's Corky has a blue-collar toughness that works perfectly in contrast with Tilly's rendering of the femme fatale. Violet uses the preconceived notions about her intelligence and manner to get what she wants — like a modern take on Marilyn Monroe. It is classic stereotyping that she uses to her advantage.

Things seem to always work out right in the end for characters in the Wachowskis' films. In *Bound*, Corky and Violet overthrow Caesar, the mob, and the straight world. The final scene feels like a correction to the ending of *Thelma and Louise* (1991), a film claimed by queer viewers despite the central characters' demise. Corky and Violet clasp hands in her brand-new pick-up, paid for with Caesar's money, but they do not drive off a cliff to their doom as Thelma and Louise do, instead setting a course to their paradise, as lovers, with nothing but the wind at their backs. It was a radical message for a mainstream queer movie in the mid-1990s, particularly in the erotic thriller, where lesbians were frequently cast as villains, such as *Basic Instinct* (1992).

Early in its release, *Bound* ran into criticisms and accusations that the Wachowskis gave the film a "male gaze" in its lesbian sex scenes. These criticisms, which also erased Susie Bright's role in the development of those scenes, hinged on the fact that the Wachowskis were perceived as men at the time. Today it has become evident that their transness influenced how their films operated, a lesson to film critics and viewers alike that basing critique on their perception of a director's gender identity can be a reductive, unhelpful exercise. *Bound* is so clearly a labor of love *for women who love women.* It is also an expression of yearning for the liberation that comes with expressing oneself clearly. It rings true as an experienced document of queerness, thanks to the input of Susie Bright, while also acting as a point of longing to be in those same queer spaces by the directors. The Wachowskis have never made another film like *Bound*, but it was a building block in wishing to break free as your true self, and that sense of expression would later be re-coded in their totemic action films.

The Matrix: A Trans Allegory Takes Flight

At the beginning of the *The Matrix*, Thomas Anderson (Keanu Reeves) is sleepwalking through life at his office job as a computer programmer. He is introduced as an introverted bedroom-dweller who moonlights as a computer hacker under the alias of "Neo." His identity is one defined by dualities in an early moment of trans coding for the character. The stagnant quality of Anderson's life is represented by a dim color palette of faded grays and greens, with rooms barely lit beyond the glow of computer screens.

On a whim, he is invited to a club by one of his customers. Everyone at the place is dressed in leather and the soundtrack pumps along to a dance remix of Rob Zombie's "Dragula." Neo could not feel more out of place. But then, a woman introduces herself in a film noir set-up that recalls *Bound*. She is Trinity (Carrie-Anne Moss), the hacker he has admired from a distance, and she is there to warn him he is being followed. He takes her seriously because she calls him Neo. He says to her, clumsily, "I just thought... um... I thought you were a guy." Trinity responds deadpan, "Most guys do," a clever way for the Wachowskis to acknowledge how presumptions of gender in internet spaces are often wrong. Trinity then whispers to Neo a cryptic message that still expresses a sense of support to him:

I know why you're here, Neo. I know what you've been doing. I know why you hardly sleep. Why you live alone and why, night after night, you sit at your computer. You're looking for him. I know, because I was once looking for the same thing, and when he found me, he told me I was not really looking for him... I was looking for an answer.

This dialogue exchange is loaded with signifiers for trans viewers. Trinity aligns the struggles and questions Neo faces as ones she has also experienced; they are words of affirmation for Neo — that his search is worth continuing. It then becomes evident that Anderson, the office worker, is the disguise. Neo is his true identity. Trinity also tells Neo about Morpheus (Laurence Fishburne), who is the resistance leader of humans against the AI system known as "The Matrix," and that Morpheus has the answers he is looking for. It becomes evident for viewers that Neo's world as Thomas Anderson is in fact a simulation.

In the lexicon of today's pop culture, no one refers to Keanu Reeves' character as "Thomas Anderson." Viewers of the film look at Reeves and simply see Neo. Anderson is the equivalent of a deadname, the name trans people are given and forsake in their transition. The most notable character who speaks to Neo strictly as "Mr. Anderson" is the villain Agent Smith (Hugo Weaving), and it is often said with a derisive, jabbing tone. In their first scene together, Smith enters Neo's workplace. Neo's hacking and his identity have been "found out," which again plays into common trans tropes of closeted trans individuals having their "secrets revealed" and being "outed." Smith comes with armed police officers and presents himself as a government official of some kind when, in reality, he is an agent of The Matrix. Smith believes Neo has information regarding Morpheus, who has been designated a terrorist. Neo refuses to cooperate and suddenly, in a moment of surreal horror, finds his mouth sealing over. He is bound to an interrogation table and Smith implants a robotic parasite into his body to track him. Neo wakes up believing it is a dream, only to realize the parasite is still inside and must be extracted by Trinity, who then takes him to Morpheus.

Neo's first interaction with Morpheus is through a phone call where he speaks cryptically and tells Neo that he is "The One." Neo initially sees Morpheus in a black trench coat with sunglasses that shield his eyes as he delivers the truth about The Matrix, revealing that he and all of humanity are slaves in bondage:

> Let me tell you why you are here. You have come because you know something. What you know, you can't explain, but you feel it. You've felt it your whole life, felt that something is wrong with the world. You don't know what, but it's there like a splinter in your mind, driving you mad. It is this feeling that brought you to me. Do you know what I'm talking about?

What Morpheus describes to Neo, the feeling that something is inexplicably amiss, can also align with gender dysphoria, where a potentially lifelong struggle for a sense of autonomy is never resolved. Morpheus presents Neo with a choice: he can take the blue pill and wake up back in his mundane daily life, or take the red pill and "stay in Wonderland" with Morpheus and his group of revolutionaries to find out more about The Matrix. The red pills themselves are significant in trans coding, with feminine hormone replacement therapy drugs often being in pill form, and Premarin, an estrogen drug in the 1990s, was maroon red.[6] While Neo's choice and the film's plot follow the traditional path of a hero's journey, the Wachowskis have this moment unfold with a degree of ambiguity, filming Morpheus in close-up with a Cheshire Cat grin and Neo's ingesting of the red pill being soundtracked by thunder and a lightning clap straight out of an old horror film.

After taking the red pill, Neo begins to touch a mirror that has taken on a liquid state. He begins to leave his digital body behind, with the red pill used by Morpheus and the others to trace him where he goes. The liquid from the mirror starts to envelop Neo, who then wakes up in his pod, revealing that he has lived cocooned in this other reality. Mirrors are used in *The Matrix* in a way that is not dissimilar from the work of surreal French film director Jean Cocteau's *Orpheus* trilogy. The mirror is a fantastical element that transforms the body in unpredictable ways, rather than imposing limitations on it. Cáel Keegan argues that the usage of mirrors in the aftermath of the red pill scene shirks the traditional mirror scene aesthetics of trans narratives, which often present limitations of the body. For Keegan,

> the fluid mirror has internally duplicated Neo's proprioceptive positions, folding his consciousness into a loop across two worlds that are not quite two. *The Matrix* thus aestheticizes transgender as a movement out of the limits of dictated form — a door forward into a supersession of the categories for embodiment in any single reality.[7]

This reading presents Neo's embodied transness as being neither in a fixed nor determinative position, as he was as Thomas Anderson, but as an experiential state of radical multiplicity.[8]

Neo is taken in by Morpheus's ship, the *Nebuchadnezzar*, with Morpheus soberly greeting him, "Welcome to the real world." It is not 1999, but closer to the year 2199, with free humans living in an underground city named Zion. Morpheus tells Neo more of the truth. The Matrix is a disruptive computer program meant to control the reality of human beings and harvest their imaginative powers for energy through a head-jacking system. Morpheus and his crew exploit the virtual reality of The Matrix by entering the program via their own primitive systems of the same technology the machines use. They do this in an effort to free other enslaved people from the pods. But saving Neo takes on a stronger significance. Morpheus believes Neo fulfills what The Oracle (Gloria Foster) prophesied, which is that "The

One" would free all of humanity and defeat The Matrix, for that is the only way humanity can truly be free.

Neo goes through rigorous training to fight against the agents and machines that are constantly chasing Morpheus and the other rebels. As Neo, Reeves's body and voice develops into a more confident figure who distances himself from the timid Thomas Anderson. He works with Morpheus in martial arts to fight in the worlds of The Matrix, but he also begins to develop skills that cannot be taught, such as stopping bullets and taking flight. Despite being told by The Oracle that he is not The One, Neo embodies his role as the hero and saves Morpheus from Agent Smith, risking his own life in the process. Morpheus and others still refer to him as The One, but more significantly, Neo starts to believe in himself and that these skills come from within, achieving Keegan's read of the character transcending the limitations of the human body through this coded trans embodiment.

The notion of choice has acted as a bridge for trans allegory in the Wachowskis' work ever since Neo took the red pill instead of the blue one. He chose to wake up and stop living a lie. He chose to become himself. Destiny and opportunity to grow from what was always within. While The Matrix is fundamentally about a disruptive computer program meant to control the reality of human beings, it also acts as a land of potential fantasy for those who have been awakened to transform themselves in any manner they please. For Neo, he was a shell of a person who needed to change and transform.

The first of The Matrix films was the fourth-highest grossing 1999 release, making over $400 million worldwide, winning four Academy Awards, and being instantly canonized in popular culture. Film audiences of all stripes were obsessed with the film, as they devoured its acrobatic fight choreography that combined wire-fu martial arts with John Woo-style gun battles. The film's aesthetics were instantly adopted into mainstream video games and filmmaking. It changed cinema almost immediately at the dawn

CORPSES, FOOLS, AND MONSTERS

of the new millennium, hitting at the perfect time. With the rise of the internet, there was a new strain of cinema that was interested in technology, and while there were several films about computer hackers, *The Matrix* — although not without its own influences from Japanese films like *Ghost in the Shell*, *Perfect Blue* (1997), and *Serial Lab Experiments Lain* (1998) — felt fresh, innovative, and prescient in how it used online life as a fulcrum for telling stories of individuality, avatars, and personal creation.

Sequels to *The Matrix* were immediately put into the works. *The Matrix Reloaded* (2003) and *The Matrix Revolutions* (2003) came out within months of each other, making over a billion dollars in box office combined. These sequels put the theoretical underpinnings of the first film on the back burner and opted for more pristine action cinema (the heist and car chase in *Reloaded* and the anime-tinged bouts in *Revolutions* are highlights). These films also play up the romantic relationship of Neo and Trinity, and this is where the trans coding manages to persist in the subsequent films. In *Reloaded*, Neo and Trinity leave a rave to have sex — their intimacy is filmed within the confines of what is allowed within a big-budget popcorn film. It is another tantalizing sex scene from the Wachowskis, which recalls their investment in relaying themes through lovemaking. They knew that Carrie Anne-Moss and Keanu Reeves bore a resemblance to one another, and leaned into that fact when composing their sex scene. When Neo and Trinity have sex, the physical differences between male and female are obfuscated, and they seem to merge into one single androgynous entity.

When Lilly and Lana Wachowski each came out as trans in the subsequent years, the idea of *The Matrix* as a trans allegory began to gain more mainstream credibility. It helped that the Wachowskis were not just vocal in approving the trans reading of the films, but also that they confirmed they had tried to smuggle in more ideas around trans identities. Lilly Wachowski would go on to talk about how the minor character Switch (Belinda McClory) was initially conceived as male in the real world and female in *The Matrix*, but the idea was nixed by Warner Bros.[9]

The success of the trilogy brought the Wachowskis other big-budget opportunities, but also a lot of unsolicited attention. Both sisters have noted that, in the making of these films, there was a lot of personal struggle around coming to terms with their transness and that, in the rare moments they were openly able to express those identities, it was not received well.[10] Lana Wachowski briefly went to film premieres of *The Matrix* sequels with an androgynous presentation, which began fueling speculation about her gender identity in the tabloids. At the height of their name recognition and fame, the Wachowskis became more reclusive. They expressed this tumultuous period through another film, this time with a less uplifting expression of trans coding.

Masking Out of Survival: The Wachowskis and Racer X

The commercial success of *The Matrix* films afforded the Wachowskis the privilege of a blank check for their next film. They first worked on producing the successful adaptation of Alan Moore's *V for Vendetta* (2005), directed by James McTeigue (an assistant director on *The Matrix* trilogy), where the titular masked revolutionary V inspires a revolt against a totalitarian regime. Much like *The Matrix*'s red pill, *V for Vendetta* and V were later co-opted by reactionaries. The Wachowskis' next directorial project was, on the surface, much lighter than Alan Moore's politically charged graphic novel — a live-action adaptation of the beloved manga and anime series *Speed Racer* (2008), which had been in production limbo for years.

Speed Racer was a critical and box office failure, but the earnest, candy-colored, pop filmmaking has earned it cult status. It also contains a trans allegory that arguably could not have existed without the filmmakers, one of whom had their gender identity become a story of interest in the run-up to the film's release. This is expressed through the Wachowskis' reworking of Racer X (Matthew Fox), another masked man, into a character who has left behind their family to shift into another identity. While the film has a vibrant, sugary sheen, it also contains moments of mourning, tied to symbolic death and familial loss.

In both the manga series and television shows, Racer X was always an elusive character, who donned a face mask and was an unpredictable driver who seemed very protective of the titular character, Speed (played in the film by Emile Hirsch). In the film, Speed's brother Rex Racer (Scott Porter), who had a falling out with their father and was never seen again, is believed to be dead, but Speed begins to believe the mysterious driver is in fact his brother. In one confrontation, Speed asks this Racer X to unmask himself, which he does, revealing a different face from that of the brother Speed has lost. But the Wachowskis add another twist: Racer X is indeed Rex Racer, but to protect Speed and other members of their family, he faked his own death, underwent reconstructive facial surgery, and assumed a new identity.

Unlike Joanne in *Come Back to the 5 & Dime, Jimmy Dean, Jimmy Dean*, who discloses her trans identity and past, Racer X withholds and denies all associations with his previous identity. Trans people who return to a place they inhabited before transition or see somebody from their past must often navigate this tension. The risk in disclosing who you once were and who you are now invites questions, some too difficult or intrusive to answer. While the risk of *not* disclosing causes there to be no potential reconciliation with your past, some trans people then feel they are left with little choice but to walk away and disown their earlier lives. The past only serves as a stifling, traumatic reminder of the limitations they experienced. Racer X, as rendered by the Wachowskis, is informed by the idea that trans people are living a double life, with a second self, and that one life must end for another to begin. Racer X does not just transform from Rex with a simple name switch, but has altered his face and extracted himself from all familial ties. To quote Cáel Keegan, Racer X's "association with surgery, disguise, and use of an adopted name mark him as symbolically transsexual."[11]

Speed Racer was made during a period in which the Wachowskis, particularly Lana, were being uncharitably judged for their decisions and appearances. Due to the films she made with her sister being lucrative properties for a major Hollywood studio, she was navigating unknown territory in the 2000s — including the risk of her gender identity becoming a story that overshadowed her work. Although *Rolling Stone* scrubbed the story from their online archive, a January 2006 print issue of the magazine featured a piece by Peter Wilkinson that outed Lana Wachowski and went into details about her personal life, her first marriage, and associations with the BDSM community and adult performers.[12] She would not officially come out publicly until the release of *Cloud Atlas* in 2012. Then, in 2016, Lilly Wachowski's disclosure of her trans identity was not voluntary, but rather her attempt to get ahead of being outed by the tabloids.[13] Though the *Rolling Stone* piece was criticized at the time, the outing of Lana Wachowski did show that even respected magazines couldn't resist the impulses of presenting transness as a spectacle to gawk over.[14]

Lana Wachowski rejected public life and sought to be reclusive to preserve her family partnership in filmmaking and the jobs of many other people tied to that enterprise. Racer X took the step of going into hiding and altering his identity to protect his family, particularly Speed. Racer X is not just an allegory of transness but also represents the sacrifices the Wachowskis made in going under the radar to live in their trans identities, offering an insight into the anxieties of the 2000s, when there was a considerable amount of risk in being open about one's gender identity, and when such private matters were widely seen as fair game for media speculation and discussion. Towards the end of *Speed Racer*, there is a montage in which Racer X witnesses his own funeral from a distance, goes under the knife for cosmetic surgery, and takes the bandages off to see his new face in the mirror. When the character Inspector Detector (Benno Fürmann) asks Racer X if he felt he made a mistake hiding this secret from his family, Racer X answers, "If I did, then it's a mistake I will have to live with..." The answer reads as firm and definitive, but Fox is filmed gazing into the distance as his voice trails off, conveying sadness and resignation. It is a poignant moment that is hard not to read retrospectively as a personal messaging from the filmmakers.

Cloud Atlas: The Limits of Transformative Humanism

While the Wachowskis proved that the trans film image was capable of elasticity and that trans-coded filmmaking was possible, they are not without their flaws as filmmakers. Their 2012 film with co-director Tom Tykwer, *Cloud Atlas*, was an ambitious adaptation of David Mitchell's science-fiction novel and the first where Lana Wachowski was credited under her trans identity, but the excitement around the film was rather short-lived. *Cloud Atlas* is a very important lesson about limits of the trans film image and trans coding: it cannot supersede specificities of race. When *Cloud Atlas* debuted at the Toronto International Film Festival in 2012, Lana Wachowski called it an "experimental" film that "speaks about human courage." The Wachowskis have sometimes been naive when it comes to their idea of universality. Their films have had diverse casts, but they, like many white filmmakers, have disregarded racial differences in suggesting that people are all one. This is utopian in theory, but in practice trivializes the experiences of minority groups, including those within their own trans community. As a result, this has led to instances of racism percolating throughout their work, such as in *Cloud Atlas*.

Cloud Atlas attempts to tell the story of an inter-connected humanity through six nested stories about six individuals, who are reincarnated across space and time. With co-director Tykwer, best known for the experimental action thriller *Run Lola Run* (1998), the Wachowskis have all the actors remain in their roles across these timelines. This involves characters at some points switching genders, nationalities, and race through reincarnation. White actors transform into indigenous islanders in one timeline and into Asian characters in the dystopian future world of Neo Soul. Rather than re-cast these roles, millions of dollars in CGI and makeup are used to alter the faces of white actors Jim Sturgess, Hugo Weaving, and Jim D'Arcy to make them appear Asian. Supporters of *Cloud Atlas* argued for the merits of the subversiveness in the film, in also having African-American actress Halle Berry and Korean actress Doona Bae transform into different races, but the Wachowskis still allowed yellowface, despite its own unsettling history in Hollywood filmmaking. This created obvious problems for the film, with many critiques excoriating it. Cultural critic Zeba Blay said of the film:

> The filmmakers labor under the misapprehension that their work resides in some sort of vacuum, free of wider cultural context, or in the domain known as the "post-racial" society. This blissfully naïve understanding proceeds from the dominant point-of-view, the white point-of-view.[15]

Blay's argument best outlines the problems inherent in applying ideas of universality to questions of transformation, and captures some of the problems in how the Wachowskis apply the trans film image. For all the good the Wachowskis have done, there is also a lesson here for white trans artists and cultural producers seeking intersectionality with other minority groups. For all the commonalities that might exist, it is essential to acknowledge that there are differences in the lived experiences of specific minority groups.

After *Cloud Atlas*, the Wachowskis reunited with Tykwer and returned to the idea of interconnectivity in their ensemble Netflix show *Sense8* (2015–2018). In *Sense8*, this idea is applied with more maturity, grace, and caution, while also introducing their first ever explicitly trans character in Jamie Clayton's Nomi Marks. Nomi follows in the footsteps of prior Wachowski characters by being a hacker, and is used by the Wachowskis to address the political and social tensions around being trans and having a trans body, while also allowing the character to express her sexuality and have her problems be reflective of the world around her. In the wake of the critical and box office disappointment of their sci-fi action film *Jupiter Ascending* (2015), the existence of *Sense8* was a reminder of the Wachowskis' gifts as storytellers.

Lilly Wachowski would go on to be a television writer and producer for the queer television show *Work in Progress* (2019), set in her native Chicago. But Lana decided to return to *The Matrix* series, writing and directing the fourth *Matrix* film, *The Matrix Resurrections* (2022), on her own. *The Matrix Resurrections* would, unsurprisingly, be much more than a major film studio trying to milk money from a pre-existing I.P. cash cow. It is a film characterized by reflexivity, with its original co-creator confronting the problematic and complicated legacies attached to the earlier trilogy by reasserting what the films meant to her.

The Matrix Resurrections: The Allegory as Decoded and Remixed

It is easy to celebrate the narrative trajectory of becoming yourself and praising the act of transition, or in Neo's case taking the red pill, but it is much more difficult to argue for continued survival and propose a trans narrative beyond initial transition. Neo's life has been about struggle from the moment he awoke into the real world. Trans people have survived such struggles through community and small but life-affirming pockets of other people like themselves. It is with that fact that trans narratives must also move beyond the initial singular discovery of oneself, something which *The Matrix Resurrections* suggests in its allegories and metaphors. *Resurrections* is a self-referential journey back to the central pairing of Neo and Trinity, while acknowledging the wider community of those who have also carved out their own identity in The Matrix.

The original trilogy played with the notion of Neo being The One, an anomaly and messianic hero, but the films also portrayed a group of like-minded individuals with a vision of freedom fighting for the greater good. *The Matrix Resurrections* remixes the whole series to make audiences actively reconsider Neo's iconography as The One and reinforce that, in fact, he was merely one of many. Wachowski rebooted the concept of Neo — the fictional Christlike savior who was co-opted by real-world reactionaries — to prevent him from being perceived as the sole trans-coded phenomenon. *Resurrections* suggests that Trinity and Neo are in some sense doubles of one another. It also presents a universe that is not at war, as it was in the initial trilogy, but one that is still a work in progress, with deeply insidious elements remaining, even after the fall of the machines.

Resurrections concedes that The Matrix is here to stay. The program retconned itself to become more accommodating and livable — and in terms of the use of color, the film looks completely different from the trilogy, representing the shift in internet aesthetics from black and green into something more multi-colored and inviting. This new Matrix represents how the internet has irreversibly been folded into day-to-day life, an open acknowledgement that, while community can be found there, it can also be the place where it is destroyed too. Wachowski has her characters voice their misgivings as a way of addressing the right-wing co-option of the film and the idea of the red pill. The character Bugs (Jessica Henwick) says to Neo, "They took your story, something that meant so much to people like me, and turned it into something trivial. That's what the Matrix does. It weaponizes every idea. Every dream. Everything that's important to us."

The Matrix Resurrections finds Neo and Trinity at a crossroads, and they must decide if they are in fact willing to save themselves again. The film follows Neo decades after the events of *Revolutions* — he is back inside The Matrix under his old name Thomas Anderson, working as a videogame designer (on a game called Binary) for a company owned by Warner Bros. He is also a minor celebrity because he made a trilogy of video games called *The Matrix*. He is unable to enjoy his fame, and is in therapy for hallucinations, post-traumatic stress, and other anxiety disorders. The story is that he attempted suicide.

There are those in Io (formerly Zion) looking for Neo, but in an echo of *Speed Racer,* his digital image has been scrubbed so that he appears different. As Thomas Anderson, his appearance is that of a balding old man with a shaggy beard, though Neo perceives himself as he always has been (as actor Keanu Reeves), unaware of these physical differences. Trinity, who has been resurrected in The Matrix as Tiffany, lives as a mother of two and is married to a man named Chad (former Matrix stunt coordinator and *John Wick* director Chad Stahelski). They cross paths again as strangers, but slowly Neo begins to remember her. It is later revealed that they have been purposely kept apart by the current programs run by his analyst (Neil Patrick Harris) to extort more power from him in energizing The Matrix. Trinity struggles with her decision to join Neo in the real world, as she has doubts about the possibilities of living freely. The dullness of her life as Tiffany gives her a false sense of security and structure. *Resurrections* is more mature than the first three films, with its central drama focused on choices, compromises, and yearning, as opposed to the broad themes of freewill versus enslavement in the original trilogy.

The Matrix Resurrections frequently includes contrasting images of flight and falling. This serves to represent a life lived on one's own terms versus one that is compromised, and in *Resurrections*, this motif is favored over the red pill-versus-blue pill dilemma of the first film. The leap of faith sequence in *The Matrix* was initially used to represent a freeing of the mind, an act of will and self-belief that would allow characters like Neo, Trinity, and Morpheus to extend the capacities of their bodies. The slow-motion frame of Neo jumping from a building in *Resurrections* recalls his original leap, but his analyst diagnoses it as a psychotic break. In the aftermath of the event, Neo finds himself in therapy for suicidal behavior and on a prescription of blue pills (an anti-depressant-like drug), which dulls everything in his life. At a later point in the film, Neo is once again in a situation of suicidal ideation and duress atop a building in the dark of night. He drunkenly mutters, "I fly or I fall," only to be pulled back from the edge of the roof by the character Bugs, who tells him he changed her life and served as a point of radicalization for her. Bugs was a window-washer when she saw Neo for the first time, and she knows what really happened in the earlier incident on the roof, telling him with a knowing smile, "You never fell." The film revisits this moment on several occasions, each time from a slightly different angle and perspective. What looks like self-destruction in the eyes of one person might look like a heroic act of self-possession to another.

In 2012, Lana Wachowski would publicly disclose that she had planned a suicide attempt, planning to jump in front of a train, but could not act on it because there was a man in a subway station who was staring at her. She would say, "I don't know why he wouldn't look away. All I know is that because he didn't, I am still here."[16] Bugs goes from an awed bystander who could not take her eyes off Neo while he was on the verge of leaping to the very person who stops him from trying to leap again. It is impossible to untangle suicide and the ghosts that come with that act within the trans community. This motif of the leap, as well as the usage of past footage from *The Matrix*, hangs over the events of *Resurrections* like a haunting. But in Bugs' version, seeing Neo's first leap becomes a call to action. Bugs is a hacker and a rebellious hovercraft captain seeking to free Neo and the others from The Matrix, but what she also represents is the viewer who saw Neo as a liberating, affirming figure. She too is a trans-coded character in the way Neo and Trinity are, a stand-in for the trans viewer who watched *The Matrix* and understood the coded messaging.

Wachowski also revisits other previous symbols of trans allegory in *The Matrix*. One central image from the series is confronted and reset in *Resurrections*: the role of mirrors in trans narratives. *Resurrections* further expands the idea of the mirror as an object in contention with transness by using it as a tool for both dysphoria and fantastic manipulation. The machines have modified Neo's avatar so he cannot be found by others. This is subtly acknowledged in a scene at a coffee shop where, in a low-angle shot, Neo can briefly be seen with this modified reflection, introducing trans concepts of a pre-transitional longing around how you are perceived versus how you may see yourself. The audience sees Neo, but the mirror says something else. Trinity is given the same effect in the same shot, seen as an older woman with long gray hair. There are numerous scenes leading up to Neo's understanding of how his image has been altered where he presses on mirrors and stares at himself with discontent, and while this is tied into the notion of how his life is now structured, rather than a physical dissatisfaction with himself, it still provokes a recognizable response in the trans audience. When he does see himself for the first time as an aging bearded man with graying hair, he does not recognize himself. He traces his hand across the mirror and looks on in astonishment and disorientation. The disorienting effect is profound as a trans film image — it is a character rejecting what he sees, and plunging his arm into the mirror so that he may become the truer version of himself once again.

The Matrix series can never be reduced to a single theme or allegorized entirely as a trans-coded film — and to do so would reduce the open-ended richness of the franchise. But there are certain images in *The Matrix Resurrections* that gesture towards trans history, embodiment, and livelihood. The idea of the leap captures many of these themes and returns in the climax. When Neo and Trinity are cornered by the agents of the Analyst, they again have a choice to fly or fall. When they jump, it is Neo who plummets and Trinity who can fly. She lifts them both up. To leap into a world as a trans person in complete isolation can be dangerous, but sharing that leap into the unknown with another becomes life-affirming and lifesaving. In *Resurrections*, The Matrix becomes theirs to control and reconceive, offering up something new and different from the false lives they have lived before. The world and the self are always there to be reclaimed and remade.

Living as yourself is not a decision that is only made once. It is continuous and re-addressed every single waking day. Red pill or blue pill. Fly or fall. The Wachowskis, through the early coding of their experiences, demonstrated an earnest humanism that has matured over time and revealed the potential of a developing and multifaceted trans cinema that is broader in themes, aesthetics, and notions of embodiment.

CHAPTER 9
Cis-As-Trans Casting

A quick look at the history of the Academy Awards reveals numerous instances of cisgender actors being awarded or nominated for playing trans or gender non-conforming characters. Even in the rare instances of a trans person playing a trans character — such as The Lady Chablis, who played a version of herself in Clint Eastwood's prestigious true crime adaptation, *Midnight in the Garden of Good and Evil* (1997) — they did not receive the same attention or critical plaudits given to cis actors in their "transformative" roles.

As we have seen throughout this book, there have often been trans people in Hollywood with very visible profiles, but almost always they were not chosen or perhaps even considered for trans roles in "respectable" films that centered on transness. For example, despite appearing in Oscar-winning films and coming from a well-known acting family, trans actor Alexis Arquette was given very few mainstream avenues where she was allowed to express her trans identity on-screen. Instead, the most notable "prestigious" representations of transness or gender nonconformity on-screen have almost always been played by cis male actors. But cis-as-trans casting has included many cis women as well — for example, Felicity Huffman as trans woman Bree in *TransAmerica* (2005), which is seen by many as a missed opportunity. Trans actress Alexandra Billings disclosed years after the film's release that she had been offered the lead role. However, writer-director Duncan Tucker said that she was not famous enough to get the film made, and instead gave the role to Huffman, who was having a career-resurgence thanks to being on the widely popular American network television show *Desperate Housewives* (2004–2012).[1] While not being trans-led or having trans authorship, Huffman and Tucker would choose to highlight that they employed trans woman Calpernia Addams, who also acted in the film, as a consultant, helping with Huffman's "look" and "voice." Additionally, trans activists Andrea James and David E. Harrison (who would later carve out a notable career in Hollywood as a television actor) had supporting parts. This was often the extent of trans involvement in film projects about trans people with Oscar aspirations.[2]

Some of these cis-as-trans performances are less egregious than others. In *The World According to Garp* (1982), for example, John Lithgow imbues his character Roberta Muldoon with warmth and verve, as the character's transness is never placed into any real conflict in the film. On the other hand, however, there is the case of *The Crying Game* (1992).

The Reveal as Phenomenon: *The Crying Game*

The Crying Game's cultural legacy and reception hangs over it like a dark cloud for many trans viewers, despite the film having a beguiling, strong performance from Jaye Davidson as trans woman Dil. It showed how, in instances of cis-as-trans casting, the cis performer could only do so much in creating a credible trans film image. The film's writing, direction, promotion, and critical reception also bear responsibility for how these images were received.

When *The Crying Game* was released, there was a great commotion about its numerous plot twists surrounding terrorism, espionage, and character detail. Roger Ebert, in a rave review, called it one of the best films of 1992, and implored readers to put down his review and go watch the movie with the advisory, "See this film. Then shut up about it."[3]

As we have seen, transness as reveal is a cheap trope that

was becoming increasingly common in Hollywood, usually reserved for tertiary characters, particularly sex workers, that stretched across film genres, be it in Paul Brickman's Tom Cruise breakout film *Risky Business* (1983), Sidney Lumet's crime drama *Q&A* (1990), or the action-comedy *Crocodile Dundee* (1986). These foolish side characters would immediately be disposed of upon the reveal, but in the case of *The Crying Game*, a film forever synonymous with its reveal, the "trap" was not somebody disposable, but instead a compelling film heroine: its femme fatale, Dil (Jaye Davidson), whose trans identity is revealed by the sight of her penis on-screen.

While Dil's gender identity is not key to the plot, which covers the relationship between Fergus (Stephen Rea), a member of the IRA, and Jody (Forest Whitaker), a British Soldier being held captive by the group, it overwhelmed the cultural image of the film from the moment it was released. The moviegoing public did not just respond to the reveal in a positive manner — it reveled in it.

To unpack this, it is necessary to return to one of the film's biggest champions, the influential American film critic Roger Ebert. In Ebert's review, his opinion of Davidson's performance is incredibly respectful, calling the character an "original." He explicitly praises Davidson's style and "delightfully dry" line delivery as possessing a type of charisma that had been missing in modern movies. But earlier in the review, he compares *The Crying Game* to *Psycho*, stating that both achieve the same effect of being a film that is "really about something else altogether." By making this comparison, Ebert cryptically presents Dil's reveal scene alongside Norman Bates'. It's also worth noting that Ebert's film industry work included being the screenwriter for Russ Meyer's cult classic *Beyond the Valley of the Dolls* (1970), which also contains a notorious reveal scene of a trans figure. The film's villain, Ronnie "Z-Man" Barsell (John LaZar), takes off his shirt to reveal breasts and declares, "I am Superwoman!" and goes on a murderous rampage when their reveal is met with disgust and repulsion. Ebert, as a viewer, was not just somebody who was programmed into the mechanics of the reveal scene trope, he was also the major engineer of one (albeit in the exploitation genre).

Miramax Films, *The Crying Game*'s American distributor, ran with the marketing tactic gifted by Ebert that recalled the methods of B-movie producer William Castle. But while Castle made profitable junk, *The Crying Game* was up for awards consideration. Due to the relentless marketing campaign of the now disgraced Weinstein brothers who ran Miramax, *The Crying Game* grossed $71 million worldwide, being dubbed a "sleeper hit." More importantly, it netted six Academy Award nominations, including Best Supporting Actor for Davidson, and Neil Jordan would be awarded the Oscar for Best Original Screenplay. Trans people were collateral damage in this cultural phenomenon — a fact that was front and center at the 65th Academy Awards Ceremony. *The Crying Game* reached a level of cultural significance few films attain and was the showcase bit in host Billy Crystal's opening monologue parody. Written by gay comedian Bruce Vilanch and set to Frank Sinatra's "(Love Is) The Tender Trap," "(Surprise) It's the Crying Game!" was the comedic twist on the trans panic reaction to the film. Rather than play along, Davidson, to his credit, reacted completely stone-faced to Crystal's trivializing performance.

In the time since *The Crying Game* was released, its central reveal has become an instant cultural movie moment, and would also be spoofed in several other films and television shows, such as with *Ace Ventura: Pet Detective* (1994). In *Ace Ventura*, Jim Carrey's character rushes to the bathroom in disgust when he realizes Lt. Lois Einhorn (Sean Young) was the disgraced Miami Dolphins place kicker Ray Finkle. Her character's villain reveal does not involve an undress as explicit as Dil's, but it does contain an extremely crass close-up of her groin area, indicating a tucked penis that makes every male character in the film vomit and gag. In *The Crying Game*, after Dil's penis is revealed, Fergus violently pushes her away to run to the toilet to vomit. Dil apologizes to Fergus, while rightfully questioning why he was at a gay bar. The reveal scene, from her perspective, was never intended to be such a shock. While not broadcasted to everyone she met, she assumed it was implicit and known in the queer spaces she would perform. Their relationship manages to survive this initial indiscretion on Fergus's part, but this scene has damaged an otherwise good film.

It is hard to blame any trans individual for rejecting *The Crying Game* outright due to this one scene, but it is worth re-examining, and trying to understand what it might have to offer beyond this twist. Films where a cisgender man and a trans woman fall in love were a rarity then, and they still are today, even if they are no longer treated like an outright taboo. This does give *The Crying Game* a charge that other modern films about trans people lack. It still feels novel to see a trans character like Dil embody a femme fatale with wit and charisma, which only further enhances the noir-tinged fable of double-crosses, shifting allegiances, and political violence.

Dil's greatest ties to the plot of *The Crying Game* are that she fell in love with two different men on separate sides of the Irish Troubles. *The Crying Game* uses Dil's gender identity as a wedge to re-introduce new elements into the plot as things shift further into espionage. But through it all, Davidson gives the character integrity. Dil's emotions and perspective are always considered. Davidson's androgyny allows him to tap into his masculinity when Fergus later shaves Dil's gorgeous ringlet hair so she can go into hiding when things intensify between the IRA and their enemies. Dil is strong-willed enough to not completely acquiesce to the plans of Fergus and has some agency in the plot-heavy espionage fallout, though her later suicide attempt feels like a betrayal of the character. Dil was many things throughout the film, but mentally fragile was not one of them.

For everything good that *The Crying Game* does, it also stumbles, making for a complicated viewing experience of wins and losses. Davidson is not at fault; his performance remains a high watermark for cross-gender casting, despite also being placed in one of cinema's most notorious cultural moments. In the end, Dil and Fergus find one another again when she visits him in prison after he takes the fall for her in the murder of Jude (Miranda Richardson), who was responsible for Jody's death. It is an ending only fit for the movies, where logic goes out the window in matters of the heart, even going against the genre conventions tied to the inherent cynicism of noir. The old-fashioned romance of Fergus and Dil perseveres. Unfortunately, people forget that part of *The Crying Game*.

Boys Don't Cry: The Passion of Brandon Teena and the Problem of a Singular Trans Masculine Representation

Given the even greater paucity of trans masculine images compared to the trans feminine, *Boys Don't Cry* (1999) has remained the placeholder of trans masculine representation in cinema since its release. However, this is not because of the resonance of its trans film image, but instead due to mainstream films remaining static in their depictions of trans masculinity.

At the time, *Boys Don't Cry* was celebrated and rewarded by the Hollywood industry, but its legacy in dramatizing the life and story of Brandon Teena — a trans man who was murdered by two men in Nebraska in 1993 — is very complicated. It is not without its knotty nuances, but much of the discord over the film for trans viewers comes back to both the casting of Hillary Swank as Brandon Teena, and Teena's portrayal by writer-director Kimberly Peirce.

Teena's murder in 1993 was initially met with hostility, condescension, and ignorance both well-intentioned and overtly malicious. This was the standard public reaction to any story of a dead trans person that hit the tabloids and talk show circuit of the time, also represented in the publicization of Billy Tipton's 1989 death. The murder of Teena and his friends Lisa Lambert and Phillip DeVine was covered in trans publications *TransSisters*, *FTM Newsletter*, and *Chrysalis Quarterly*, who actively followed the case along with other reports of trans hate crimes, but there was also a fair amount of coverage from a lesbian perspective too, as found in films such as the DIY black-and-white short *Cuz It's a Boy* (1994) by Catherine Gund, who interviewed butch lesbians in New York City about the story.

The true crime version of the story, Aphrodite Jones' 1996 book *All S/he Wanted*, further obfuscated Brandon's trans identity and was met with hostility by the trans community after Jones insisted on writing Teena as a woman. The trans community felt betrayed by Jones, who had been invited to trans conferences and community gatherings while she wrote the book.[4] When John Lotter and Tom Nissen were sentenced for the murders in 1996, the story recirculated and was used as an opportunity to punch down at Brandon Teena's trans status through cheap jokes, such as in a "Weekend Update" segment on a February 1996 episode of *Saturday Night Live*, when anchor and comedian Norm MacDonald said of the 1993 triple murder:

> In Nebraska, a man was sentenced for killing a female cross-dresser who accused him of rape and two of her friends. Excuse me if this sounds harsh, but in my mind, they all deserve to die![5]

The segment aired, and was re-aired in syndication, without any later apology from MacDonald or *SNL*, with Transexual Menace's campaign of handing out flyers in New York City outside NBC headquarters barely registering in the mainstream media.

Then came the attempts to dramatize Teena's story. *Boys Don't Cry* (which had an early working title of *Take It Like a Man*) was in a race into production against another Brandon Teena project by Mark Christopher (writer-director of *54*).[6]

Another Teena film was also attached to Drew Barrymore in the Brandon role, with actress-director Diane Keaton as producer.[7] *Boys Don't Cry* would be produced by Killer Films, the independent film production company spearheaded by Pamela Koffler and Christine Vachon, who had previously found themselves embroiled in controversy over Todd Haynes' film *Poison* (1991), due to conservative outrage over an explicitly gay film receiving funding from the National Endowment of the Arts.[8] It became the bedrock production house of the New Queer Cinema movement of the 1990s, with such titles as *[SAFE]* (1995), *Velvet Goldmine* (1998), *Go Fish* (1994), *Swoon* (1992), *I Shot Andy Warhol* (1996), and the 1995 dramatization of *Stonewall*. Being produced by Killer Films gave *Boys Don't Cry* credibility, despite the film being Peirce's first feature (although she had made a 1995 short of the story with the same name).

There was a broadly inclusive casting search for the role of Brandon that included butch lesbians and trans men, but according to a 1999 interview with Pierce for *The AV Club*, these aspiring performers "couldn't carry it off on-screen" or "couldn't pass as a boy."[9] In a twentieth-anniversary retrospective of the film, Peirce revealed that Harry Dodge and Silas Howard, the creative team who would later make the trans masculine buddy film *By Hook or by Crook* (2001), were among the trans individuals (although both at the time were tied to the butch lesbian community), who tried out and sent tapes to play the role of Brandon.[10] In the same interview, Peirce reflects on coming across Hillary Swank, who is described as an "unknown" — despite the fact that Swank had a considerable mainstream resume in network television, including a stint on the very popular *Beverly Hills, 90210* (1990-2000) and as a lead in a theatrically released *Karate Kid* film sequel. Without directly naming her, Pierce simply describes Swank as "a beautiful androgynous person [who] floated across screen — cowboy hat on, sock in the pants, gorgeous boy jaw, boy ears, boy eyes, boy nose, boy mouth, Adam's apple. Finally, a girl who had all the traits that begin to blur the gender line."[11] Peirce would reiterate this line verbatim about Swank's features during major media appearances like *The Charlie Rose Show*.[12]

Peirce's attachment to Brandon Teena has always been evident, recently framing the film as autobiographical.[13] Her defenders will note she did "the work" in terms of talking to trans people and hiring trans people to work on the film, including trans activists and the group Transexual Menace.[14] How she speaks of the film has evolved over the years, speaking more affirmingly about Brandon with male pronouns, something related perhaps to the fact that she now identifies as a trans butch, describing herself as part of an "ever-changing middle."[15] However, it is crucial to look back at her earliest description of Teena when the film came out in 1999:

> Well, Brandon told his mom he was a lesbian when he was 14 years old, and his mom put him in an institution, so that eradicated "lesbian" as an identity. So, Brandon now thinks that gay is bad. Brandon then thinks, "I will be straight. Straight is good." Brandon wants to be straight, and he still likes women, so he says, "I want to be straight. I like women. I look like a guy. Oh, I'll be a straight guy." Then it's, "I want to go to New York. You can't be a straight guy in New York looking the way I do. I'll stay right here, where it's much easier to pass as a boy. Then I get to stay home because I really want to live in a trailer park and basically live the way I live."[16]

Peirce's armchair psychology echoed some of the tensions and discord between the lesbian and FTM communities regarding the story at the time, when it was still up for debate who Brandon Teena was and which community had a "claim" over him. Even in Peirce's affectionate takes on Teena, there is a lot of class condescension around Brandon's upbringing and presumptions that such an upbringing meant he had no masculine reference points or role models.

"I fell in love with this trailer-park girl who didn't have any money and didn't have any role models, yet took this imaginative leap and transformed herself, which is extraordinary," she says in that same *AV Club* interview.[17] In more sober terms, Teena's institutionalization by his mother ended with him being discharged from a crisis center, where a medical professional saw him as trans and referred him for outpatient treatment that he never received, and which could have saved his life.

This side of Teena's story and the role of the state, medical gatekeepers, and carceral institutions is downplayed in *Boys Don't Cry*. Instead, the film introduces Brandon as taking that "imaginative leap" of transformation with a haircut and change of dress. After doing so, he struts from his trailer park to a local roller rink and hooks up with a girl with incredible ease due to his charm. The rest of the film, after this opening, follows the beats of his romantic courtship with Lana Tisdel (Chloë Sevigny) after he arrives in Fall City. His interactions with Lana's family and friends place him opposite to the volatile smalltown troublemakers Lotter (Peter Sarsgaard) and Nissen (Brendan Sexton III), who have an inkling there is something different about Brandon. His trans identity is found out and he is subsequently raped by Lotter and Nissen, who later murder him for trying to take his assault case to the police. The opening of *Boys Don't Cry* creates a false sense of security for Teena in terms of him passing and socially transitioning. The childlike optimism that Peirce and Swank have Teena imbue make him one of the ultimate trans cinematic martyrs, defined by his differences and othered in one of the most brutal reveals of a trans body on-screen.

There had been praise of *Boys Don't Cry* from the trans community at the time of its release. Those who saw it even as a brutal story saw optimism in having the story retold; a trans person finally not framed as a joke. It also received a lot of critical weight from queer and trans academics. Jack Halberstam, in his book *In a Queer Time and Place*, used the film to build on feminist academic Laura Mulvey's famous formulation of the "male gaze" by claiming that Peirce created a "transgender gaze" by allowing cisgender spectators to adopt Brandon's perspective. For Halberstam, *Boys Don't Cry* "signaled something much more than the successful interpretation of a transgender narrative for a mainstream audience," by "hijacking" the common modes of viewing.[18]

Halberstam ignores a central reason for why *Boys Don't Cry* would be such an accessible film for a mainstream audience. True crime as a popular narrative genre in America fueled a lot of interest in *Boys Don't Cry*, and even Halberstam wrote with great ambivalence of the proliferation of what he would call "The Brandon Industry."[19] At the time of *A Queer Time and Place*, in 2005, Halberstam was also anticipating the film would usher in a new age of mainstream trans film images, and especially trans masculine images, pointing to "recent explosions of transgender films."[20] Halberstam also puts a lot of faith into the spectator's perception of trans people in presenting this notion of a transgender gaze, especially when the audience is shown Teena's social transition from the outset, and Halberstam admits within the same piece that the film cannot sustain this theoretical mode when the story shifts into its dark dramatizations of rape.[21]

Even before the vicious trans reveal and punishment Brandon sustains in *Boys Don't Cry*, Peirce engages in other common trans tropes and signifiers that highlight Brandon's trans body. The mirror scenes, for example, prove to be a punishing reminder of Teena's otherness, as seen in a close-up of Hilary Swank's flat crotch in a pair of white cotton briefs. During this scene, Brandon creates himself piece by piece, and it is filmed in a way that cisgender audiences from the period could understand. Brandon uses an ACE bandage to tape his breasts down — also with the camera in close — and wears a baggy flannel shirt so as not to draw attention to that area. Swank plays the scene not as a character dressing up as he pleases, or even experimenting with compromises around what looks can be pulled off, but as if Brandon was donning a disguise. This choice is tied into Pierce's insistence on creating tension in the film around whether Brandon will be found out. The camera also lingers long enough on Swank for the audience to take stock of Brandon's body and inspect it. Prior to this mirror scene, Brandon is shown at a gas station stealing tampons — a scene that serves no narrative function in the film, except to remind audiences of Brandon's biology. This scene is not a moment that causes dysphoria, contemplation, or empathy, but exists only to further the tension of Brandon's eventual reveal that he is not a cis man.

Swank's performance also emphasizes Teena's jitteriness and looming anxiousness of being "found out," even in the privacy of his room. The film's primary investment in this character is of martyrdom and audience pity of the other. *Boys Don't Cry* situates itself for those later scenes of punishment, cruelty, and senseless violence by highlighting how Brandon is different and presenting his survival tactics of check-forging that have yielded a criminal record into a murky, cumbersome merging of his trans identity with being an ex-con with something to hide.

When Brandon's reveal scene happens against his will, another mirror scene emerges. While in a haze of disassociation, Brandon's conscience produces an image of himself among the crowd of people staring back at him that makes this moment more devastating and isolating. As Cáel M. Keegan writes, this becomes a moment of "transforming the mirror from a space of becoming to a portent of destruction."[22] The image he has cultivated as Brandon Teena is staring back at him: somebody who is stripped down, exposed, and violated. Brandon's terrible fate becomes inevitable, like Icarus flying too close to the sun, as Roger Ebert conjured in the conclusion to his rave review of the film.[23] This is what the film tells viewers, but the real story of Brandon Teena leading up to that night in Humboldt is more complex.

The Brandon Teena Story (1998), by lesbian partners Susan Muska and Greta Olafsdottir, is a necessary film supplement to *Boys Don't Cry*, but is also not without its own imperfections. The documentary fills in the blanks of Brandon's life in the movie. For example, in *Boys Don't Cry*, Lana Tisdel is portrayed as Brandon's one true love, but *The Brandon Teena Story* more accurately portrays her as Brandon's last girlfriend, with several of Brandon's former girlfriends also interviewed, including one who stated she received a marriage proposal from Brandon. Their testimonies state that he did discuss wanting to take hormones and get gender-affirming surgeries, but had also once identified as intersex to explain his physical presentation. The presence of Brandon's mother, JoAnn Brandon, in the documentary is of a parent in denial, grieving, unable to reconcile her child's trans identity. Instead, she is adamant that Brandon was just a girl caught up in the wrong crowd. A photograph of Brandon as a teen, a more "feminine" version that his mother prefers the world to see of her dead child, is present in the interviews. This is not an unusual thing to see from an unsupportive parent of a trans person, and often leads people in the trans community to find chosen families among one another. But Teena never had that community. In that respect, Keegan is right to call works like *Boys Don't Cry* "overburdened."[24]

Boys Don't Cry cannot act as a substitute for the people and systems that failed Brandon in his life. But when resituating Brandon Teena's story to the modern understanding of trans masculinity, correcting the record remains important. In 2018, journalist Donna Minkowitz wrote an apology piece for her misreporting on the Brandon Teena story in her 1994 article "Love Hurts" in *The Village Voice*.[25] Writing for *The Village Voice* again, Minkowitz declared her original piece as "the most insensitive and inaccurate piece of journalism I have ever written," in how she characterized Brandon Teena as being more representative of a butch lesbian — a community that Minkowitz was a part of —

than a trans man.[26] Minkowitz also states that the failing of the piece was not going deep enough into the story of the third murder victim of Lotter and Nissen, who was omitted completely from *Boys Don't Cry*: African American Phillip DeVine.

DeVine remains an erased smudge within *Boys Don't Cry*. Lisa Lambert, the other victim, is represented in the film, albeit under a different name, as Candace (portrayed by Lecy Goranson), whose housing and kindness towards Brandon made her collateral damage for Lotter and Nissen. *The Brandon Teena Story* abbreviates DeVine's life to a news report bulletin, where his race is presented but not remarked upon. DeVine was a disabled black man from Iowa romantically involved with Lana Tisdel's sister Leslie (who also is scrubbed from the film). Him being black and in an interracial relationship easily could have been a point of tension for Lotter and Nissen, with the latter reported to have been in a white supremacist group, noted in John Gregory Dunne's 1997 reporting of the case for *The New Yorker*.[27] But Teena's relationship to a male figure like DeVine — who did him no harm — stood in the way of the story Peirce preferred to portray about Brandon's dynamics to traditional masculinity. It is an omission of convenience for Peirce, who insisted she could not do DeVine's story justice and had no room for another character, even though he was among the slain.[28] Halberstam found DeVine's absence in the film to be a decision that "reduces the complexity of the murderous act."[29] The specter of racism is avoided out of cowardice.

Boys Don't Cry has only become more polarizing in the years since its release, an emerging dividing line among those in an older age group who see the film, however flawed, as an important work in bringing this story to light. A younger generation, however, whose earliest trans reference point was *Boys Don't Cry*, find the brutalization of Brandon Teena to be more harmful than factual and are put off by the casting of Swank and her characterization — Oscar statue be damned. This shift in discourse was most magnified during the 2016 protest of a *Boys Don't Cry* screening at Reed College in Portland, Oregon.[30] The student body made posters and banners with extremely inflammatory attacks against Peirce. Cáel M. Keegan saw the incident as *Boys Don't Cry* being a work that "continues to be a battle in the generational narrative of transgender community formation."[31]

But back in 1999, the film was considered a success in making a "difficult," "important" movie and was nominated for two Academy Awards: Swank as Best Actress in a Leading Role and Chloë Sevigny as Best Actress in a Supporting Role for her portrayal of Brandon's girlfriend Lana Tisdel, with Swank winning. Swank's acceptance speech from that night contains an oft-used soundbite: "We have come a long way!," as if to earmark on-screen progress for trans people. But the soundbite is misleading. In fact, "We have come a long way!" was instead Swank referencing the film's long journey from pre-production to the award. Brandon Teena was only referenced late in the speech, with no other mention of trans people or the trans activists who helped assist in the research of the film. As Chase Joynt and Morgan M. Page note:

> It is uncomfortable in 2021 to listen to Swank thank a murder victim, essentially for being murdered, without any call for action on the structures and circumstances that made his death possible. The audience was not urged to stop killing trans people or even to support the rights of trans people, but rather to join Swank in praying for a future in which diversity is celebrated — a politically empty liberal fantasy with no enduring bite.[32]

Whether people believe *Boys Don't Cry* needs to be "dethroned" from the so-called "trans canon," or if people believe it should be given grace for the period in which it was made, the weight it has had to carry through the years was never sustainable. *Boys Don't Cry* can only stand to benefit in no longer being perceived as the *only* film to center a trans masculine film image. Today, there are more voices and stories telling trans masculine stories, not to mention well-known actors inhabiting trans masculine roles, like Elliot Page. What remains to be seen is if the mainstream will ever give contemporary and future works that center trans masculinity the same platform it gave *Boys Don't Cry*. That is where the onus needs to be ultimately placed. The mainstream needs to demonstrate that the images of transness on-screen do not need to be compromised or told in a way where trans humanity is in a trade-off with trauma, violence, humiliation, and death.

The Martyred Fools: *The Danish Girl* and *Dallas Buyers Club*

Jean-Marc Vallée's *Dallas Buyers Club* (2013) fashions itself as an *Erin Brockovich*-like tale for the AIDS era, and stars Matthew McConaughey as Ron Woodroof, a partying, homophobic womanizer who learns the error of his ways when he finds out he has AIDS. Woodroof was a real person who took it upon himself to illegally distribute drugs that helped those with HIV when the disease was being actively ignored by the Reagan administration. On paper, it was a noble story to make a narrative around, and Vallée was an accomplished director, but with the inclusion of a trans woman character named Rayon, played with simpering frailty by Jared Leto, the film undoes whatever goodwill it could have accumulated.

The problems begin at the script level, where Rayon is described confusingly with he/him pronouns: "Sitting on an examining table, meet RAYON, a cross-dresser in his early 30s, in long eyelashes, earrings, painted nails with a pink scarf tied around a full brown curly wig."[33] It was common in the 1980s for the line between cross-dressing and transsexuality to be obfuscated, because these groups of people often settled in the same spaces, and cross-dressing is often a bridge for transsexuals to medical transition if it is the right option. However, *Dallas Buyers Club* has scenes where Rayon states that she wishes her breasts were real and that she were prettier. There are moments in the script that offer Rayon potential humanity through her vulnerability that could have been embodied with the right touch and care, making sure the character was not consigned to tropes of queer death. But Leto's performance is calibrated less to delivering a multilayered and credible performance, and more to what appeals to industry award bodies.

Leto's performance is embarrassingly sculpted around try-hard modes of bodily transformation and over-acting. His Rayon is a pathetic waif resigned to death. When Leto is not leaning on these typical indicators of queer misery, he indulges in a basic type of cattiness. He approaches the character as a victim of AIDS first and a trans woman second, interested strictly in the miserable martyrdom of both character tropes. In moments where Rayon struts down the street, it is as a momentary respite until the clock strikes midnight on her life. Many mainstream depictions of the AIDS epidemic myopically focus on the death and often minimize why the life of the character and their queer identity was so important, and *Dallas Buyers Club* is no different.

The film also finds time to punish and drag her through the worst of her trauma by including a scene where she visits her father, looking frail, wearing men's clothing and begging him for money. Rayon, when not put in this vulnerable position, primarily exists as a prop for McConaughey's Woodroof to learn the error of his ways, and thus the heterosexual, cisgender audience does as well. Once Rayon serves that purpose, she perishes. There has been some controversy around whether Rayon was intended to be a trans woman or a cross-dresser, but in 2013, the mainstream still found those gender lines hazy. In the film's press tour, Leto always asserted that Rayon was transgender.[34] And so Rayon became another exquisite corpse tossed onto a pile of bodies, all the dead trans characters before her, with the exchange of this martyred trans film image being in the form of Oscar gold for Best Supporting Actor.

The Danish Girl, David Ebershoff's historical novel about Lili Elbe, had been a sought-after project since its publication in 2000. The novel had gone through numerous film development attempts before finally moving forward with Tom Hooper (*The King's Speech*, 2010) after Swedish directors Tomas Alfredsson and Lasse Hallstrom had each been attached at different points. Nicole Kidman had also long been attached to play Elbe, essentially attempting what Tilda Swinton did in Sally Potter's *Orlando* (1992) and Vanessa Redgrave had done in *Second Serve* when playing tennis player Renée Richards before and after transition. But it did not come to pass. How the role ended up being played by Eddie Redmayne was simple: he had won an Oscar for playing Stephen Hawking in *The Theory of Everything* (2014).

Redmayne was also nominated for an Oscar for the role of Elbe, largely thanks to an aggressive campaign by the film's distributor, Focus Features. But Redmayne has in recent years expressed regret in taking the role.[35] His portrayal of Elbe in *The Danish Girl* (2015) is a worse performance than Leto's Rayon in *Dallas Buyers Club*. Rayon was just a mere composite of a character; Lili Elbe was a real, brave, pioneering figure whose life story gets botched by Redmayne's performance, Hooper's direction, and Lucinda Coxon's script. Redmayne plays Elbe like an alcoholic with a sensory disorder and a paraphilia for stockings and lingerie. His conception of womanhood is orgasmic, with heaving moans, trembling, and breathy vibrato. The performance can best be viewed through the lens of camp.

Alongside Redmayne's Elbe is Alicia Vikander in the role of the real-life artist Gerda Wegener (also known as Gerda Gottlieb). who guides Lili along the surfaces of womanhood as a costume and social role. This mentorship of femininity has a sexual component to it too, with consequences that get out of control for Elbe. Redmayne acts like Elbe has been "infected" with femininity after the triggering moment of Wegener insisting that she pose with a dress for a painting. This origin is fetishist rather than a scenario where her gender identity was innate. *The Danish Girl* is devoid of any real eroticism or romantic chemistry between the two characters, despite the fact that the film is about artists and being in love with somebody who shifts from spouse into muse. There are scenes of "role play," but it is rendered into a child's game of "playing house" that ends in a "shocking" conclusion when Elbe expresses her trans identity. Wegener is portrayed as a "suffering wife" who ultimately must leave Elbe for a man. The film manages to trivialize their relationship and turn these two real-life Bohemians, who were interested in queerness in both their art and lives, into extremely traditional modes of femininity for their period.

Redmayne's idea of gender dysphoria for Elbe is contorting in ways that feel like a bad 1960s sci-fi TV serial. There is one scene where Elbe goes to a peep show and mimics the cis women performer, but when she reaches down below her waist, she trembles in agony and shame. It is laughable and infuriating all at once. Elbe's social transition involves uncomfortable propositions from male suitors, and a scene where she's seen wearing an androgynous pantsuit out in the park whilst being trailed by two gawking men, who act as though they are straight out of a Tex Avery cartoon.

In real life, Elbe was a trailblazer in the field of medical transition as she was willing to take risks with her body that helped pave the way for others in learning what was possible. In 1930, she went to Germany for sex reassignment surgery, which was highly experimental at the time, and a series of four operations were carried out. The first of these was an orchiectomy (removal of the testes) that was overseen by Dr. Magnus Hirschfeld in Berlin and performed by Dr. Erwin Gohrbandt. The second operation attempted to implant an ovary into her abdominal musculature, and the third removed her penis and scrotum. In 1931, she had vaginoplasty surgery and was allowed to change her sex and legal name on her passport to match her gender identity. During these operations, she gave up painting, which the film couples with her newfound submissive understanding of womanhood, but it was more likely she did not have time to create art as she was in constant recovery from surgeries. Elbe died of a heart attack after her body rejected an attempted uterine transplant months after it was implanted, and while this surgery has not been re-examined for trans women with any serious consideration, vaginoplasty has since become commonplace.[36]

The Danish Girl, however, is only interested in the result of these surgeries — death — to make Elbe a martyr, which is telegraphed with a foreboding gloom that sours the viewer in how to perceive the risk of these surgeries. Hooper and Coxon reduce her into a submissive, stereotypical gender role that diminishes her creative pursuits and later patronizingly imagines her as a scarf blowing in the wind once she passes. Redmayne treats the character on these terms as well, and his broad, expressive acting makes Elbe take on the appearance of a pathetic, unstable fool, who dared to believe that she could ever become a woman in the first place.

Progress?: A Christmas Miracle in *Tangerine* and the Evolving State of Cross-Gender Casting

Transgender actress Laverne Cox was on the cover of the May 29, 2014, issue of *Time Magazine* accompanied by the headline: "The Transgender Tipping Point." It was just a year removed from "gender identity disorder" being dropped from the 2013 publication of the *DSM-V*, subsequently re-termed "gender dysphoria."[37] In the cultural mainstream, Cox became a mainstream avatar of transness after a few years in which notable trans figures like Janet Mock, Lana Wachowski, and Laura Jane Grace received mainstream coverage after publicly disclosing their trans status in magazines and published memoirs.

Cox had become a prominent figure due to her role as hairstylist and inmate Sophia Burset in the popular Netflix show *Orange is the New Black* (2013–2019). While its attempts at telling stories of transness were at times clumsy and didactic, it presented transness to a global audience. At the same time, trans leads and co-leads were also becoming more visible at major film festivals like Sundance. There were films like *Drunktown's Finest* (2014), featuring an indigenous trans woman played by Carmen Moore, which was written and directed by Navajo trans filmmaker Sydney Freeland. In 2015, there was Sean Baker's *Tangerine*, which starred two trans women of color.

But the hyper-visibility of transness that followed in the years since Cox's *Time Magazine* cover has proven to be fool's gold in terms of aligning newfound trans celebrities to trans rights advancements. The piece itself also fell into the common trap of regurgitating things trans people already knew for the sake of "educating" its cis readership. Objectively, trans people *had* made progress culturally, and the attention surrounding the blowback that accelerated against the industry-praised performances of Jared Leto in *Dallas Buyers Club* and Eddie Redmayne in *The Danish Girl* would have been unimaginable a decade before.

Backlash from the trans community often had to function as a last line of defense in addressing the failures of film and film culture in instances of cis-as-trans casting. Trans people are usually told to accept these practices, as these films would not have been produced otherwise. Alexandra Billings was told directly that, for a trans narrative to be made, it could not be her or any trans woman in the lead trans role.[38] Trans people were being robbed of work opportunities in film — a situation not limited to Hollywood or independent films, but a problem with world cinema in general. There is an inequity in the way film culture treats the rare film with the trans lead versus those that have a cis performer as the trans lead — Sebastien Lifshitz's *Wild Side* (2004), which featured trans lead Stéphanie Michelini, struggled to get global distribution despite winning prizes like the Teddy Award at Berlinale. The deck of cards has been stacked against trans people to enter and grow within these film spaces, which has only intensified the discussions that surrounded the practice of cis-as-trans casting and the cynical motivations that drove cis performers who took these opportunities. In the 2015–2016 film awards season, there was a notable shift in how cross-gender casting was discussed. Part of this was because television and films were featuring more roles played by trans people, making films like *The Danish Girl* look even more regressive.

Sean Baker's *Tangerine* (2015) debuted the same year as *The Danish Girl* to a completely unsuspecting crowd of cinephiles and critics at the Sundance Film Festival. The film had buzz through strong word-of-mouth about its daring use of the iPhone 5s as a camera, and the fact it starred two trans women of color who gave strong performances as Los Angeles sex workers: Mya Taylor and Kitana Kiki Rodriguez.

Taylor's performance as Alexandra earned praise from the outset. She was the emotional heart of the film and her poignant vocal performance of the holiday song "Toyland" in this scrappy, Christmas-set story was a breathtaking moment of beauty and longing for her character. Taylor had the critical push during awards season, which ended with her winning an Independent Spirit Award for Best Supporting Actress, the first trans woman to win an award (Harmony Santana was the first known trans woman nominated in the same category by that awards body for 2011's *Gun Hill Road*). *Tangerine* was overwhelmingly favored by trans people in the year of its release, with a lot of that favorability rooted in its casting and the fact that its story felt authentic to the reality of a lived trans experience, while films like *The Danish Girl* came off fraudulent and cynical.

Tangerine did not shy away from extremely contemporary topics, such as the realities of sex work, cis male "trans chasers," incarceration, housing insecurity, and everyday harassment — not to mention portraying two very different trans women in demeanor and personality on-screen, and how they play off each other. Rodriguez and Taylor were a dynamite on-screen pairing and the closing scene of Alexandra giving her wig to Sin-Dee, after she gets her own wig destroyed in a transphobic hate crime, is one of the most powerful images of trans sisterhood and solidarity that American film has offered. *Tangerine* is not a slick market-correction of prior Hollywood misdeeds; it is an independent film about friendship featuring two trans women just trying to make it through their day.

Tangerine's impact was felt among trans viewers immediately and was representative of the overall positive trends happening in independent and arthouse cinema spaces — for example, Daniela Vega's star turn in *Una mujer fantástica* (*A Fantastic Woman*) (2017). While the film's characterization of Marina (Vega) was tied to her interactions with transphobic individuals and systems in Santiago, Chile, it did showcase Vega's training as a performer and singer. *A Fantastic Woman* was a didactic, overdetermined, well-intentioned, issue movie, but precisely the kind that would win mainstream awards, which it did at the 90th Academy Awards for Best Foreign Language Film. With its accessibility and plaudits, perhaps this was the trans film image to close the discussion on cis-as-trans casting once and for all. That sense of symbolic victory and relief, however, was short-lived, when Lukas Dhont's *Girl* (2018) debuted at Cannes later that year.

Dhont's feature-length debut, *Girl*, was criticized in two respects: first, the casting of male ballet dancer Victor Polster as Lara, a teenage trans feminine ballerina, which Dhont defended through his "gender-blind" casting approach;[39] and second, in the film's climactic scene, the deeply dysphoric Lara performs a botched attempt at self-surgery with industrial-sized scissors to near fatal results, a scene that strongly mirrors Wendy Ross's last-ditch attempt to salvage her trans femininity in the climax of *I Want What I Want*. While *Girl* was loosely inspired by a real-life trans ballerina, the film cynically unfurled various plot devices in the service of traumatizing the lead character that were not based on that ballerina's lived experiences. The infamous scissors moment never happened.[40] The film had low credibility and an overall hostile reaction among trans viewers, despite winning prizes at Cannes and recirculating at major film festivals across the world. *Girl*'s prominence reinforced the idea that film culture's expectations of trans narratives in casting and content were not going to go away immediately.

Cis-as-trans casting is an anachronism. Broader film culture must evolve beyond expecting these common tropes and inaccurate depictions of transness on-screen. There has been headway, with performers like Trace Lysette being in the ensemble film *Hustlers* (2019) and telling her own trans narrative with *Monica* (2022). Hari Nef has been in films that include the high-profile indie *Assassination Nation* (2018) and box-office sensation *Barbie* (2023). Laverne Cox featured in *Promising Young Woman* (2020) where, fascinatingly, her trans status is not explicitly stated or at any point remarked upon in the film's plot. But beyond just labor opportunities for these performers, progress must also be made in trans authorship, production, exhibition, distribution, and curation within these systems of film culture that can broaden the trans film image with more authentic and original narratives.

CHAPTER 10
Towards a New Cinematic Language of Our Own: The 1990s into the 2000s

Building a Trans Film Culture of Our Own

The 1990s and 2000s were a period when, among high-points in non-fiction like *Paris Is Burning* and the mixed bag of dramatized narratives from works like *Boys Don't Cry*, other trans film images were emerging, particularly from trans performers and trans filmmakers. Some of these films have been rediscovered by trans viewers years after the fact, and so their places in any broader "film canon" are still at an embryonic stage as an awareness of them within cinephile film culture grows.

Systems and institutions in the form of queer and even trans film festivals, for the purpose of uplifting trans voices in film, were also starting to emerge. In 1997, three different trans film festivals popped up in London (1st International Transgender: Film & Video Film Festival), Toronto (Counting Past 2), and San Francisco (Trannyfest).[1] But these festivals, films, and filmmakers did not receive regular coverage in the main trans publications like *Transgender Tapestry*.

In general, the trans community that ran IFGE and AEGIS at the time were not always paying close attention to trans film images in the arthouse or independent cinema scene, much less the experimental film scene in the way *FTM Newsletter* and the DIY zines were. *Transgender Tapestry* generally paid attention to mainstream cinema, writing about films like *To Wong Foo, Thanks for Everything! Julie Newmar* (1995), *The Birdcage* (1996), and *The Adventures of Priscilla, Queen of the Desert* (1994) — even putting characters from the films on their covers — rather than, say, a Pedro Almodóvar film that featured trans characters and trans performers. There was a general feeling in the 1990s that these mainstream films could signify a shift in perception, where cross-dressing and transness as a topic would not be immediately treated as a joke or be perceived as fatal to an actor's career. Publications like *Tapestry* also paid specific attention to films like *Southern Comfort* and *Transexual Menace*, as they featured their own work and advocacy. Given the thorniness around the mainstream reaction towards trans people from *The Silence of the Lambs* and *The Crying Game* to schlocky comedies like *Ace Ventura: Pet Detective*, it was understandable why trans publications monitored and paid more attention to what came out of Hollywood. But within these communities of newsletters, zines, and magazines, there were filmmakers who were creating works and pushing to establish film festivals specifically about and for their community, knowing full well that their work would not necessarily serve as breakthroughs into the mainstream, but rather as respites from it.

There were a few notable examples of trans people who made films for their community with very little consideration of whether cis people would be put off by the content of their work. Canadian trans filmmakers Jeanne B. (the *nom de plume* of Mirha-Soleil Ross) and Xanthra Phillippa (MacKay), who also edited the trans zine *Gender Trash from Hell*, made the DIY video short *Gender Troublemakers* (1993) to express their desires and intimacies with each other on-screen. The film presents their t4t relationship, which went against all the mainstream conventions surrounding trans people as desired bodies. Even as a short film that only features dialogue among these trans women and a love scene, it is a truly radical work of trans amorous desire that celebrates their shared struggle rather than wallow in it. Beyond filmmaking, Ross was an organizer within film spaces, organizing Counting Past 2: Performance-Film Video-Spoken Word with Nerve!, a film festival in Toronto, Canada, in the 1990s and early 2000s.[2]

Another example is Christopher Lee's films (in collaboration with Elise Hurwitz), such as *Christopher's Chronicles* (1996) and *The Trappings of Transhood* (1997), which received festival interest but had limited audience potential due to their explicit content — something that also received criticism from sectors of the community, particularly the full-length presentation of trans male pornography, *Alley of the TrannyBoys* (1998). Lee co-founded Trannyfest: Transgender and Transgenre Cinema, now known today as the San Francisco Transgender Film Festival, which, although it skewed predominantly experimental, gave opportunities for trans filmmakers and films presenting the trans film image to be seen by a wider audience. Lee, who died in 2012, believed his output of trans film images was part of an aesthetic of gender continuum beyond the traditional "before and after" mode of transition, and he was eager to take part in the next millennium of radical trans art.[3] This spoke to the way the 1990s were shifting in a broader discussion of gender and queerness beyond previously more binary categories and towards a different kind of filmmaking that would be required to present these broader notions of identity.

Flat Is Beautiful and the Pixelvisions of Sadie Benning

One director from the New Queer Cinema scene of the 1990s, whose experimental films were never able to re-circulate the way other titles were, was Sadie Benning. The *wunderkind* child of famed experimental filmmaker James Benning, Sadie, who identifies as a trans non-binary person, was embraced not just by New Queer Cinema luminaries but also third-wave feminism due to their associations with the riot grrrl punk scene and being a founding member of the Kathleen Hanna-fronted band Le Tigre.

In their teens, Benning had already become a film festival sensation for the unorthodox way they were using a type of toy camera. Receiving a Fisher-Price PXL 2000 as a Christmas gift, Benning created film diaries about growing up in blue-collar Milwaukee, Wisconsin. "Pixelvision," an image that is heavily primitive and distorted, was designed to be interpreted through the eyes of a child, and Benning became one of its most significant users and has been credited with inventing a new type of experimental film.[4] Benning's use of it in their work also served as a forerunner to online self-documenting, which has been one of the biggest characteristics of queer and trans expression from millennials and Gen Z through YouTube and TikTok. While self-documenting was obviously not limited to queer and trans people, this style would be the way many would use online spaces to navigate their lives, such as coming out and transitioning, and finding community. This foreshadowing of future self-documentation techniques for queer people, through a camera designed to be used for children, is why *Flat Is Beautiful* (1999) remains Benning's greatest work — a trans film image that shows a pre-teen beginning to absorb and react to the world around them.

Flat Is Beautiful stands out as Benning's longest film, at around 49 minutes, and is their most concerted effort to do a narrative story. Aesthetically, it also incorporates Super-8 film cameras in addition to Pixelvision. It is a *bildungsroman* of autofiction that speaks to how one can cultivate their gender expression and gender identity regardless of where they come from, and show an adolescence of gender questioning that is not at all pathologized, but instead part of the innate curiosity of that accruing sense of self-realization.

All the characters in the film wear cartoon paper masks,

an aesthetic Benning had used in their other short, *The Judy Spots* (1995). The masks conceal the identity of the performers, but the crudeness of the masks is at once an abstraction and works well within the dilapidated exteriors of blue-collar Milwaukee. A bunch of kids walk out of school and Benning focuses their camera on Taylor, a classic "tomboy," in pants and a Milwaukee Brewers baseball ringer T-shirt. Taylor lives with their mother, who supports them, and has a male roommate, a gay man named Quiggy. Taylor's father (a stand-in for James Benning) is not quite out of the picture, but his interest in being in his child's life appears to conflict with his career in the art world, which has him traveling all over the world. Taylor is a latchkey kid who has their after-school routines down to a science: come home, check if their mother is home, check if Quiggy is home, put the TV dinner in the microwave, and eat it while watching television. What Taylor sees on television proves to be significant.

On this day, they watch a talk show featuring a trans man talking specifically about not identifying as a girl. Regardless of the crudeness or hostilities those individuals may have encountered on these shows, there were many viewers who would ultimately find these appearances valuable when coming to terms with their gender identity. The talk show moment is not explicitly remarked upon, yet its presence is an essential part of their gender-non-conforming child's observation.

Taylor's mother clearly loves them, but is overworked and cannot really mother her child due to economic circumstances. Quiggy is simply a roommate, never presenting as a parental figure, and through Taylor's eyes, he becomes another expression of non-traditional masculinity and gender-play. Quiggy is shown lip-syncing in drag to Heart's "Crazy on You" and also invites men over for sex. Taylor's awareness of Quiggy's sexuality is unspoken and their exploration of what Quiggy is drawn to is shown in Taylor sneakily reading his dirty paperback books and smutty gay magazines. Benning attaches no judgment or moralism to these sequences of Taylor skimming through the pages and images. It is a realistic depiction of what children and teenagers would get up to when exploring media deemed too adult and explicit with minimal supervision. There is nothing consequential nor traumatic about these encounters, and Taylor is otherwise a typical Gen X kid, with posters of Michael Jackson and Madonna in their room, playing video games, watching baseball, drawing, and making scenes out of their action figures and dolls. But they are not without some sense of loneliness and solitude. Their lucid bad dreams of being chased by aliens are taken at face-value by their mother, but it speaks to some unspoken anxiety about feeling different in ways that are unexplainable.

Orlando: A Fantasy of Change and Incidental Trans Film Images

"Do not fade. Do not wither. Do not grow old."

Sally Potter's *Orlando* (1992) all but clinched its status as a New Queer Cinema classic in the moment when Tilda Swinton, who has transformed from an androgynous male nobleman to an Elizabethan-era Lady, says to the camera, "The same person, not different at all, just a different sex." An adaptation of Virginia Woolf's 1928 novel, it diverts in crucial ways from the source material, pulling it into the modern era and subverting the text as well as period filmmaking. However, even if not consciously, Potter's film also subverts the often miserabilist social realist presentation of trans lives.

Woolf's *Orlando: A Biography* was written as a tribute to her lover, Vita Sackville-West. Potter had characterized it as a "spoof biography" of Sackville-West,[5] but it is apparent Potter was not looking at the novel in terms of its reputation as quite possibly the first trans novel ever written, or as a precursor to the trans memoir in presenting its subject's life before and after transition. The novel was published in 1928, predating cases like Lili Elbe but after Dr. Magnus Hirschfeld's studies on trans people were published and known.

There had been film treatments prior to Potter's version, the most notable being Ulrike Ottinger's *Freak Orlando* (1981), which emphasized the character's misfit status by having them join a punkish circus (in the book, the circus troupe is of Romani people). While actress Magdalena Montezuma as Orlando is not remotely androgynous-looking, even with short hair, the film does create audacious trans film images, such as a trans Jesus Christ on a cross. Potter's *Orlando*, while being consciously playful around artifice and gender dynamics across multiple time periods, ultimately serves as a statement on feminism, class, and the British Empire. As a man, Orlando is awarded property, fortune, and the "gift" of becoming ageless by Queen Elizabeth I, played by Quentin Crisp. Crisp was seen as a subversive piece of cross-gender casting at the time — something that becomes even more intriguing in recalling that Crisp claimed a trans identity in later years.[6] Somewhat reductively, Potter characterizes Orlando's impetus for shifting from man to woman as rooted in a "crisis of masculine identity," due to seeing death on the battlefield. When Orlando wakes up as a woman, she has lost her status in the gender hierarchy, removed as owner of the property bestowed to her by the Queen. This forfeiture of property, fortune, and status parallel trans experiences. Society tends to pull the rug out from under trans people, with many, especially during the 1990s, being fired or losing housing if outed. Orlando is no different.

Another legacy of *Orlando* is Tilda Swinton's "gender-bending" performance. Having been the muse of Derek Jarman for years, her being the lead gave the film instant queer film bona fides. Swinton's natural androgyny is a point of interest, and in the years since *Orlando*, she has pointed to David Bowie's Ziggy Stardust genderplay as a formative influence on her whole acting career.[7] She had engaged in cross-gender castings dating back to her earliest performances in theater,[8] and there was always something a little more credible and engaging in her portrayals that made *Orlando* feel fundamentally different to the stunt casting of gender-play roles throughout the 1990s. One of the rather disappointing changes Potter makes is opting to not include other characters in the text who experience these gender shifts. Swinton is peerless as a performer, but *Orlando* easily could have been populated with more trans film images in line with Woolf's text.

Nonetheless, as critic So Mayer notes, "I think it is a trans text and a gender-fluid text, a queer text and, importantly, a feminist text."[9] Orlando is the same person, but in addition to living in a different gender, is now one gifted with immortality. After balking at a marriage proposal, she escapes through a garden maze and within a single cut has entered a new time, the Edwardian age, in a new dress.

The film ends in the then modern age of 1992, with Orlando seeing her daughter — another Potter revision; Woolf gave Orlando a son — in a field filming her surroundings with a movie camera. She points her daughter to an angel suspended in air singing a hymn. The angel is played by Bronski Beat frontman Jimmy Somerville, whose work was often the soundtrack for gay AIDS activists and was situated, according to Potter, "somewhere between heaven and earth in a place of ecstatic communion with the present moment."[10] This moment of a queer figure transcending time takes on a specific poignancy in the aftermath of a global AIDS crisis that had decimated a generation. Trans people, who were also particularly ravaged by the AIDS crisis, often search for the types of worlds that Potter describes. The real world often fails them, but trans people always persist in chasing that ecstatic communion, and for that, *Orlando* still resonates as a trans film image.

"And the world is how I want it": *Ma vie en rose*

Perhaps one of the more enduring and painfully relevant films about growing up trans is Alain Berliner's 1997 *Ma vie en rose*. Although it made significant headway internationally, winning a Golden Globe Award for Best Foreign Language Film, and was deemed a crowd-pleaser by American critics, the ratings system in America gave it an R, killing its commercial prospects and broad audience potential, particularly among youth and families. *Ma vie en rose* was not trying to spark systemic change and discussion around trans people or trans youth, yet it is all the better for avoiding the didactic, programmatic trappings that social issue dramas on transness have often opted to be.

Ma vie en rose is about trans child Ludo Fabre (Georges DuFresne), whose yearning to be seen as a young girl makes her and her family the target of transphobic attacks and exclusion. Ludo's parents start the movie reaching their bourgeois aspirations of a nice home in an affluent community, but they are threatened when others take offense to Ludo's gender presentation at a school play and in public. The Fabre family are forced to move due to transphobic incidents, which take a toll on everyone in the family. Systemic and cultural transphobia does not just harm the trans individual, but also influences how family and loved ones are dissuaded by society from affirming or respecting the ways in which somebody, particularly a young child, can explore their gender. This drama surrounding Ludo and their family does not even include the medical side, which speaks to how transphobia can manifest through transness being seen as an upending of cultural and societal norms. Ludo is sent away to live with her grandmother, which offers her the opportunity to further express and explore who she is. Her imagination brings to life her affection for the world of the Barbie-like doll called Pam.

Building worlds as an outlet for safety is common to the trans adolescent experience and Ludo's method of escape is

CORPSES, FOOLS, AND MONSTERS

not at all dissimilar to Taylor's in *Flat Is Beautiful*. But where Benning's diary-like "Pixelvision" remains constant, *Ma vie en rose* becomes candy-colored in its imaginative visions of an idyllic Belgium, giving lightness to a tale otherwise full of trauma, bigotry, and ignorance. But even the colors of the film start to become muted as Ludo's light is dimmed by the actions of others.

Ludo's mother (played by Michele Laroque) is the family member who has the strongest negative reaction to Ludo's attempts at social transition, cutting Ludo's androgynous bob into a buzzcut and slapping Ludo after catching them and another child playing dress-up. The film conceivably could have continued that path, where the parental control over the child's autonomy in their gender expression ended with death or a total repression of their innate identity to avoid being bullied. Berliner, mercifully, avoids going down that path by allowing Ludo's mother to step into the world her child wants. This moment of magical realism pays off: a mother finally sees her child as the child wants to be seen. There is ultimately a reconciliation, and it is not taken as something that was simply accepted but as slow, stubborn, and not without tension. Ultimately, Ludo's mother realizes that she would rather have a child that is happy and alive above all else.

Trans children are often the first victims in the culture and legislative wars surrounding their existence. Even in instances where they reach a self-understanding that involves a trans identity, they are told that they are merely "confused." Ludo's spirit and high character resonate. Her rebellion and imagination show her self-possession as a trans individual that needs to be protected, not suppressed.

By Hook or by Crook: A New Moment for the Trans Masculine Trans Film Image

Harry Dodge and Silas Howard, the directors of *By Hook or by Crook* (2001), first had ties to the San Francisco lesbian community around the time of third-wave feminism, when DIY zine culture was in full swing. The documentation of this era of queer life is best shown in Chloe Sherman's photography of 1990s San Francisco. In Sherman's photo, "The Heist," Silas Howard can be seen walking the streets of San Francisco's Mission District wearing sunglasses and an embroidered Western shirt rolled up with tattoos on his forearms that imbues butch masculinity. Harry Dodge is seen in "The Backseat," with him in the driver's seat of a car coiffed with dapper trappings in a fine suit, his hair brushed back with gel and a cigarette in his hand. His image recalls the grittiness of 1970s-era Dustin Hoffman or Al Pacino.

These butch presentations, which have since recirculated online and at art galleries across the world as part of Sherman's program *Renegades: San Francisco, the 1990s*, openly presented the fluidity of gender expression and identity. A few of the other subjects in *Renegades* would also later identify as trans masculine, such as actor Daniel Sea (*The L Word*, 2004–2009), but at this time, they represented a new wave of San Francisco outsiders and artists that emerged in the aftermath of HIV/AIDS, which had ravaged the city. Howard and Dodge each had bigger ambitions than being San Francisco legends — they had already co-founded the performance space Red Dora's Bearded Lady café together, and Howard was a member of the queercore punk band Tribe 8 under the stage name "Flipper." They were inspired by the no-budget success of Kevin Smith's *Clerks* (1994) and other indie films of the era, looking to make a movie in which they could put themselves in front of the camera.

"It was an era where if you didn't see something reflecting you, you needed to make it happen," Silas Howard would tell *Filmmaker Magazine* in a 2022 retrospective.[11] The process of making *By Hook or by Crook* took almost three years. The final product is of an uncommon authenticity and scrappiness that intervenes in the trajectory of trans film images by taking matters into its own hands.

Howard and Dodge wanted to make a buddy movie, but

one in which these two buddies did not have to explicitly state who they were in identity terms — being trans, butch, or even passing as cis men. Howard and Dodge believed the way to circumvent tropes is in gender ambiguity, which allows for a more universal story where viewers do not feel like they must withhold identification based on gender identity. This active "disidentification process," as Dodge put it, did seemingly work in terms of exposure and film festival reach.[12] Yet *By Hook or by Crook*, as much as it can be a universal tale about friends and journeys of self-discovery, has an undeniable queer spirit, one that immediately earned it comparisons to Gregg Araki's work and John Schlesinger's *Midnight Cowboy* (1969).

Shot on MiniDV, *By Hook or by Crook* was hailed by Jack Halberstam as marking a "real turning point for queer and transgender cinema."[13] It is very nearly the trans equivalent of Dennis Hopper's *Easy Rider* (1969), in the way that it is languid and comfortable in its own looser expressions of masculinity on the open road. This spirit places it in conversation with a tradition of cinematic depiction of masculinity that is definitively American in its posture, but given new meaning through a depiction of queerness that is bold even in comparison to roughly contemporaneous films like Gus Van Sant's *My Own Private Idaho* (1991). *By Hook or by Crook* deserves to take its place alongside other canonized movies because it has a lot to say about masculine expression and, through the specificity of gender nonconformity, remains fresh, provocative, and exciting.

The film follows Shy (Howard), who hails from Kansas, hitting the road head-to-toe in denim, heading out west to San Francisco, already following a pilgrimage of many queer people before him. He is mourning the death of his father and has accepted entering a "life of crime." Given the parameters of the ways gender is and is not spoken about in detail in the film, the question of what the "life of crime" exactly entails could easily mean being a gender outlaw. Shy's butch androgyny makes him a target of a hate crime by a cis man

— something both Dodge and Howard experienced in real-life — which leads to the introduction of the character Val (Dodge), short for Valentine, who saves Shy's life. The scene is pivotal but not gratuitously violent, and clearly informed by the shared experience of its creators.

Val's presentation of a street-smart, wise butch with a scraggly beard catches Shy's attention. As they run away from the scene of the attack, he realizes that he and Val are of the same stripe. Val is also dealing with the absence of a parent but in reverse from Shy's scenario, trying to seek out the mother he has never met who put him up for adoption. Their bonding in brotherhood, in their gender outlaw status, and in their lack of blood family make them each other's chosen family. It also has them forge ahead in committing small-time crimes, in which their trust of the other is tested. But their understanding of one another, and who they trust, keeps them afloat.

The film is scrappy in its style, which centers these two rag-tag heroes who never stop to explain themselves to the audience. Early on, a child, in what appears to be an ad-libbed scene, asks Shy about his gender, and even then Shy refuses to give a direct response. Shy is not even sure himself. Yet identity is never a point of struggle for these characters. It is never pathologized or given conflict through reveals, coming-outs, forced outings, or how the outside world perceives them. Shy explicitly expresses gratitude to Val for being able to express himself truthfully with a like-minded soul. They are doubles, partners in crime, brothers in arms. It is a far cry from the common narrative of a trans character as an isolated figure who faces humiliation or death.

Howard and Dodge did not immediately jump into more narrative films, despite *By Hook or by Crook* playing at major festivals like South By Southwest (SXSW) and Sundance. After the film, Howard wanted to refine his craft and went to UCLA Film School, and has since been one of the most consistent trans filmmakers, primarily with trans-centered television for programs like *Transparent* (2014–2019) and

CORPSES, FOOLS, AND MONSTERS

Pose (2018–2021), but he has also been instrumental in documenting trans elders, like with his beautiful documentary short *Sticks & Stones* (2014), about the late San Francisco trans icon Bambi Lake. Dodge had briefly appeared in John Waters' *Cecil B. Demented* (2000) before the release of *By Hook or by Crook*, but he did not do any acting work after that. Instead, he went to art school at Bard College, and while he has made experimental shorts, his concentration has been in the modern art world and teaching, rather than mainstream filmmaking. Dodge did, however, lend his voice to Jenni Olson's experimental feature about San Francisco, *The Joy of Life* (2005).

By Hook or by Crook created an alternative universe and narrative around trans and gender non-conforming characters being on the margins and fringes of society's morals and gender system. It deserves to be hailed in the same space as other canonized New Queer Cinema movies and has endured as a fresh, provocative, and exciting work of DIY cinema. A respite from the nomenclature of trans tropes of narrative filmmaking, it achieves its appeal by being a universal story while showing a seldom represented expression of trans masculinity on-screen.

Hedwig and the Angry Inch: A New *Rocky Horror* with Its Own Complex Legacy

As *By Hook or by Crook* showed, there were American independent films still being put out in the 2000s that could be seen as a spiritual extension of New Queer Cinema. Another successor to that film movement was John Cameron Mitchell's 2001 adaptation of his own hit off-Broadway musical, *Hedwig and the Angry Inch*. The off-Broadway show was developed at the Squeezebox, a famous drag and rock club in New York City. While the film did not break even in its initial theatrical run, it became a cult hit, winning critical plaudits and awards at film festivals, and was ultimately put out on home video by the Criterion Collection, with the stage musical officially opening to great success on Broadway in 2014. Beyond New Queer Cinema, *Hedwig*'s most obvious antecedent in terms of both the stage and film version gaining a devoted following is *The Rocky Horror Show*. But *Rocky Horror* seems restrained compared to the provocative lyrics and story of East German-born rockstar Hedwig, whose trans identity remains a contentious and controversial subject even for Mitchell, *Hedwig*'s co-creator and the performer most associated with the character.

In a positive retrospective, film critic Sam Moore highlighted the provocative nature of the text as a positive:

> In a way that directly challenges the expectation for easy, comfortable queer and trans narratives, from her botched surgery onward, Hedwig embraces her life in-between, and refuses to censor herself around those who might be uncomfortable, or might not understand."[14]

But Mitchell, who has identified as non-binary in the years since the stage show's debut and film's release, has repeatedly stated he does not view Hedwig as a trans story, and his reasoning is rather curious. In a 2021 interview with *The Advocate*, Mitchell spoke of the character's origin story saying:

> The trauma wasn't really a trans choice of finding yourself and defining yourself because the character was raped and mutilated and forced into a gender reassignment against their will, which is not exactly a trans fairy tale... it's more like someone having a forced medical procedure from a communist government.[15]

In another interview a year later, Mitchell would prefer to call what happens to Hedwig a "patriarchal mutilation," which the eponymous character climbs out from under using drag and rock.[16]

In the last decade, the musical had been embroiled in

controversies around casting, since cis man Neil Patrick Harris played the role in the 2014 Broadway run. International productions of the musical have also had protests and even cancellations over Hedwig often being performed by cis actors.[17] There have also been cis actresses like Ally Sheedy in the stage role, but Hedwig has often been seen as a drag role for men, not unlike the role of Dr. Frank N. Furter in *Rocky Horror*. Mitchell and his co-creator Stephen Trask initially issued a statement in 2020 that the role of Hedwig is "open to anyone who can tackle it, and more importantly, anyone who needs it."[18] Essentially, the show should not and would not be exclusionary against anyone who tried out for the title role. But Mitchell's statements as to why Hedwig is not trans obfuscates the clear connections the work has to trans narratives, something which Mitchell, in the film version, visually underscores and explicitly lays out by referencing the character as "transsexual."

The stage and film versions of *Hedwig* present the effeminate Hansel, who supposedly could pass as a woman even without female hormones, but who nonetheless has to get bottom surgery in order to go to America with her GI husband, Sergeant Luther Robinson, in order to "pass" through immigration (which requires a physical examination) and have a legal heterosexual marriage. She is encouraged by her own mother, but things do not go as planned — beyond the botched surgery, Hedwig's marriage to Robinson immediately sours. Hedwig's origin story may express typical anxieties around "forced femininity" and body horror, but it also presents a failed attempt at assimilation, with Hedwig now having a gender non-conforming body due to this botched procedure.

The musical and film smash-cuts from the initial plans for her operation to Hedwig unleashing the primal scream that opens the title song, which details her "mound of flesh" and "Barbie-doll crotch," where her "penis used to be" and where her "vagina never was" — anatomy that is simply now "an angry inch." It is an effective, provocative, and

punk moment of badassery. While Hedwig clearly has misgivings about what happened to her, she does not wallow
in victimhood. Hedwig gets called a "faggot" by an uncomfortable male audience member during the performance,
but her band has her back and turns the finale of the song
into a chaotic fracas. She is a loud, shameless, and confrontational force of nature. She may have entered this part of
her life through trauma, but she has filtered it through her
art and performance.

Hedwig was not unanimously embraced by trans people,
which is underscored in the deeply ambivalent academic
reaction to the film by Jordy Tackitt-Jones called "Gender
Without Genitals: Hedwig's Six Inches" in the Susan
Stryker-edited omnibus *The Transgender Studies Reader*. It is
an overall unkind critique, but Tackitt-Jones' classification
that *Hedwig* functions as an "overt citation of a transsexual
woman"[19] would be the more accurate characterization of
what Mitchell did in this story, if taking his declarations in
earnest. This character and story would not exist without
the component of transsexual identity, but Mitchell articu-
lating the cumbersome aspects of the narrative in relation
to transness articulates earlier critiques of the work.

It is fair to acknowledge who Mitchell believes Hedwig
is, but audience perceptions of who the character is have
shown there is a significant amount of people who see the
character as trans. As *The Silence of the Lambs* showed —
which Mitchell references as a tease when Hedwig extends
out her butterfly-wing-like cape evoking "Goodbye Horses"
— declaring the character not trans, even within the text,
does not necessarily stop the viewer's perception of transness. Mitchell has his character experience things that are
incredibly close to the trans experience, even if they are not
directly synonymous. This is particularly notable through
how the character's notoriety in America as an artist is
formed.

Hedwig's relationship and adjacency to fame is present
throughout the story. In one sequence, Hedwig playing to

an audience of one at a music festival is contrasted with the packed house for a Sarah MacLachlan-type performer — a sly reference to the ways that gender non-conforming and trans musicians were often not given the same staging nor considerations in ostensibly "inclusive" music events, such as the all-female festival Lilith Fair. Hedwig would play in kitschier settings and at dive bars while serving as the babysitter, which leads her to cross paths with a teenager named Tommy (Michael Pitt), a 1990s *Tiger Beat*-type of male beauty whose soft features recall Hedwig's own adolescence as Hansel. Hedwig begins to write songs like "Wicked Little Town" and attempts a relationship with Tommy until she has a "reveal" moment that leaves Tommy disgusted. Instead of Tommy fading away like any other temporary lover, he becomes famous. It creates a rivalry between the characters. Hedwig certainly believed that Tommy was her other half at a certain point. Instead, Tommy is living the life Hedwig wants as an artist.

There is a brief reunion between these exes in New York City, when Hedwig has her band shadow Tommy's tour. This leads to a rendezvous in a car that, due to an accident, creates a paparazzi frenzy. The tabloid headlines the next day read: "Tommy Gnosis' Gay Transsexual Lover: 'I wrote every song on that album!' and 'Who is Mystery 'Woman?'" Tommy attempts to play down his association with Hedwig, such as not realizing she "wasn't a real woman." This leads to Hedwig being portrayed as a salacious object of tabloid fodder, defined by her gender being in scare quotes. Hedwig once again gets discarded by Tommy, but rather than forgotten, she gets played off as a "cheap fling" and a "mistake," as opposed to the creative lodestar for Tommy's art and persona.

According to Mitchell, Hedwig was constructed as an amalgamation of glam rock heroes like Bowie, Iggy Pop, and Lou Reed — who, although not trans, had varied associations with transness.[20] Mitchell would also say that it was Squeezebox's notoriety as a drag club that was the impetus for creating a female character, even though he had no prior history in performing in drag. Trans punk rocker and previous trans film image Jayne County would later wonder if her "scare queen" makeup look, along with her connections to David Bowie and being a performer at Squeezebox, made her a possible inspiration for the character, which Mitchell has never publicly confirmed.[21] Mitchell would also later say that he modeled Hedwig on the babysitter of his Army brat adolescence in Kansas.[22] More recently, he stated the text's allegory of German reunification and the fall of the Berlin Wall, representing the breakdown of sexual and gender borders, came from trans woman Charlotte von Mahlsdorf's *I Am My Own Woman*.[23] However, one influence Mitchell has discussed as the backbone for *Hedwig* as a text has remained consistent. The play and film were also built on Aristophanes' speech known as "The Origin of Love," which became the obsession of *Hedwig* co-creator Stephen Trask — who, like Mitchell, identifies as non-binary and goes by both male and female pronouns.

Recorded in Plato's *Symposium*, Aristophanes posits that there were three sexes: man/child of sun, woman/child of Earth, and man-woman/child of the moon. The third sex, an androgynous being with male and female characteristics, was a threat to the Gods and so these beings were split in half. The song "The Origin of Love" becomes the emotional heart of the film's soundtrack, with Hedwig singing the song alongside a projected animated sequence (done by animator Emily Hubley), which presents the creation of these beings and how the children of the moon — now split — are in search for their other half. Hedwig connects this with her own story, and even has a tattoo on her hip of two split half-moons to represent her sense of identity. Trask and Mitchell are enamored with the splitting metaphor, presented in both the story in the split (and reunification) of Germany and the splitting of Hedwig's body in a physical and emotional sense. This again runs closely with common trans narratives — even beyond bodies cut open in invasive

surgeries, these stories are defined by lives that are bifur-
cated, divided into a series of before and after. Much like
Hedwig's experience, trans people often do leave something
behind when they make their "change," in their pursuit to
become a whole person.

Hedwig attempts to seize this celebrity to advance her
own career, which presents in a montage that has her
perform on national talk shows and in clubs. While still
nowhere near Tommy's crowds, these spaces are worlds
better than the bars and diners she used to play. However,
even as Hedwig gets a small taste of mainstream recognition, with its positives and negative transphobic drawbacks,
she breaks down. She rips off her wig and fake breasts while
performing the most hardcore song on the soundtrack,
"Exquisite Corpse." The scene is a violent debasement,
as if enacting trans violence on the self, with Hedwig's
self-loathing and shame feeling all-consuming in a moment
that carries allusions of detransition or trans death. After
this moment, when entering the film's finale of "Midnight
Radio," Hedwig's presentation shifts from a Farrah Fawcett wig to a look that mirrors Tommy Gnosis but remains
androgynous, and which she retains through to the end of
the film.

Yitzhak (Miriam Shor), Hedwig's beleaguered ex-drag
queen bandmate and partner from Eastern Europe, is both
one of the more fascinating and frustrating aspects of the
show and the film. Yitzhak represents a more interesting
kind of gender-play: a woman in heavy male drag — a bandana, leather jacket, and fake beard — only to transform
into a blonde feminine vixen by the end. Yitzhak's longing
glances at Hedwig's wigs and costumes, and their general
eagerness to please Hedwig, who serves as their inspiration,
still feels untapped. Even with the backstory about Yitzhak's
past as a drag queen, this on-screen transformation happens in a matter of seconds and with Hedwig's assistance.
In the way Dolores Fuller gives the angora sweater to Ed
Wood in *Glen or Glenda*, Hedwig gives over the blonde wig

to Yitzhak. Yitzhak's character arc is never centered; they never sing a solo song, and they are not the most consequential lover of Hedwig. Yet their transformation into a woman as they crowd-surf to "Midnight Radio" is, nevertheless, absolutely spellbinding.

After "Midnight Radio," Hedwig, a child of the moon, walks under the moonlit skies naked. Her tattoo is now of a whole child of the moon to show she has finally found and merged back with her other half. She is leaving behind her life for new, different horizons, with many potential shifts and transformations to follow. It is possible to look at Hedwig still waiting to find a label to better express herself, or, perhaps better still, not needing any label at all.

Hedwig and the Angry Inch was a trans film image for many who came of age in the early 2000s. It is complicated, but not at all a work that should be discarded. Mitchell might not see trans people as the subject of this story, but he has also accepted that trans people can certainly inhabit the character in the stage versions. The stage musical productions of *Hedwig* have become broader in casting, with drag queens, non-binary, and trans people assuming the main role, as well as the stage productions themselves having trans directors.[24] The film and musical will always be held with reverence among a broader queer audience, as well as by many trans people who have found solace in songs like "The Origin of Love" and "Wig in a Box." Hedwig as a character absolutely embodies a truthful and multi-valent trans film image — one tied to being a media spectacle, outing gender non-conforming bodies, and becoming a folk hero and celebrity due to being perceived as a music and gender phenomenon. Hedwig as a character and as a work gestures to broader identities beyond even those Aristophanes could imagine.

Maggots and Men and the Remixing of Political Cinema for Trans Masc DIY Images

Cary Cronenwett's films cast a mix of utopian urges and circumspect resignation. His experimental works *Phineas Slipped* (2002) and *Maggots and Men* (2009) recast trans masculine and gender non-conforming individuals into environments associated with traditional masculinity and all-male ensembles: an all-boys boarding school (*Phineas Slipped*) and the navy (*Maggots and Men*).

Maggots and Men is a dramatization of the 1921 Kronstadt Rebellion, a pastiche of Soviet cinema not far off from the films of Guy Maddin. Beyond aesthetic and technical pantomiming, the film is a major achievement in both DIY filmmaking and trans cinema for the sheer number of trans people involved in the project, including dozens of non-professionals as well as known trans performers, such as Max Wolf Valerio (*Max*, 1992 and *You Don't Know Dick: Courageous Hearts of Transsexual Men*, 1997) and Texas Starr (*Gendernauts*, 1999). The film took several years to make, shot in California and Vermont on 16mm and Super-8 cameras, and bankrolled by a mix of grant money and low-budget ingenuity in the form of sourcing from Craigslist and dumpster-diving for sets and props. Casting call bulletins looking for people who were willing to work for free were posted at trans health clinics. Susan Stryker, who herself has a small role, serving as a rare feminine presence in the film, said the recasting of trans bodies in *Maggots and Men* "evokes the poignant sense that our present world is haunted by radical potentials that have yet to be fulfilled."[25]

After *Phineas Slipped*, Cronenwett had wanted to make a film about sailors. From Kenneth Anger's *Fireworks* (1947) to Rainer Werner Fassbinder's *Querelle* (1982), there was a rich lineage of films filled with homoeroticism featuring sailors. But Cronenwett did not want to present American sailors on-screen.[26] The film was being made in the mid-2000s, during the Bush administration's increasingly unpopular wars in Iraq and Afghanistan, with reports circulating of the torture of detainees at the Guantanamo Bay Naval Base. Cronenwett ultimately decided on the true story of the radical sailors in the Soviet Union who, due to disappointment in Lenin's Bolshevik government on anarchist and leftist grounds, staged an insurrection that lasted several days until the Red Army overpowered the rebels in the port city of Kronstadt on Kotlin Island.

Maggots and Men takes its title from the opening chapter of Sergei Eisenstein's masterpiece *Battleship Potemkin* (1930), "The Men and the Maggots". The title connects to the failed promises of revolution wherein the sailors, who were among the strongest believers in collective struggle, are being stripped of their humanity and are placed in intolerable conditions that are infested with maggots. The "maggots" also represent the significance of the trans masculine bodies now in these roles. It goes beyond the provocation of imagining these trans bodies as rebellious sailors from the Russian Civil War, and also serves as a commentary for how trans people are often in constant struggle with both the state and media for how they are treated, perceived, and represented.

Cronenwett had initially conceived of *Maggots and Men* in a shorter version, one built upon vignette after vignette, each retelling the story of the rebellion. Early sections of the film do tease a more fragmented direction, such as the scene of a Mad Scientist (played by San Francisco and underground film legend George Kuchar) in a laboratory with a human patient, which is never referenced again. After shooting the winter scenes in Vermont, and having a full-length feature' amount of material, Cronenwett decided post-shooting to add narration and an epistolary conceit, which served as the connective tissue between these sequences. Cronenwett retells the story of the Kronstadt Rebellion through letters and a voiceover from one of the real-life leaders of the rebellion, Stepan Petrichenko (portrayed on-screen by Stormy Henry Knight, with the narration of the letters spoken in

Russian). In these fictional letters to his sister, Stepan gives a brutally honest assessment of the deteriorating political situation, the events that led to the rebellion, and why the rebellion could not hold. The letters, which Stepan begins to suspect have been intercepted by Soviet authorities, represent a counter-narrative of unvarnished truth against the other forms of media that circulate throughout the film, but perhaps none more so than the movie camera, of which Lenin himself says in the film: "Cinema for us is the most important of the arts."

There is a fascinating moment in the film where the characters are shooting a film of the sailors performing their exercise routines. Cronenwett shoots this scene from a distance, featuring these sailors being filmed for propaganda purposes. But then the propaganda camera asserts itself and the style of how these sailors are filmed shifts. The propaganda camera presents these sailors at different, varied angles, including the classic "hero shot" low-angle camera placement and immersive close-ups. The sailors have their forms of media, but they cannot compare to the potency of cinema and the power the government has over them. And once Kronstadt was retaken by the Red Army, the truth and the stories of these sailors would soon be suppressed and altered, with Stepan and the other survivors left to live as exiles in Finland.

Cronenwett depicts cinema's power and the power of institutions — in this case, the state — in how stories of the past are often told, and particularly in what gets left out or twisted to fill a point of view that often simplifies things for the sake of upholding the status quo. Ultimately, Cronenwett connects the story of the Kronstadt rebels to how trans people are often not the ones telling their own stories — their histories are suppressed or erased, they fall under constant surveillance, and are often at the mercy of institutions and their media. Yet, even when finding this connection between these marginalized, overmatched communities of past and present to be sobering, there is still a

lot of tenderness within Cronenwett's image; the trans masculine bodies presented are diverse and sensual. This makes
Maggots and Men one of the most original and overtly political works that center trans masculinity.

Interconnected: Brief Snapshots Twenty-First-Century Trans Online Visibility

The increasing visibility of transness from the 2000s onward
is undoubtedly tied to the rise of the internet. The creation
of online forms like Susan's Place and TGForum gave rise
to greater interconnectedness, and were places to discreetly
share thoughts, opinions, photos, and information with
like-minded individuals, with a common grasp of slang,
niche acronyms, and pseudonyms. At the same time, vid-
eo-sharing websites like YouTube also offered new avenues
for trans film images.

The most common of these were the vlog diaries of trans
people coming out and being transparent about struggles
related to dysphoria, transphobia, rejection, exclusion, and
medical transition, and particularly how they progressed
on hormones. YouTube did not just democratize filmmaking, but also made available information on matters of
trans health and procedures that was previously not widely
shared. As Morgan M. Page and Chase Joynt noted, this
"first-wave" of YouTubers

> were untrained and unmonetized, relying primarily on
> iMovie, early smartphones, and grainy webcams to produce
> DIY content for each other. Though their work is largely
> forgotten, these YouTubers constructed the now-ubiquitous
> trans vlog format.[27]

In doing so, as Laura Horak notes, these users created their
own series of cliches and tropes of the transition timeline
within the vlog space.[28] In many ways, as Horak framed it,
"Instating transition as a norm" arguably helped accelerate

the ways in which trans audiences were able to articulate their dissatisfaction and fatigue with the fictionalized transition narratives appearing in mainstream culture. Most trans people had already seen many of these stories before on their own computer through authentic real-life images and experiences.

YouTube was also used as an archive to connect with trans elders' testimonials. One such popular case was the Trans Oral History Project, whose subjects included Stonewall veteran Miss Major, trans elder Ben Power, and testimonies about spaces like The Stroll in New York, which became synonymous with trans women and sex work. In 2014, trans elder Dallas Denny interviewed Andrea Susan Malick at a hospital about her role in documenting the Casa Susanna retreat. Susan's presentation in the hospital is male — a negotiation of the risks of being sick at a certain age and requiring care in a hospital full of strangers — despite having socially and privately presented as a woman for many years. Susan recalls stepping out in her female presentation on the red carpet for Harvey Fierstein's Broadway play *Casa Valentina*, a work inspired by her Casa Susanna photos, not wanting to lose the authorship and association with the work, as she had done when the photos had recirculated in art galleries without crediting her. It was an especially poignant moment, as she would pass away a year later.

However, while opening a democratized space of connection and self-documentation, YouTube has also created additional vulnerabilities as a forum for personal disclosure. On the one hand, people who need and want to see certain images can do so, but on the other, *everybody* can see them and pass judgment, expressing ignorance, hate, or worse, repurposing images to engage in targeted doxxing and violence. This was never going to be a digital utopia or have the safeguards and discretion of older groups and communities, but trans visibility through YouTube offers something perhaps not unlike the way talk shows provided trans imagery for the generation before. The possibilities of discovery that came with flicking through TV channels for an unsuspecting viewer turned into scrolls and internet rabbit holes that helped to inform the self-actualization of their gender identity.

CHAPTER 11
Trans Filmmakers and Authorship: Where We Are Now

We're All Going to the World's Fair: Dysphoria as a Living Ghost Story

The internet was initially conceived in film in conceptual terms. Numerous films used computer video games as a basis for images, like *Johnny Mnemonic* (1995) or David Cronenberg's *eXistenZ* (1999). The other approach was to conceive of online spaces as distant, surreal places, which introduced alternative realities, like *Pulse* (2001) through the lens of horror, or *The Matrix* in science fiction. While initial examples of the internet in filmmaking took a cautious, concerned approach about the growing technology, there is little to no resistance in the way Millennial and Gen-Z filmmakers conceive of the internet as a natural extension of everyday life. The way that this has interacted with transness is a vast flooding of visibility through social media channels. In earlier decades, it was more difficult for a trans person to organically find their community or relatable images, but now they only need to go online.

In Jane Schoenbrun's *We're All Going to the World's Fair* (2021), the internet is intimate, personalized, and evolving for people who call it their home. Schoenbrun is strongly influenced by the work of David Cronenberg, particularly in the way his filmmaking takes the human body and collapses it inside new realities and possibilities for definition through surreal uses of technology. With *eXistenZ*, Cronenberg tried to understand how things like video games and the internet were beginning to become like a prosthesis for the human body. *We're All Going to the World's Fair* builds on this idea with specificity, as the internet acts as a type of virus that is induced by shared loneliness and a longing for community.

In *We're All Going to the World's Fair*, this is foregrounded through a blood oath. To participate in the "World's Fair Challenge," a user must cut themselves and wipe the blood on their screen. After enacting this blood oath, transformations are supposed to occur, and the participant is required to document their experience of those changes, which echoes the popularity of YouTube transition timeline videos that date back to the 2000s. Teenager Casey (Anna Cobb) becomes obsessed with the transformations and eagerly joins this online community, where she spends her evenings on YouTube listening to others chart their symptoms. These transformations unfurl into the realm of the uncanny. Casey watches a video of a young woman's skin becoming like plastic, or that of a boy whose arms are being overtaken with a fungus. The language of the "World's Fair" is built upon the backbone of body horror, analogous to dysphoric transness. In Schoenbrun's director's notes, released alongside the film at Sundance, they state that *World's Fair* is an attempt to "use the language of cinema to articulate the hard-to-describe feeling of dysphoria."[1] Schoenbrun elaborates further that their adolescence was a "constant feeling of unreality, one cut with an ambient sense of shame, self-loathing and anger."[2]

World's Fair is staggeringly unique in construction and exciting for what it offers in telling stories of coded transness, free of the burden of medical queries dominating narrative and representative images. Casey's experience with the "World's Fair" and the way the film utilizes dysphoria is like a secret handshake of transness that is deliberately for trans people, because it is not conceived of in the way it is normally shown. There are not any broad depictions of anguish that are present in more traditional transition narratives, but rather a quiet unease and the dispossession of Casey's subjective experience of herself.

Casey's internet seems to exist under the shield of a perceived anonymity. It feels haunted in the style of Kiyoshi Kurosawa, but unlike the characters in Kurosawa's films, like *Pulse*, Casey is completely at ease with giving herself and her body to the internet, and in fact, she cannot realistically exist without the contours of what it promises in dominating her life. Schoenbrun treats algorithmic loading screens like a séance and lingers on them for long periods of time before someone or something is summoned for Casey during her lonely nights. Sometimes, she is accompanied by a positive force, like an ASMR video telling her that nightmares are not real, which rocks her gently to sleep, but in one instance, she comes across a video that acts as a direct warning that she is in trouble for reckoning with the horror of the "World's Fair" and its curse of transformation. Is any of this real? Or is it a type of viral participatory chain-letter of the body? It hardly matters for Casey, whose isolation and discomfort with her own existence have made her look for kinship in the waiting arms of the internet, and this community of people who may or may not be charlatans, and whose body morphing videos may or may not be fake.

When Casey does begin to experience symptoms, such as feeling outside of her own body, a kind of disassociation, an older man who goes by JLB (Michael J. Rogers) introduces himself. He speaks to her through an internet avatar, revealing it was him who made the video warning Casey. The horror elements are most strongly present in the potential danger of this relationship. Casey's videos also have taken a darker turn, which have involved her destroying a childhood teddy bear and wearing homemade corpse paint when online.

Casey is never characterized as someone with a great

home life. Viewers are never shown her parents, with their only representation being an angry paternal voice heard from downstairs ordering her to go to bed. There is no indication she has any friends, and she appears to be an extremely solitary, introverted person, which makes her vulnerable to the community promised in online spaces and potential predators alike. JLB is ultimately benign and is shown to care about Casey, but it is hard to parse that through their initial interactions, which gesture towards something more sinister and predatory in his intentions. Casey never gives JLB her real name, but she is also interested in the recklessness of continuing their communication. For her, it is all part of the experience.

The online mythmaking of the "World's Fair" resembles the online paranormal subgenre of "Creepy Pasta," which Schoenbrun documented in her film about internet lore, *A Self-Induced Hallucination* (2018). Casey's experiences are built upon this type of internet legend. Found-footage horror is also a major reference point, with Casey mentioning a fondness for the *Paranormal Activity* movies — representative of how the film features numerous unbroken, static scenes. In one of her videos, Casey is lit with only the glow-in-the-dark adornments on her bedroom walls and a single lamp. She stands in the middle of her bedroom, wearing glowing paint make-up, staring into the lens for an unreasonably long time, taking on the appearance of someone possessed or experiencing disassociation. She then rips apart a childhood teddy bear in a trance. A few minutes later, she becomes conscious of her surroundings and cries over what she has done. It is an unnerving and upsetting scene.

World's Fair poses the following question: Does this habit of internet usage contribute to loneliness, or does it help stave off complete isolation? Schoenbrun does not answer this question and the film is better off for it. *World's Fair* is not a tragic story, or even one that comes from a moral place in positioning the internet as an inherently negative experience. It is far more nuanced. For younger Millennials and Gen-Z, the internet is not a bogeyman, but as natural as the air they breathe. The communities that a person can form online can change someone's life astronomically for the better, and this is especially true of trans people who are closeted or isolated in smaller towns, with poor mental health, or conservative families. Schoenbrun's film has sympathy for people like this, who seek these online connections. Casey needed the "World's Fair" to survive, even with her frightening reactions to it, and for today's generation of young adults, they have very likely had similar experiences in their chosen internet spaces and personas. Casey's story introduces a type of dissonant, trans-adjacent narrative where viewers can see and feel the desperation in wanting to transform, find others like yourself, and how the internet can make that a possibility. It is a cinema influenced by how people live with the internet, which is also undeniably and textually informed through the lived experience of transness.

A Trans with a Movie Camera and Transgressive Allusions

Experimental filmmaker Frances Arpaia and transgressive artist Louise Weard are looking for new answers to what a trans film image implies. The title of Arpaia's short *A Trans with a Movie Camera* (2018) echoes Dziga Vertov's landmark experimental film *A Man with a Movie Camera* (1929), but with a "fuck you" attitude to cinema of the past.

Beginning with a track by the influential trans punk band G.L.O.S.S. as the film's thesis statement, *A Trans with a Movie Camera* seeks to light ablaze the tragic martyr myth that has so long dogged transgender representation, and creates something entirely free and without the baggage of the past, by focusing on trans people living loudly in the present. As Sadie Switchblade of G.L.O.S.S. screams: "Lined lips, spiked bats / Gotta take femininity back." In this film, trans women are seen topless or in the arms of another woman, with the blistering euphoria of free bodies and open sexuality. Arpaia also chronicles things like gender dysphoria through spoken word poetry, and the closeted spaces of trans women with language and symbols that trans people coined for themselves, such as the literal cracking of an egg. These images exist as a foundation and a future to a more definitive trans film image that is direct and confrontational, and built out of trans feminine culture and language. In *A Trans with a Movie Camera*, one trans woman drinks gasoline and spits fire — one of the most liberating images of transness in this new age.

Weard's *100 Best Kills: Texas Birth Control, Dick Destruction* (2022) is a film of wild pandemonium that creates a montage of genital destruction as a transgressive point of endurance, until castration almost seems natural. Watch the film long enough and a split scrotum suddenly starts to elicit the vaginal allusions of a Georgia O'Keeffe painting. Weard's *Computer Hearts* (2015), which she co-directed with Dionne Copland, is a natural extension of Cronenbergian interests in the eroticism of new technologies, and alludes to disc-drives being their own vaginal orifice for the sexually stunted lead character, who Weard plays herself. Weard co-directed *Computer Hearts* prior to transitioning, but always intended it to be for trans women, and the *Tetsuo: The Iron Man* (1989)-isms of its final bodily transformations, which echo the castration of Shinya Tsukamoto's own mingling of technology and the body, proposes transness as an evolutionary, separate expansion of new flesh and imagistic ideas of death and rebirth. Weard is unburdened by any respectable ideas of what a trans film image should be, and that makes her work appealing and liberating.

Angelo Madsen Minax's Cinema of Personal Reflection and Familial Bonds

In the experimental film space, Angelo Madsen Minax meditates and explores the ways in which trans masculinity interacts with the modern world. He has often faced push back for his work not being seen as "trans enough" to be deemed as part of trans cinema,[3] a bizarre claim as his output in his shorts and installation work contains rich nuances of trans masculinity, from his own experience and the experiences of others. Some of Minax's best work presents trans people in dialogue with the ways in which the perceptions of trans bodies have shifted and evolved in the modern era. In his installation short, *No Show Girls* (2012), a trans masc guy performs a striptease. It is something of a deconstruction of a stage performance that is synonymous with sex work, with there being no music or spectators viewing this beyond Minax himself, who gives the performer direction while in the periphery of the screen. The trans performer is dressed in a ball cap, jeans, and a flannel. They begin to strip, revealing their trans body. The performer has signs of a masculinized face from hormones, with facial hair and other body hair on their chest, but they do not have top surgery, which is a notable difference from many trans men. It is a fascinating display of bodily autonomy that is not underscored with anything beyond the unbroken trust the performer has with the director.

In *The Eddies* (2019), which is scripted but based on real-life encounters, Minax uses the since-defunct Craigslist personal page when visiting Tennessee to seek out a man who is willing to jerk-off on camera while also clutching a gun. The loaded phallic metaphor seems lost on the potential Eddies (the pseudonym he gives to every man he meets) that he approaches for this project. But one particular Eddie takes a sexual interest in him and wants them to both jerk off. Minax discloses his trans status to Eddie, who is surprised but still wants to engage with Minax, who does agree to jerk off together. Minax based this encounter on the changes he saw on gay hookup sites like Adam4Adam — that shifted from transphobia to desire — when encountering queer men who expressed sexual attraction to his trans masculine body. It is one of the more radical showcases of modern desire that has yet to be fully replicated in more conventional narrative features that feature trans masculinity.

Minax's overall experimental film output functions like a scattered collage of YouTube deep dives and dating apps that are contemplative about the present. His feature-length film *North by Current* (2021) is a more personal non-fiction work, but one where his tendencies to divert from conventional trans narratives are clarified. Minax comes from a conservative part of the state of Michigan, where his trans identity becomes an unavoidable topic of discussion when interacting with family members. In *North by Current*, he discovers that his coming out as a trans man is treated by his parents as a symbolic death for them. His parents equate his decision to transition to the tragic death of his infant niece. This floors Minax, who thought he and his parents had reached an impasse in accepting his transition. But these types of behaviors are familiar to many trans people when interacting with family members who, while not outright rejecting their decisions to transition, do often incrementally drop microaggressions and guilt trips against their trans children in the aftermath.

Minax is also confronted with a much tougher revelation to gauge, which is the fact his troubled sister, Jesse, felt his avoidant behavior and selfishness did not help her in their adolescence, leaving her to feel like she had no sibling to help her through life. Despite their tempestuous relationship, Minax is incredibly empathetic and protective of his sister, whose life has been especially troubled since the death of her child.

Minax is not interested in filming a navel-gazing exercise, but makes himself and his identity vulnerable alongside other delicate facts about his family, and does so with unconventional editing choices, structuring, and voiceover. Transness can often be centered as a force of tension within narratives in both fiction and non-fiction filmmaking. Trans people, by existing, no matter how passive they are as individuals, still often upend the societal expectations of parents, friends, and loved ones. Minax presents family trauma and the systemic trauma wielded against him and his sister over the years, showing that, despite once feeling like strangers, he understands and finds kinship in how his and his sister's lives have altered through the years, and how they walk through the world on eggshells in the judgment of others. *North by Current* is gut-wrenching in several moments, but seeks to uncover, reveal, and mend old wounds.

Similarly, Yance Ford's *Strong Island* (2017) does not have the director's transness foregrounded in the narrative, focusing instead on how his masculinity and sense of family were informed by his older brother, William Ford, whose 1992 murder remains an unresolved injustice. The film was made from pain and hurt over the fact that his brother's murderer was not even indicted with the crime, because an all-white jury believed the killer's claim of self-defense. The memory that Ford carries of his brother is seen in the provocative closeups of his face when speaking directly to the camera and telling people that, if they do not like what they are going to hear about him and his family's thoughts on the American criminal justice system, as well as Long Island's history of systemic racism, then they should stop watching. *Strong Island*, in many ways, is a *détournement* of true crime tropes, with Ford purposely avoiding showing the image of the teenage mechanic — his brother's murderer — on screen and simply revealing the stonewalling he faces in asking questions to those who worked on the case. Ford's sense of brotherhood with William is shown through home videos, remembrances, re-readings of his brother's journals, and a phone message from William that he kept for years. While his brother never got to see Yance as a trans man, their relationship showed an implicit acceptance that, for a trans person, can mean the world.

Strong Island is both a clear-eyed film about seeking answers and about the ways in which individuals who have

had their friends and loved ones harmed in their marginalized communities are often forced to suppress their pain
and grief. Ford ultimately allows himself to be filmed in
a very raw moment where he lets out a primal scream in
response to the effect William's death has had on himself
and his family. William and the Ford family did at one point
believe in upward mobility, having dreams and ambitions
not just for themselves but of helping others in their work
and altruism. Ford shows how that belief completely rup-
tured and altered everyone's perspective, notably his parents, after William's death.

Strong Island, along with *North By Current*, remains the
high point in recent non-fiction films that show different
sides of loss, the salvageability in fractured familial bonds,
and the wounds that will never heal.

Cross-Generational Trans Histories on Film

Transgender activist and filmmaker Tourmaline has
emerged as an essential figure for trans people of color
reclaiming their influence in discussions of trans and
LGBTQ rights. Her research of pre-twentieth-century
trans history informs much of her work on film, particularly her narratives of sex workers, such as Egyptt LaBeija,
whose story is told in *Atlantic is a Sea of Bones* (2017), and
her 2018 short with Sasha Wortzel on the life of Marsha
P. Thompson, *Happy Birthday, Marsha!* (starring Mya Taylor
as Thompson). Perhaps her most daring work, however, is
Salacia (2019), an experimental short and hybrid film about
Mary Jones, a real-life trans woman of color from the early
nineteenth century.

Salacia is a reparative narrative, telling the story of Jones,
a trans sex worker who was outed when she was accused by
a john of robbery, resulting in a five-year prison sentence in
Sing Sing, with caricatures of her featuring the abject label
of "Man-Monster" posted and passed around New York
for her alleged crime.[4] Tourmaline immediately knew she

wanted to make this story and tell it as one of black folklore, collaborating with cinematographer Arthur Jafa, who had worked for the likes of Julie Dash and Spike Lee. The results are sumptuous and mysterious, shot in 16mm, with literary allusions to the work of Toni Morrison and Virginia Hamilton's *The People Who Fly: American Black Folktales* (1985) (which is directly quoted in the film). But it is also a film that is political to its core. Jones (played by Rowin Amone) is treated like a freak, monster, and a phenomenon, cornered and isolated by the world around her, even though she was initially framed as a desirable body by a white male john. Tourmaline inserts a clip of Sylvia Rivera saying words of encouragement, "You gotta keep fighting, girly," reframed as encouraging Jones from the future, which results in forging a trans sisterhood that stretches over a century. It is a powerful moment of solidarity and a doubling of two trans women whose images were often morphed and othered by the people and systems of the period.

Cross-generational trans narratives like this are an emerging element in trans fiction and film, such as Jordy Rosenberg's novel *Confessions of the Fox* (2018), which reframes the "Mack the Knife" figure Jack Sheppard as a trans man whose memoir and personal testimony is uncovered in an archive by a contemporary trans academic. While Rosenberg's story plays more from dramatic license than historical fact, this method offers the potential to see beyond the present, deepening the past and highlighting trans authorship as a driver in connecting these otherwise disparate narratives and images. Tourmaline's *Salacia* — later expanded into the installation piece called *Mary of Ill Fame* — runs, as Ayanna Dozier puts it, as a "visual counter-archive" about black trans women and sex workers that provides "a template of alternative and informal tactics" of not just the creators of these counter-archives, but the ways in which these trans film images as *characters can operate with these tactics as tools for survival.*[5] Mary Jones is not made simply a martyr, but part of a lineage that highlights the ways trans women of color and trans sex workers are regularly dehumanized by society at large.

The lineage of the harm society does in action and reaction to the fear of a trans body offers incredible potential for reframing trans tabloid subjects and other degraded figures in history. For Aisling Chin-Yee and Chase Joynt, the directors of No Ordinary Man (2020), which interrogates the story of Billy Tipton, a former jazz musician and stealth trans man whose outing in death became a tabloid sensation, it became a collaborative community project. Joynt, in a discussion with trans academic and filmmaker Jules Rosskam, would state that collaboration in film, for him, was "itself about making and unmaking pre-existing categories and forms of knowledge in pursuit of a shared story."[6] Rosskam, in this same discussion, would note that making and unmaking such categories and forms was itself an essential aspect of transness.[7] In using Tipton's life story, No Ordinary Man makes collaboration essential to the making of what a trans narrative can be but also the concerted effort to underscore how many of the trans narratives that have been previously told need to be unmade. Part of the film critiques the very television programs that made a sideshow of Tipton's life and how Tipton's biographer, Diane Wood Middlebrook, had major blind-spots and unchecked transphobia in telling his story in her 1998 book, Suits Me: The Double Life of Billy Tipton. No Ordinary Man goes beyond the talking-head documentary format and instead holds open auditions for trans actors for the role of Tipton, which are shown in the film. This immerses trans people in the narrative and allows each performer to bring their own trans experiences to Tipton's story. This film within a film functions as a critique of Hollywood's failures in representing trans masculinity.

Archival histories on film present the power of connecting past and present images of transness. Tourmaline remains perhaps the best example of a trained archivist who did a reparative work of a castigated figure of the past through making Mary Jones a trans film image and reclaiming her humanity in the process. *No Ordinary Man* sought to do the same for Billy Tipton. These films are a part of a long lineage of trans people independently creating revisionist and reparative works to reframe trans histories. This seeking to repair and rehabilitate the stories of trans ancestors and contemporaries is not new, but how trans filmmakers reframe these stories on-screen, and how that produces more truthful trans film images that can get a wider viewership beyond the trans community, is a new development.

The Films of Isabel Sandoval: The Trans Film Image in the Visual Grammar of Classical Form

Isabel Sandoval is one of the most important figures to emerge in the wider scope of the trans film image.[8] Her influences come from classic international arthouse cinema, with a keen focus on sensuality. She is a self-taught filmmaker, whose film education comes from her cinephilia and watching pirated DVDs of world cinema masters such as Ozu and Fassbinder. The influence of Fassbinder, in particular, can be felt on her work in her portrayal of disempowered or disadvantaged women navigating the social structures of their lives as they attempt to make life-altering decisions that could have any number of catastrophic or, indeed, hopeful effects. Her film *Lingua Franca* (2019) feels particularly indebted to Fassbinder's *Ali: Fear Eats the Soul* (1974). But Sandoval's films have a certain specificity as trans narratives — they fill in the gaps of the trans film image in the classic, narrative form, which has been missing from direct trans representation and authorship.

Sandoval had a goal of presenting trans women as fully realized three-dimensional characters, because the trans depictions that she had been familiar with in her native Philippines were caricatured and stereotyped. She made the feature *Senorita* (2011) prior to identifying publicly as a trans woman, and considers the film to be what ultimately led to the self-realization of her trans identity. In that film, she plays Donna, a trans sex worker in Manilla who relocates to the small town where her son (who believes she is his aunt) lives. The look and feel of Donna were heavily inspired by Bree Daniels (Jane Fonda) in *Klute* (1971). After *Senorita*, she made *Apparition* (2012), which followed a group of Catholic nuns caught in the tensions of an important political decision during the years of Ferdinand Marcos dictatorship in the Philippines. *Apparition* has much more camera movement, a better feel for texture in color, and a stronger sense of blocking and framing than *Senorita*, which showed Sandoval's progression as a director. *Lingua Franca*, from 2019, is the culmination of her talents both behind and in front of the camera.

In *Lingua Franca,* Sandoval plays a Filipina trans woman named Olivia who wants a green card and stability in her life. She is ensnared in the bureaucratic red tape of the American immigration system, which is made more fraught because she is a trans woman. Olivia's passport is outdated, listing her gender as male and containing her birth name. It is not rare for trans people to let government identification expire and contain outdated information, as often within those systems there is no acceptance or understanding. To further drive how much has changed between the identity in her passport identity and who she is now, we learn that she has already undergone a vaginoplasty in a quietly revolutionary scene of her performing a post-surgical dilation in quotidian detail. The dilation scene has not been widely utilized in trans narratives, but is a fact of life for numerous trans women post-surgery. There have been instances of trans surgery on-screen and the immediate post-op aftermath, but rarely have there been explorations of what post-surgery recovery entails, which, in the case of a vaginoplasty, is consistent dilation for the remainder of that person's life. Such a moment in *Lingua Franca* rings as immediately significant to a trans viewer, and it is depicted with a quiet grace by Sandoval because it is simply an extension of Olivia's everyday experience. Olivia is rendered with these specific touchstones that are familiar to any trans person or immigrant, but it is the way in which Sandoval tells this story that it feels new.

Sandoval gestures towards the transphobia her character may face, but the threat is two-fold with her immigration status. The hanging threat of deportation is underscored by bombastic soundbites on televisions heard off-screen of ICE raids and Donald Trump's hate-mongering. Sandoval chooses to shoot her character with several close-ups that trace the lines of her weary, tired face. Sandoval's filmic grammar is traced from her influences in how she frames her characters and the world around them. The way she shoots exteriors in Brooklyn and through the interior spaces of kitchens where women hold conversations recalls Chantal Akerman's domestic chamber pieces that centered female characters and their interiority. While *Lingua Franca* is politically minded, it is also very domestically focused through Olivia's labor as a caregiver for Olga (Lynn Cohen), an elderly Russian-Jewish woman with dementia.

Olivia is sending installment plans to an American-born man named Matthew who is willing to marry her for a green card, but she soon finds herself falling for Olga's grandson, Alex (Eamon Farron), who has moved in with his grandmother after a stint in rehab. Through their romance — he is not immediately aware of her trans status — the film becomes something daring, electrifying, and novel: a genuine melodrama of a complicated relationship between a cis man and a trans woman, who are each flawed individuals burnt out by life.

Alex is a recovering alcoholic who has a precarious job at a meat-packing plant. He is a self-destructive figure who is genuinely trying to put the pieces of his life back together and make something of himself. He sees Olivia as his chance for redemption, and through her, he wants to become a better man. It is a classic storyline and there is burning sexual tension between the characters. Sandoval uses lots of dissolves when Olivia and Alex share scenes, merging their reciprocated romantic and sexual desires for one another before they act on it. One of the more romantic scenes is a long, uninterrupted take of the two dancing to a rendition of "Smoke Gets in Your Eyes," a song rich in film history, previously featured in films by Edward Yang and Fassbinder, among others. There is a sequence of Olivia masturbating to the thought of Alex wrapping his arms around her that develops the emerging sensuality between the two even further. Sandoval's choice to glide her camera along Olivia's body in a moment of pure need gives us a new image of a trans woman as a sexual being without the cis gaze making a fetish out of the trans body. Her orgasm is under her control and directed by her imagination, something extraordinarily unusual in cinematic depictions of transness.

When the two eventually have sex, it is nearly as great as her conjured fantasy. Alex fixates on numerous parts of her body before he gives her oral sex. Olivia is largely motionless during this scene, but not disconnected — there is a degree of self-consciousness visible on her face, but it fades with her growing pleasure. In this scene, Sandoval is as engaging as an actress as she is a director. It is absorbing and exhilarating to watch Olivia loosen up and achieve real pleasure, and it is rare that trans people get to experience this much orgasmic joy in a film framework that is not pornography. Sandoval has amusingly dubbed herself a "Queen of Sensual Cinema,"[9] and those sequences make a great case for her claim. But in classic melodrama fashion, there is no happy ending for Alex and Olivia as a pair.

Alex has lied and withheld important information from Olivia. He has found out she is trans after allowing a friend of his to steal money from her purse. Olivia, who had given him so much grace, cannot ignore this indiscretion that threatens her livelihood and safety. She has much more to lose than Alex. Sandoval does not vilify Alex when he makes mistakes, but asks viewers to understand why Olivia would find certain things more unforgivable than others. This is not a film where lives are crushed, but one where disappointment emerges from what was once seen as hope, which is a far more complicated emotion to sit with than misery.

Sandoval's work is classically influenced, but she finds new images and routes for storytelling, with transness permeating the form of her films rather than merely presenting a didactic narrative around transness. Her short film *Shangri-La* (2021) is a sensual delight where Sandoval plays a trans woman in an interracial relationship who speaks of her erotic fantasies in a church confessional booth during the Great Depression. Taking its cues from Wong-Kar Wai through romantic cross-dissolves, Sandoval creates an invigorating visual palette by introducing images of beautiful, erotic transness into modes of melodrama. Sandoval inserts herself where trans women had previously been absent through a classical framework of history and cinematic fantasy. Sandoval's films are empathetic character studies in the grand tradition of great movies about women — where trans femininity intersects with race, class, and politics non-didactically. Her filmography is far from finished, but what she has already created is among the finer oeuvres of any trans filmmaker in the history of the medium, with *Lingua Franca* a movie that will endure as an important trans narrative.

When a Film Can Save a Life: *T Blockers*

By the time she was 18, trans teenage *wunderkind* Alice Maio Mackay already had multiple feature and shorts credits to her name, like DIY slasher films *So Vam* (2021) and *Bad Girl Boogey* (2022), where anti-trans bigotry is just as much a feature of the horror as the blood and gore. But her most recent feature, *T Blockers* (2023), quite remarkably fulfills the legendary film critic Manny Farber's designation of "termite art" as a film work that "eats its own boundaries... leaves nothing in its path other than the signs of eager, industrious, unkempt activity."[10] *T Blockers* shows the potential in the future of trans cinema that Mackay imbues with incredible cinephilic vigor, ingenuity, and limitless imagination.

T Blockers earned the Australian filmmaker international attention and major festival play from horror and LGBTQ film festivals alike. The film presents contemporary trans struggles, but also meditates on genre conventions, midnight-movie film aesthetics, allegory that tips its hat to New Queer Cinema, and posits how making a discovery of trans history, more specifically trans film history, can be an act of service to not just trans people, but to everyone.

T Blockers focuses on Sophie (Lauren Last), a trans teenage filmmaker in Australia who aspires to make a genre horror film while working with her friends at a movie theatre. She clearly functions as Mackay's stand-in, but there is a brutal honesty in Sophie's everyday life. Viewers see her navigating casual trans misogyny on dating apps, dealing with more confrontational misogyny and transphobia at bars, while wanting to express her art in a fiercely independent way without censorship or paternalistic oversight from powerful film producers. The film is not overburdened with trauma or anxieties, which often engulf those lived experiences on-screen. Instead, Mackay gives an honest portrayal about her life and her contemporaries, who make art about their lives and are in constant search of a better world.

The film's central conflict is not garden-variety transphobia, medical gatekeeping, or fascistic legislative overreach that seeks to destroy trans existence. Mackay instead presents a threat to her protagonists in the form of parasites that emerge after an earthquake. The parasite latches specifically onto men and further amplifies and weaponizes their aggression. This is found among the very transphobic and homophobic antagonists that Sophie and her friends cross paths with. Think of it as a remix of Cronenberg's *Shivers*, where the plague is not built upon the carnal urges of perverse humans who behave like zombies, and is instead contained exclusively among those who have allowed bigotry to transform them into monsters. *T Blockers* also shares the touchstones of B-horror films with a Rod Serling social-horror twist. Mackay's metacommentary posits that the effect the parasites have on the safety of her characters is not too out of step with real-life dangers for trans women. Nevertheless, these parasites further inflame the treacherous terrain for Sophie and her friends who seek out movies as a labor of love and escape.

A consistent motif in the film is the Elvira-like movie channel hostess that plays on the television named Cryptessa (played by the non-binary drag performer Etcetera Etcetera), who speaks directly to the camera, assuring the audience, "It's only a movie." But Cryptessa also imparts this for the viewers of her program within the world of *T Blockers*: "The film you are about to see is a work of fantastic fiction... but it's realer [sic] than you think!" It is revealed that the parasites are not some new threat to this modern world, but are in fact ancient and have struck humans before. Essentially, Mackay is presenting that, for as long as trans people have existed, their lives have been under threat of violence. Yet Mackay does not present futility in this situation for her characters. In fact, she shows a path to resistance through Sophie's curiosity in trying to thread together her work as a trans filmmaker in the present to the mysterious, marginalized past of trans filmmakers that came before her.

Sophie becomes obsessed with an underground trans filmmaker from the 1990s named Betty VO. This element recalls Cheryl Dunye's New Queer Cinema classic *The Watermelon Woman* (1996), where the lead character Cheryl (also played by Dunye) becomes obsessed with the old Hollywood African American lesbian actress Fae Richards, who she discovers among the tapes at her local video store. Like Richards in *The Watermelon Woman*, Betty VO did not exist in real life. Instead, the character serves as a larger composite of trans artists from that period who never could break into the mainstream and resided strictly in the niche spaces of genre and DIY cinema. Sophie finds out that Betty VO had taken her own life, but not before her own run-in with an earlier strain of parasites. It is Betty VO's film, *Terror from Below*, that documents these events for Sophie and her friends, allowing them to combat the parasites of now and honor the late filmmaker's legacy by making a sequel to recirculate Betty VO's resistance and help others against the parasites.

Much like with other trans artists, Mackay has made a work — a fictional one — about the intergenerational dialogue between trans people of the past and present who often face the same problems. These characters realize that their art can function in a lineage to help people like them move through a difficult world. *T Blockers* is not about identity politics in terms of respectability or the assimilation of fading into the mainstream. It is clear-eyed about the realities of day-to-day trans struggles while creating a work that can be quite literally lifesaving. Even without the connection to the parasites, Betty VO's mere existence as a trans filmmaker of the past surely would still inspire Sophie as a filmmaker, with Betty VO's lived existence no longer obfuscated and on the margins of film history. Mackay goes for it all in ways that are admirable, playful, and refreshingly unpretentious, making the trans figure of the past hold the key to a trans person's guide to survival today.

Mackay's film is emblematic of how up-and-coming trans Gen-Z filmmakers are shifting away from typical trans narratives. They are not bound to older narratives and tropes, conservative studio filmmaking, or the sense they must placate an audience unable to grapple with trans identities without hand-holding. *T Blockers* is still accessible to the average moviegoer because of Mackay's incredibly light panache in making a very stylized, colorful genre film that manages to foreground so many of these ideas about transphobia, trans history, and trans film images with incredible confidence. Mackay as a filmmaker and storyteller shows the inquisitiveness of trans people wanting to mine through film history to find a North Star, while also creating a very contemporary pop cinema that is formed on her own terms and is exciting and inspiring. Mackay's consistent aims turn the tables and show the true monsters as the reactionary bigots against her trans heroes, offering a long overdue trans counter-narrative.

CONCLUSION
The New Frontiers of the Trans
Film Image

As it currently stands, there is not an agreed-upon wider trans canon of films, which are listed and discussed in the same way that film experts typically categorize different genres and subgenres. This speaks to the compromised nature of the trans film image in the twentieth century, but as we have seen, there have been trans film images throughout the history of cinema. These films have undeniably shaped mainstream perceptions of transness, in ways that were well-intentioned and others that played upon ignorance and fear of the trans body. They are all worth considering, because they give us the full scope of how transness has been conceived in film up to this point.

Trans people remain in pursuit of bodily autonomy and the ability to live with dignity and respect for their social and medical decisions. It is why it is so important to look back at how transness and the trans film image has played out in popular culture. It is valuable in understanding how the lack of autonomy and decision-making filtered into the community's mistreatment and misunderstanding from the mainstream. If we forget our past, then our future will be fought for in repetition, and trans history has been shown to fall into these patterns before. These films, as harrowing or uncomfortable as they play today, show us who we were and how we were perceived and portrayed, and that must be reckoned with going forward.

The trans film images of the past have informed the

potency of the current movement of trans filmmakers, through either unconscious or direct commentary. These historically harmful images, which have rendered trans people as corpses, fools, and monsters, should not be forgotten, and to do so would be negligent. It would be an undue burden to expect a new generation of trans filmmakers to completely exorcize these elements. Instead, many of these filmmakers have shown intelligence in making art on their own terms. The broader scope of the trans film image previously had created an inelegant portrait, but there was beauty to be found nonetheless. With these new filmmakers, and with the availability of filmmaking technology at the fingertips of many through cell phones and an internet connection, there is hope for a more authentic, organic filmmaking that transforms the trans film image by introducing new ways of communicating transness on-screen.

The trans film image is a concept that is still developing. Trans artists and performers who have centered their work around trans embodiment and experiences have shown the importance of authorship and collaboration in yielding a more truthful image. Trans cinema can become a subgenre that presents transness in all its varied manifestations without obfuscation. The trans film image has undergone a trajectory towards a fuller, richer tapestry of presenting what it means to have a trans body in the world. Despite the compromised nature of the trans film image of the past, there are many new horizons possible for the trans film image of the future, and that canvas, with all these images, will tell our story in cinema.

NOTES

Preface: What Are Trans Film Images?

1 Maclay, Willow, and Caden Mark Gardner. "Body Talk: Conversations on Transgender Cinema with Caden Gardner Part Three." *Curtsies and Hand Grenades*, 26 March 2018: <http://curtsiesandhandgrenades.com/index.php/2018/03/26/body-talk-conversations-on-transgender-cinema-with-caden-gardner-part-three/>.

2 Stryker, Susan. "My Words to Victor Frankenstein Above the Village of Chamounix: Performing Transgender Rage." *GLQ*, vol. 1, no. 3, 1994, pp. 237–254: <https://doi.org/10.1215/10642684-1-3-237>.

Chapter 1: The Legend of Christine Jorgensen

1 Kemp, Peter H. "Bi-Polar Gender-Blender: *Sylvia Scarlett.*" *Senses of Cinema*, no. 22, October 2002.

2 Queersighted: Breaking Taboos." *The Criterion Channel*, 30 June 2021: <https://www.criterionchannel.com/videos/queersighted-breaking-taboos>.

3 Ibid.

4 Alron Productions. "Christine Jorgensen." Ron's In Laguna, created by Ron Niles, 1986.

5 "Magnus Hirschfeld." *Holocaust Encyclopedia*: <https://encyclopedia.ushmm.org/content/en/article/magnus-hirschfeld-2>.

6 Green, David B. "1868: The 'Einstein of Sex' Is Born (and Dies)." *Haaretz*, 14 May 2015: <https://www.haaretz.com/jewish/2015-05-14/ty-article/.premium/1868-the-einstein-of-sex-is-born-and-dies/0000017f-dc83-df62-a9ff-dcd72e1b0000>.

7 Horton, Kami. "Meet Oregonian Dr. Alan Hart, Who Underwent the First Documented Gender-Confirming Surgery in the US."

Oregon Public Broadcasting, 30 June 2022: <https://www.opb.org/article/2022/06/30/oregon-us-gender-affirming-surgery-history-dr-alan-hart-lgbtqia-history/>.

8   Ibid.

9   Meyerowitz, Joanne J. *How Sex Changed: A History of Transsexuality in the United States*. Harvard Univ. Press, 2009. pp. 42–43.

10 Stryker, Susan. *Transgender History: The Roots of Today's Revolution*. Seal Press, Berkeley, 2017, pp. 62–63.

11 Ryan, Hugh. "25 Years Ago Today Christine Jorgensen, 'America's First Transsexual,' Died of Cancer." *VICE*, 3 May 2014: <https://www.vice.com/en/article/exmbdp/a-bathroom-of-ones-own>.

12 Craig, Rob. *Ed Wood, Mad Genius: A Critical Study of the Films*. McFarland & Co., Jefferson, North Carolina, 2009, p. 25.

13 Nutrix Co. *Letters from Female Impersonators*, Vol. 3, pp. 10–16. 1961. *Digital Transgender Archive*: <https://www.digitaltransgenderarchive.net/files/c247ds10z>.

14 Jorgensen, Christine. *A Personal Autobiography*. Bantam Books, Toronto/London, 1973, p. 193.

15 Doyle, Peggy. "The Real Christine Approves 'Jorgensen Story'." Clipping. 1970. *Digital Transgender Archive*: <https://www.digitaltransgenderarchive.net/files/kd17cs96z>.

16 Athitakis, Mark. "Saluting 'Myra Breckinridge' on its 50th Anniversary." *Los Angeles Times*, 23 February 2018: <https://www.latimes.com/books/la-ca-jc-myra-breckinridge-20180223-story.html>.

17 "Books: Myra the Messiah." *Time Magazine*, 16 February 1968: <https://content.time.com/time/subscriber/article/0,33009,837914,00.html>.

18 *Transvestia*, vol. 9 no. 53. p. 65. Periodical. 1968. *Digital Transgender Archive*: <https://www.digitaltransgenderarchive.net/files/9k41zd84c>.

19 Daly, Steven. "Myra Breckinridge: Swinging Into Disaster." *Vanity Fair's Tales of Hollywood: Rebels, Reds, and Graduates and the Wild Stories behind the Making of 13 Iconic Films*. Penguin Books, New York, 2009, p. 253.

20 Ibid., p. 246.

21 United Artists Pressbook. "'The Christine Jorgensen Story' Movie Pressbook." Press Release. 1970. *Digital Transgender Archive*: <https://www.digitaltransgenderarchive.net/files/4b29b615v>.

22 Ibid.

Chapter 2: On the Cusp of Stonewall

1 Hughes, Paul. "The Surgeon Who Changes Men Into Women." Clipping. 1976. *Digital Transgender Archive*: <https://www.digitaltransgenderarchive.net/files/tm70mv25x>.

2 Stryker, Susan. "We Who Are Sexy: Christine Jorgensen's Transsexual Whiteness in the Postcolonial Philippines." *Social Semiotics*, vol. 19, no. 1, March 2009, p. 85: <https://doi.org/10.1080/10350330802655551>.

3 Stryker, *Transgender History*, pp. 84–87.

4 Ibid., p. 68.

5 Ibid., p. 145.

6 Ibid., p. 76.

7 Ibid., p. 68.

8 Ibid., p. 77.

9 Wilson, Steve. "The Queen." *Ransom Center Magazine*, 2020, pp. 22–25.

10 Bullock, Michael. "Flawless Sabrina." *Apartamento Magazine*, 2017.

11 Zahlten, Alexander. "The Prerogative of Confusion: Pink Film and the Eroticization of Pain, Flux and Disorientation." *Screen*, vol. 60, no. 1, 11 March 2019, pp. 25–49.

12 Abrams, Simons. "Funeral Parade of Roses." *RogerEbert.com*, 9 June 2017: <https://www.rogerebert.com/reviews/funeral-parade-of-roses-1970>.

Chapter 3: Post-Stonewall Transness from the Underground to Mainstream Cinema in the 1970s

1 Harris, William. *The Transvestite: The Magazine for and about Transvestism*, Vol. 4, p. 39. Periodical. 1973. *Digital Transgender Archive*: <https://www.digitaltransgenderarchive.net/files/fn106x98v>.

2 Lee, Linda. *Drag*, Vol. 2 No. 6. Periodical. 1972. pp. 26, 31. *Digital*

Transgender Archive: <https://www.digitaltransgenderarchive.net/files/0z708w44g>.

3 *Arena: Tales of Rock and Roll — Walk on the Wild Side*. Directed by James Marsh, BBC, 1993.

4 Smith, Patti. *Just Kids*. Ecco Press, London, 2010, p. 130.

5 Woodlawn, Holly, and Jeffrey Copeland. *A Low Life in High Heels: The Holly Woodlawn Story*. HarperPerennial, New York, 1992.

6 Davis, Allison P. "A Look at Holly Woodlawn's Warhol Days." *The Cut*, 7 December 2015: <https://www.thecut.com/2015/12/look-at-holly-woodlawns-warhol-days.html>.

7 Wiegand, David. "Candy's Fairy-Tale 'Face'; Diaries Reveal Longing For Identity." *SFGate.com*. 28 July, 1997: <https://www.sfgate.com/books/article/books-candy-s-fairy-tale-face-diaries-2832156.php>.

8 Brewster, Lee G. *Drag*, Vol. 2 No. 6 (1972). pp. 8–12. Periodical. 1972. *Digital Transgender Archive*: <https://www.digitaltransgenderarchive.net/files/0z708w44g/>.

9 Getlen, Larry. "The Bizarre True Story That Inspired 'Dog Day Afternoon'." *The New York Post*, 3 August, 2014: <https://nypost.com/2014/08/03/the-man-who-inspired-dog-day-afternoon/>.

10 Jahr, Cliff. "The 'Dog Day' Bank Robber Learns Moviemaking, Like Crime, Does Not Pay." *The Village Voice*, 24 January 2020: <https://www.villagevoice.com/2020/01/24/the-dog-day-bank-robber-learns-moviemaking-like-crime-does-not-pay/>.

11 Kluge, P.F., and Thomas Moore. "The Boys in the Bank." *LIFE Magazine*, 22 September 1972, pp. 66–74.

12 Jacques, Juliet. "Disclosure Review: The Progress and Missteps of Trans Representation on Screen." *Sight and Sound*, 28 September, 2020: <https://www.bfi.org.uk/sight-and-sound/reviews/disclosure-trans-lives-screen-sam-feder-documentary-representation-progress-missteps/>.

13 *Dog Day Afternoon*. Directed by Sidney Lumet, written by Frank Pierson, Warner Bros., 1975.

14 Brewster, Lee G. *Drag*, Vol. 5 No. 17 (1975), p. 9. Periodical. 1975. *Digital Transgender Archive*: <https://www.digitaltransgenderarchive.net/files/08612n580>.

15 Bray, James. "Richard O'Brien and the Rocky Horror Fairy Tale." *Newsnight*, BBC, 8 September 2015.

16 Gilbey, Ryan. "Rocky Horror's Richard O'Brien: 'I Should Be Dead. I've Had an Excessive Lifestyle'." *The Guardian*, 5 November 2020: <https://www.theguardian.com/stage/2020/nov/05/richard-obrien-interview-rocky-horror-trans-crack-stroke-70s>.

17 Bakkila, Blake, and Mariah Haas. "Laverne Cox Talks about Singing 'Sweet Transvestite' in 'Rocky Horror' Remake." *People Magazine*, 2 December, 2020: <https://people.com/tv/laverne-cox-rocky-horror-role/>.

18 Russo, Vito. *The Celluloid Closet: Homosexuality in the Movies*, Perennial Library, New York, 1987, p. 178.

19 Ibid., p. 52.

20 Ibid., p. 53.

21 Katz, Robert, and Peter Berling. *Love Is Colder than Death: The Life and Times of Rainer Werner Fassbinder*. Paladin, London, 1989, p. 142.

22 Vicari, Justin. "Speaking for Others: Manifest and Latent Content in In a Year with Thirteen Moons." *Senses of Cinema*, no. 37, October 2005.

23 Ibid.

24 Fassbinder, Rainer Werner. "In a Year of Thirteen Moons." *Anarchy of the Imagination: Interviews, Essays, Notes*. The Johns Hopkins University Press, Baltimore, 1992, pp. 177–195.

25 Vicari, Justin. "Speaking for Others."

26 Fassbinder, "In a Year of Thirteen Moons." p. 195.

27 Ibid.

28 Marcus, Eric. (Host) 2018, December 28. "Reed Erickson". Season 4: Episode 7. *Making Gay History*: <https://makinggayhistory.com/podcast/reed-erickson>.

29 West, Rebecca. "Conundrum." *The New York Times*, April 1974: <https://www.nytimes.com/1974/04/14/archives/conundrum-by-jan-morris-a-helen-and-kurt-wolff-book-174-pp-new-york.html>.

30 West, "Conundrum."

31 Ephron, p. 201.

32 Russo, *The Celluloid Closet*, pp. 184–185.

33 Brewster, Lee G. *Drag*, vol. 5 no. 17, pp. 17–18 (1975).

34 Raymond, Janice G. *The Transsexual Empire: The Making of the She-Male*. Beacon Press, Boston, 1979, p. 178.

35 Ibid., p. 104.

36 Szasz, Thomas. "Male and Female Created He Them." *The New York Times*, 10 June 1979: <https://www.nytimes.com/1979/06/10/archives/male-and-female-created-he-them-transexual.html>.

37 Prince, Virginia. *Transvestia*, vol. 17 no. 101, pgs. 34–38. Periodical. 1979. *Digital Transgender Archive*: <https://www.digitaltransgenderarchive.net/files/qf85nb60x>.

Chapter 4: Weathering the Storm

1 Stryker, *Transgender History*, p. 139.

2 Russo, *The Celluloid Closet*, pp. 236–237.

3 Ann, Robyn. "The Cross-dresser's Movie Guide." Periodical. 1989. *Digital Transgender Archive*: <https://www.digitaltransgenderarchive.net/files/8910jt87k/>.

4 Whittle, Stephen. *Chrysalis Quarterly*, vol. 1 no. 7, p. 17. (Spring, 1994). Periodical. 1994. *Digital Transgender Archive*: <https://www.digitaltransgenderarchive.net/files/nv935286k/>.

5 Sullivan, Louis G. "Information for the Female-to-Male Cross-dresser and Transsexual." Book. 1985. *Digital Transgender Archive*: <https://www.digitaltransgenderarchive.net/files/g158bh442/>.

6 Alter, Levi Ethan, and Anderson-Minshall, Jacob. *FTM International* #63. Periodical. 2007. *Digital Transgender Archive*: <https://www.digitaltransgenderarchive.net/files/xd07gs80t/>.

7 Callahan, Dan. *Vanessa: The Life of Vanessa Redgrave*. Pegasus Books, New York, 2015, pp. 171–172.

8 Ibid., p. 171.

9 Sullivan, Lou. *FTM Newsletter* #5. p. 13 Periodical. 1988. *Digital Transgender Archive*: <https://www.digitaltransgenderarchive.net/files/rf55z796z/>.

10 Raj, Rupert. Gender Networker, Vol. 1, No. 2, p.11, Newsletter. August 1988. *Digital Transgender Archive*: <https://www.digitaltransgenderarchive.net/files/pn89d667r>.

11 "Lee Grant, Arthur Miller, Elia Kazan and the Blacklist: None Without Sin." *American Masters Digital Archive* (WNET). 11

January 2002: <https://www.pbs.org/wnet/americanmasters/
archive/interview/lee-grant-2/>.

12 Pauly, Ira B., and Sullivan, Lou. *Female to Gay Male Transsexualism:
I — Gender & Sexual Orientation*. Motion Picture. 1988. *Digital
Transgender Archive*: <https://www.digitaltransgenderarchive.net/
files/4x51hj25d/>.

Chapter 5: Trans Grotesquerie

1 "Lawyer Urges Early Sanity Test for Gein." *The Daily Telegram*, 21
November 1957, p. 1.

2 Vallely, Jean. "Brian De Palma: The New Hitchcock or Just Another
Ripoff?" *Rolling Stone*, 16 October 1980: <https://www.
rollingstone.com/tv-movies/tv-movie-news/brian-de-palma-the-
new-hitchcock-or-just-another-rip-off-76019/>.

3 Vallely. "Brian De Palma."

4 7 Beecroft, Carol. *Femme Mirror*, vol. 4–5 no. 5–1 (December-
February, 1980). Periodical. 1980. *Digital Transgender Archive*:
<https://www.digitaltransgenderarchive.net/files/h128nd85z/>.

5 Vallely. "Brian De Palma."

6 Phipps, Keith. "The Night 'The Silence of the Lambs' Devoured
the Oscars." *The Ringer*, 23 March 2022: <https://theringer.com/
oscars/2022/3/23/22991780/silence-of-the-lambs-oscars-sweep-
academy-awards-big-five/>.

7 Weinraub, Bernard. "A Day to Demonstrate Affection for the Stars
and Some Dismay." *The New York Times*, 31 March 1992: <https://
www.nytimes.com/1992/03/31/movies/a-day-to-demonstrate-
affection-for-the-stars-and-some-dismay.html>

8 Kinane, Ruth. "*Clarice* Showrunner, Writer, and Actress Jen
Richards on Addressing Buffalo Bill's Transphobic Legacy in
Upcoming Episodes." *Entertainment Weekly*, 13 May 2021:
<https://ew.com/tv/clarice-writers-address-buffalo-bill-harmful-
legacy/>.

9 Harris, Thomas. *The Silence of the Lambs*. St. Martin's Press, New
York, NY, 1988, p. 286.

10 Brody, Jane E. "Benefits of Transsexual Surgery Disputed as
Leading Hospital Halts the Procedure." *The New York Times*, 2
October 1979: <https://www.nytimes.com/1979/10/02/archives/

benefits-of-transsexual-surgery-disputed-as-leading-hospital-halts.html>.

11 Allen, Samantha. "Can Trans People Trust Johns Hopkins's New Clinic?" *The Daily Beast*, 5 May 2017: <https://www.thedailybeast.com/can-trans-people-trust-johns-hopkinss-new-clinic>.

12 Brody, "Benefits of Transsexual Surgery Disputed as Leading Hospital Halts the Procedure."

13 Lynn, Merissa Sherrill. *The TV-TS Tapestry* Issue 49 (1986), p. 45. Periodical. 1986. *Digital Transgender Archive*: <https://www.digitaltransgenderarchive.net/files/fx719m53g/>.

14 Lynn, Merissa Sherrill. *Transgender Tapestry* Issue 100, p. 32. (Winter, 2002). Periodical. 2002. *Digital Transgender Archive*: <https://www.digitaltransgenderarchive.net/files/8g84mm35j/>.

15 Ibid.

16 Bowman, Edith. "BFI LIVE Jodie Foster." *BFI*, 16 November 2017: <https://www.youtube.com/watch?v=ZETEx_uAq9g>.

17 Demme, Jonathan, director. *Inside the Labyrinth: Making of "The Silence of the Lambs"*. Metro Goldwyn-Mayer, 2007.

18 Truitt, Jos. "My Auntie Buffalo Bill: The Unavoidable Transmisogyny of Silence of the Lambs." *Feministing*, 10 March 2016: <https://feministing.com/2016/03/10/my-auntie-buffalo-bill-the-unavoidable-transmisogyny-of-silence-of-the-lambs/>.

Chapter 6: To Be Real

1 Purchell, Elizabeth, "Audio Commentary," disc 3, *Diary of a Nudist*, BluRay, directed by Doris Wishman. American Genre Film Archive, 2022.

2 *I Am Not This Body* (28 minutes, color, 1972). Produced and distributed by the Erickson Educational Foundation, P.O. Box 185, Kendall Post Office, Miami, Florida 33156. Rental, $35. *Psychiatric Services*, 23(10), p. 32.

3 Awad, Nadia, Moore, Rusty Mae, and Goodwin, Chelsea. "Chelsea Goodwin and Dr. Rusty Mae Moore Oral History." *Oral History*. 2017. *Digital Transgender Archive*: <https://www.digitaltransgenderarchive.net/files/7d278t25f>.

4 "Let Me Die a Woman." *American Genre Film Archive Theatrical Film*

Catalog: <https://www.americangenrefilm.com/theatrical-film-catalog/let-me-die-a-woman/>.

5 Maclay, Willow Catelyn. "Jennie Livingston on *Paris Is Burning* 30 Years Later." *Hyperallergic*, 29 February 2020: <https://hyperallergic.com/544265/jennie-livingston-interview-paris-is-burning-criterion-collection/>.

6 Green, Jesse. "Paris Has Burned." *The New York Times*, 18 April 1993: <https://www.nytimes.com/1993/04/18/style/paris-has-burned.html>.

7 Gardner, Caden Mark. "Two Fly-on-the-Wall Documentaries Chronicle Trans Life in the Shadows." *The Criterion Collection*, 22 October 2021: <https://www.criterion.com/current/posts/7574-two-fly-on-the-wall-documentaries-chronicle-trans-life-in-the-shadows/>.

8 Rovinelli, Jessica Dunn. "Quarantine Reading: *I Am My Own Woman* and *Never, Ever Ever, Coming Down*." *Filmmaker Magazine*, 2 April 2020: <https://filmmakermagazine.com/109489-quarantine-reading-i-am-my-own-woman-and-never-ever-ever-coming-do/>.

9 Denny, Dallas. *Transgender Tapestry* Issue 93. pp. 13–15 (Spring, 2001). Periodical. 2001. *Digital Transgender Archive*: <https://www.digitaltransgenderarchive.net/files/k3569444k>.

10 "Transy House." NYC LGBT Historic Sites Project, Fund for the City of New York: <https://www.nyclgbtsites.org/site/transy-house/>.

11 Allen, Mariette Pathy. *Transgender Tapestry* Issue 103, pgs. 36–37 (Fall, 2003). Periodical. 2003. *Digital Transgender Archive*: <https://www.digitaltransgenderarchive.net/files/fj2362157>.

12 Ibid., p. 39.

Chapter 7: David Cronenberg, Body Horror, and Empathizing with the Artificial Other

1 Power, Tom. "David Cronenberg on *Crimes of the Future* and Why He Sees Body Horror as 'the Body Beautiful'." *Q Radio*, CBC Radio, 3 June 2022: <https://www.youtube.com/watch?v=uQ06od3TYiQ>.

2 "Viggo Mortensen, Léa Seydoux & David Cronenberg Break Down

'Crimes of the Future' Surgery Scene." *Vanity Fair*, 9 June 2022: <https://www.youtube.com/watch?v=mIIfKwL43Cg>.

3   Benedict, Christianne. "The World Made Flesh: Sex and Identity in the Films of David Cronenberg." *Film and Fishnets*, 15 February 2019: <http://filmandfishnet.com/the-world-made-flesh-sex-and-identity-in-the-films-of-david-cronenberg>.

4   Allen, Samantha. "What Science Can Tell Us about Trans People's Brains-and What It Cannot." *The Daily Beast*, 11 April 2017: <https://www.thedailybeast.com/what-science-can-tell-us-about-trans-peoples-brainsand-what-it-cannot>.

5   Conroy, Ed. "A Sexual Revolution in 64,000 Watts.," *Retrontario*, 27 September 2019: <https://retrontario.substack.com/p/a-sexual-revolution-in-64000-watts>.

6   Haraway, Donna J. *Simians, Cyborgs, and Women: The Reinvention of Nature*. 1st ed. Routledge, 1991, p. 152: <https://doi.org/10.1515/9783839413272-086>.

7   Bodrojan, Sam, et al. "Body Talk: A Cronenberg Roundtable." *Reverse Shot*, 1 July 2022: <https://reverseshot.org/features/2946/cronenberg_body_talk>.

8   Ibid.

9   Tenreyro, Tatiana. "A Different Kind of Monster Movie: Writer Karen Walton Reflects on 'Ginger Snaps' 20 Years Later." *Bloody Disgusting!*, 25 September 2020: <https://bloody-disgusting.com/interviews/3633638/different-kind-monster-movie-writer-karen-walton-reflects-ginger-snaps-20-years-later/>.

10 Rea, Steven. "'Under the Skin': Mysterious Femme Fatale Roaming Scotland." *The Philadelphia Inquirer*, 18 April 2014: <https://www.inquirer.com/philly/entertainment/movies/20140418__Under_the_Skin___Mysterious_femme_fatale_roaming_Scotland.html>.

11 Johnson, Kjerstin. "The Two Halves of 'Under the Skin'." *Bitchmedia*, 9 June 2014: <http://www.bitchmedia.org/post/under-the-skin-review-feminism-scarlett-johansson>.

12 Greiving, Tim. "From Kubrick to Spielberg: The Story of 'A.I.'." *The Ringer*, 29 June 2021: <https://www.theringer.com/movies/2021/6/29/22553929/ai-artificial-intelligence-steven-spielberg-stanley-kubrick>.

13 Kursztejn, Fran. "Utopia(s)." *Light Moves*, 17 December 2022: <https://frankursztejn.substack.com/p/utopias>.

14 Dong, Kelley. "Review: Far from Heaven-Robert Rodriguez's 'Alita: Battle Angel.'" *MUBI*, 26 February 2019: <https://mubi.com/notebook/posts/review-far-from-heaven-robert-rodriguez-s-alita-battle-angel>.

Chapter 8: Subversion of Fate

1 "Why The Matrix Is a Trans Story According to Lilly Wachowski." *Netflix: Behind The Streams*, 4 August 2020: <https://www.youtube.com/watch?v=adXm2sDzGkQ>.

2 Keegan, Cáel M. "Mirror Scene: Transgender Aesthetics in the *Matrix* and *Boys Don't Cry*," p. 495.

3 Lee, Seijin. "Lana Wachowski Discusses Bound at the Music Box 1 of 3." *YouTube*, 28 June 2018: <https://www.youtube.com/watch?v=MxynlbNKyu8>.

4 Bright, Susie. "My Handiwork in 'Bound.'" *Susie Bright's Journal*, 21 February 2006: <https://susiebright.blogs.com/susie_brights_journal_/2006/02/my_handiwork_in.html>.

5 Bright, Susie, "Audio Commentary," *Bound*, BluRay, directed by Lana and Lilly Wachowski. Olive Films, 2018.

6 Long Chu, Andrea. "What We Can Learn About Gender From *The Matrix*." *Vulture*, 7 February 2019: <https://www.vulture.com/2019/02/what-the-matrix-can-teach-us-about-gender.html>.

7 Keegan, "Mirror Scene," p. 503.

8 Ibid.

9 "Why *The Matrix* Is a Trans Story According to Lilly Wachowski."

10 Heffernan, Dani. "Director Lana Wachowski Gives Moving Acceptance Speech for Visibility Award." *GLAAD*, 24 October 2012: <https://www.glaad.org/blog/director-lana-wachowski-gives-moving-acceptance-speech-visibility-award/>.

11 Keegan, Cáel M. *Lana and Lilly Wachowski*. University of Illinois Press, Urbana, 2018, p. 82.

12 Wilkinson, Peter. "The Mystery of Larry Wachowski." *Rolling Stone*, 26 January 2006.

13 Baim, Tracy. "Second Wachowski Filmmaker Sibling Comes out as Trans." *Windy City Times*, 8 March 2016: <https://www.

windycitytimes.com/lgbt/Second-Wachowski-filmmaker-sibling-comes-out-as-trans-/54509.html>.

14 Elliott, Stephen. "*Rolling Stone* Slanders the Transgender S&M Community." *HuffPost*, 13 January 2006: <https://www.huffpost.com/entry/rolling-stone-slanders-th_b_13776>.

15 Blay, Zeba. "Ethnic Cleansing: Colorblind Casting in Cloud Atlas." *Hyperallergic*, October 2012: <https://hyperallergic.com/58869/ethnic-cleansing-colorblind-casting-in-cloud-atlas/>.

16 "Lana Wachowski Reveals Suicide Plan, Painful Past in Emotional Speech (Exclusive Video)." *The Hollywood Reporter*, 24 October 2012: <https://www.hollywoodreporter.com/news/general-news/lana-wachowski-reveals-suicide-plan-382169/>.

Chapter 9: Cis-As-Trans Casting

1 Villarreal, Yvonne. "Sunday Conversation: Alexandra Billings on Her Expanding Role on 'Transparent' and What She'd Say to Trump." *Los Angeles Times*, 19 November 2017: <https://www.latimes.com/entertainment/tv/la-ca-st-sunday-conversation-alexandra-billings-20170929-htmlstory.html>.

2 Lynn, Merissa Sherrill. *Transgender Tapestry* Issue 110, p. 34 (Fall, 2006). Periodical. 2006. *Digital Transgender Archive*: <https://www.digitaltransgenderarchive.net/files/8910jt66t>.

3 Ebert, Roger. "Movie Review: *The Crying Game*." *Roger Ebert*, 18 December 1992: <https://www.rogerebert.com/reviews/the-crying-game-1992>. Originally published in *The Chicago Sun-Times*.

4 Manley, Dion. *FTM Newsletter* #45. Periodical. 1999. *Digital Transgender Archive*: <https://www.digitaltransgenderarchive.net/files/h989r3246>.

5 The Transexual Menace. "Send NBC a Message: Murder Is No Joke! Flyer." *Ephemera*. 1996. *Digital Transgender Archive*: <https://www.digitaltransgenderarchive.net/files/xk81jk42v>.

6 Richards, Kymberleigh. *Cross-Talk: The Transgender Community News & Information Monthly*, no. 75, p. 3 (January, 1996). Periodical. 1996. *Digital Transgender Archive*: <https://www.digitaltransgenderarchive.net/files/z029p479v>.

7 7 Halberstam, Jack. *In a Queer Time and Place: Transgender Bodies,*

Subcultural Lives. New York University Press, New York, 2005, p. 62.

8 Richter, Paul. "The NEA Defends Funding of Controversial Film: Arts Endowment: NEA Chief John Frohnmayer Terms the Avant-Garde Work 'Poison' 'Neither Prurient nor Obscene' in a Move to Head off Swelling Criticism from Conservative Groups." *Los Angeles Times*, 30 March 1991: <https://www.latimes.com/archives/la-xpm-1991-03-30-ca-972-story.html>.

9 Tobias, Scott. "Interview with Kimberly Peirce." *A.V. Club*, 27 October 1999: <https://www.avclub.com/kimberly-peirce-1798208065>.

10 Dry, Jude. "As 'Boys Don't Cry' Joins National Film Registry, Kimberly Peirce Addresses Its Complicated History." *IndieWire*, 13 December 2019: <https://www.indiewire.com/2019/12/kimberly-peirce-interview-boys-dont-cry-transgender-1202196536/>.

11 Tobias. "Interview with Kimberly Peirce.,"

12 "*Boys Don't Cry*." *The Charlie Rose Show*, hosted by Charlie Rose, PBS, 5 November 1999.

13 Kleinmann, James. "Exclusive Interview: Kimberly Peirce Revisits Her Oscar-Winning *Boys Don't Cry* for TCM's Reframed Series 'I've Been Protective of Brandon's Story since the Moment I Heard It.'" *The Queer Review*, 26 November 2022: <https://thequeerreview.com/2022/11/21/interview-kimberly-peirce-revisits-boys-dont-cry-for-tcm-reframed/>.

14 Joynt, Chase, and Morgan M. Page. *Boys Don't Cry*. McGill-Queen's University Press, Montreal, 2022, p. 82.

15 Kleinmann. "Exclusive Interview."

16 Tobias. "Interview with Kimberly Peirce."

17 Ibid.

18 Halberstam, *In a Queer Time and Place*, p. 83.

19 Ibid., pp. 62–63.

20 Ibid., p. 96.

21 Ibid., p. 89.

22 Keegan, Cáel M., et al. "Mirror Scene: Transgender Aesthetics in *The Matrix* and *Boys Don't Cry*." *The Oxford Handbook of Queer Cinema*, Oxford University Press, New York, NY, 2021, pg. 499.

23 Ebert, Roger. "*Boys Don't Cry* (1999)." *RogerEbert.com*, 22 October

1999: <https://www.rogerebert.com/reviews/boys-dont-cry-1999>. Originally published in *The Chicago-Sun Times*.

24 Keegan, et al. "Mirror Scene," p. 498.

25 Minkowitz, Donna. 1994. "Love Hurts." *The Village Voice*, 19 April 1994. *Digital Transgender Archive*: <https://www.digitaltransgenderarchive.net/files/tx31qh69s>.

26 Minkowitz, Donna. "How I Broke, and Botched, the Brandon Teena Story." *The Village Voice*, 20 June 2018: < https://www.villagevoice.com/how-i-broke-and-botched-the-brandon-teena-story/>.

27 Ibid.

28 Harrison, Eric. "A Filmmaker Fictionalizes to Get at Difficult Truths." Clipping. 2000. *Digital Transgender Archive*: <https://www.digitaltransgenderarchive.net/files/8049g52>.

29 Halberstam, *In a Queer Time and Place*, p. 91.

30 Dry, Jude. "'Boys Don't Cry' Protests: Why We Should Listen to Trans Activists Criticizing the Milestone Film." *IndieWire*, 14 December 2016: <https://www.indiewire.com/features/general/kimberly-peirce-boys-dont-cry-reed-transgender-1201757549/>.

31 Keegan, et. al. "Mirror Scene," p. 492.

32 Joynt and Page, *Boys Don't Cry*, pp. 83–84.

33 Borten, Craig and Melisa Wallack. "Dallas Buyers Club." *Dallas Buyers Club*, p. 30.

34 Features, Focus. *Making Rayon Real*. YouTube, 9 January 2014: <https://www.youtube.com/watch?v=Hyfh5tW4rvk>.

35 Reed, Betsy. "Eddie Redmayne: Playing a Trans Character in *The Danish Girl* Was 'a Mistake'." *The Guardian*, 22 November 2021: <https://www.theguardian.com/film/2021/nov/22/eddie-redmayne-playing-a-trans-character-in-the-danish-girl-was-a-mistake>.

36 Meyer, Sabine (2015). *"Wie Lili zu einem richtigen Mädchen wurde": Lili Elbe: Zur Konstruktion von Geschlecht und Identität zwischen Medialisierung, Regulierung und Subjektivierung*, pp. 271–281.

37 Stryker, *Transgender History*, p. 18.

38 Villarreal, "Sunday Conversation."

39 Fagerholm, Matt. "Lukas Dhont on *Girl*, the Film's Controversial Casting, What Representation Means to Him and More." *RogerEbert.com*, 14 January 2019: <https://www.rogerebert.com/

interviews/lukas-dhont-on-girl-the-films-controversial-casting-what-representation-means-to-him-and-more>.

40 Piepenburg, Erik. "Is a Film about a Transgender Dancer Too 'Dangerous' to Watch?" *The New York Times*, 2 January 2019: <https://www.nytimes.com/2019/01/02/movies/girl-netflix-film-transgender-debate.html>.

Chapter 10: Towards a New Cinematic Language of Our Own

1 Horak, Laura. "Tracing the History of Trans and Gender Variant Filmmakers." *Spectator: The University of Southern California Journal of Film & Television*, vol. 37, no. 2, 2017, p. 15.

2 Steinbock, Eliza. *Shimmering Images: On Transgender Embodiment and Cinematic Aesthetics*. Duke University Press, Durham and London, 2019, p. 9.

3 Bell, Jed. *FTM Newsletter* #39, pp. 6–7. Periodical. 1997. *Digital Transgender Archive*: <https://www.digitaltransgenderarchive.net/files/r207tp43x>.

4 5 Dixon, Wheeler Winston, and Gwendolyn Audrey Foster. "Introduction: Towards a New History of the Experimental Cinema." *Experimental Cinema: The Film Reader*. Routledge, London, 2007, p. 1.

5 "Orlando." Press Release. Sony Pictures Classics. 26 May 2010.

6 Pronger, Rachel. "*Orlando*: The Most Subversive History Film Ever Made." *BBC Culture*, 20 September 2022: <https://www.bbc.com/culture/article/20220913-orlando-the-most-subversive-history-film-ever-made>.

7 Stern, Marlow. "Tilda Swinton on David Bowie: He 'Looked Like Someone From the Same Planet As I Did'." *The Daily Beast*, 11 January 2016: <https://www.thedailybeast.com/tilda-swinton-on-david-bowie-he-looked-like-someone-from-the-same-planet-as-i-did>.

8 "Orlando." Press Release.

9 Pronger, "*Orlando*."

10 "Orlando." Press Release.

11 Keogan, Natalia. "'Our Plan for Financial Security Is, We'll Become Famous Hollywood Filmmakers': Silas Howard and Harry Dodge

on *By Hook or By Crook*," *Filmmaker Magazine*, 20 July 2022: <https://filmmakermagazine.com/115591-interview-silas-howard-harry-dodge-by-hook-or-by-crook/>.

12 Ibid.

13 Halberstam, *In a Queer Time and Place*, p. 92.

14 Moore, Sam. "Why 'Hedwig and the Angry Inch' Is More Vital Now than Ever." *INTO*, 17 October 2021: <https://www.intomore.com/culture/hedwig-angry-inch-vital-now-ever/>.

15 Masters, Jeffrey. "John Cameron Mitchell Explains Why He Believes Hedwig Is Not Trans." *Advocate.com*, 23 February 2022: <https://www.advocate.com/people/2019/7/02/john-cameron-mitchell-explains-why-he-believes-hedwig-not-trans>.

16 Publika, Liz. "John Cameron Mitchell on Writing, Directing and Starring in *Hedwig and the Angry Inch*: An Interview." *ARTpublika Magazine*, 29 August 2022: <https://www.artpublikamag.com/post/john-cameron-mitchell-on-writing-directing-starring-in-hedwig-and-the-angry-inch-an-interview>.

17 Burke, Kelly. "'It's Not about Cancel Culture': *Hedwig and the Angry Inch* Postponed after Trans-Led Petition." *The Guardian*, 18 November 2020: <https://www.theguardian.com/culture/2020/nov/18/its-not-about-cancel-culture-hedwig-and-the-angry-inch-postponed-after-trans-led-petition>.

18 Ibid.

19 Tackitt-Jones, Jordy, et al. "Gender Without Genitals: Hedwig's Six Inches." *The Transgender Studies Reader*. Routledge, London, 2006, p. 451.

20 Pincus, Adam. "All of Me." *Filmmaker Magazine*, Spring 2001: <https://filmmakermagazine.com/archives/issues/spring2001/features/all_of_me.php>.

21 Taylor, Trey. "Jayne County, the Trans Rock'n'roll Star Who Influenced David Bowie, in Her Own Words." *Interview Magazine*, 19 April 2018: <https://www.interviewmagazine.com/culture/jayne-county-trans-rocknroll-star-influenced-david-bowie-words>.

22 Masters, "John Cameron Mitchell Explains Why He Believes Hedwig Is Not Trans."

23 Publika, "John Cameron Mitchell on Writing, Directing and Starring in *Hedwig and the Angry Inch*: An Interview."

24 Ibid.

25 "*Maggots and Men.*" *Cary Cronenwett*: <https://www.
    carycronenwett.com/maggots-and-men>.

26 CrimethInc Ex-Workers' Collective. "Kronstadt As Gender
    Anarchy." *CrimethInc*, 31 March 2021: <https://crimethinc.
    com/2021/03/31/kronstadt-as-gender-anarchy-an-interview-
    with-cary-cronenwett-director-of-maggots-and-men-i>.

27 Joynt and Page, *Boys Don't Cry*, p. 1.

28 Horak, Laura. "Trans on YouTube: Intimacy, Visibility." *TSQ:
    Transgender Studies Quarterly*, vol. 1, no. 4, Fall 2014, pp. 573–574:
    <https://doi.org/10.1215/23289252-2815255>.

Chapter 11: Trans Filmmakers and Authorship

1 "We're All Going to the World's Fair." Director's Statement.
   Lightbulb Film Distribution (UK). 2021.

2 Ibid.

3 Rosskam, Jules, editor. "Making Trans Cinema: A Roundtable
   Discussion with Felix Endara, Reina Gossett, Chase Joynt, Jess
   Mac and Madsen Minax." *Somatechnics*, vol. 8, no. 1, 2018, p. 17.:
   <https://doi.org/10.3366/soma.2018.0234>.

4 Simonoff, Cyrus. "Earthly Delights: Tourmaline Talks about
   Pleasure, Freedom Dreaming, and Her New Solo Show." *Artforum
   International Magazine*, 14 January 2021: <https://www.artforum.
   com/interviews/tourmaline-talks-about-pleasure-freedom-
   dreaming-and-her-new-solo-show-84900>.

5 Dozier, Ayanna. "Surveilling Bodies: Archives and Sex Work."
   Surveilling Bodies: Archives and Sex Work, 8 February 2022:
   <https://pioneerworks.org/broadcast/surveilling-bodies-ayanna-
   dozier>.

6 "Toward a Trans Method, or Reciprocity As a Way of Life."
   Feminist Media Histories, vol. 7, no. 1, 2021, p. 19: <https://doi.
   org/10.1525/fmh.2021.7.1.11>.

7 Ibid.

8 "Isabel Sandoval Interview: Meet the Filmmakers." *The Criterion
   Channel*, 2021: <https://www.criterionchannel.com/meet-the-
   filmmakers/videos/isabel-sandoval-interview>.

9 Marine, Brooke. "Isabel Sandoval, 'Queen of Sensual Cinema,'" Embraces Ambivalence." *W Magazine*, 26 March 2021: <https://www.wmagazine.com/culture/isabel-sandoval-lingua-franca-freeze-frame-interview>.

10 Farber, Manny. "White Elephant Art Vs. Termite Art." *Film Culture*, no. 27 (Winter 1962–63), p. 242.

INDEX OF FILMS

ACKNOWLEDGMENTS

These authors are indebted to the works of Susan Stryker, Eliza Steinbock, Laura Horak, and Cael M. Keegan, whose writing and research paved the way for us to build the historical context and mine through the diversity of the trans film image. *Corpses, Fools, and Monsters* would not have been able to cover the amount of titles it has without the help and assistance from archivist, researcher, and programmer Elizabeth Purchell whose encouragement and generosity made the book what it is. Filmmaker Jessie Dunn Rovinelli for making such singular film work and whose fearless outspokenness on why cinema has often failed trans people greatly influenced this book. Additionally, the trans and gender variance scholarship of Zagria Cowan who made much of her research accessible in online spaces and K.J. Rawson, whose work in bringing to life The Digital Transgender Archive has allowed these authors, who do not come from academic spaces, to be able to have access to important materials of the past to help build and broaden their discussions for this book. We also wish to thank Sheila O'Malley whose written film criticism and conversationalist style of obsessive deep dives of films, actors, and directors would ultimately be what would inform the structure of the trial run for this book's general idea about transness on-screen: *Body Talk*. Lastly, we would like to thank Carl Neville and Repeater Books for getting into contact with us to make this possible.

Caden Mark Gardner wishes to thank Kyle Turner, Michael Koresky, K. Austin Collins, Miriam Bale, Ashley Clark, K.J. Shepherd, Juan Barquin, Jenni Olson, Keith

Uhlich, Daniel Lavery, Emily St. James, Mackenzie Luken-bill, Sam Bodrojan, Tyler Thomas, Daniel Kasman, Girish Shambu, Elena Gorfinkel, Dan Schindel, Jake Mulligan, Catherine Stebbins, Andrew Chan, Peter Labuza, Kristen Sales, Davey Davis, Drusilla Adeline, Millie De Chirico, Davi Barrios, Moonhawk River Stone, Ellis Martin, Michael Sicinski, Juan Barquin, Kate Rennnebohm, Oliver Whitney, Margot Stacy, Dallas Denny, and the late Jim Gabriel for the direct and indirect ways they have each helped push forward and inform much of the text for this book. Personally, he would like to thank his parents, surviving grandmother, and his departed grandparents who helped foster his love of cinema.

Willow Catelyn Maclay would like to thank Carol Grant, Kiva Reardon, Sara Elizabeth, Danny King, Daniel Kasman, Tina Hassannia, Kier-la Janisse, Scout Tafoya, Alan Scher-stuhl, Adam Nayman, Michael Koresky, Courtenay Stall-ings, Jake Mulligan, Ashley Clark, Matt Zoller Seitz, Monica Castillo, David Jenkins, Juan Barquin, Kelley Dong, Miriam Bale, Justine Smith, Esther Rosenfield, Dan Schindel, Alice Stoehr, Peter Labuza, Lena Frances Houst, Michael Sicinski, Girish Shambu, Louise Weard, Kaila Hier, Pete Volk, Alex-andra Heller-Nicholas, Christina Newland, Christianne Benedict, Sally Jane Black, and Erin Pronovost for helping make the creation of this book possible. In addition to those listed above she would also like to honour those who have made her transition feasible and sustaining: Casey Plett, Empy, Maureen Gibbons, Mari-Lynne Sinnott, Chris Mallay, Ashton Quinn, Vanessa Quinn, Victoria Graham, Alexander Semidey, Victoria Marcocelli and Kasey Coady. Lastly, she would like to thank her husband Trevor Dobbin for his sup-port, encouragement and love, and for the sacrifices he has continually made to make her writing career possible.

REPEATER BOOKS

is dedicated to the creation of a new reality. The landscape of twenty-first-century arts and letters is faded and inert, riven by fashionable cynicism, egotistical self-reference and a nostalgia for the recent past. Repeater intends to add its voice to those movements that wish to enter history and assert control over its currents, gathering together scattered and isolated voices with those who have already called for an escape from Capitalist Realism. Our desire is to publish in every sphere and genre, combining vigorous dissent and a pragmatic willingness to succeed where messianic abstraction and quiescent co-option have stalled: abstention is not an option: we are alive and we don't agree.